Life IN THE AFTERLIFE

Life
IN THE
AFTERLIFE
EMBRACE WHERE WE GO IN
Spirit ON THE *Other Side* AND
THE UNBREAKABLE *Bond*

MELINDA K LYONS

Copyright © 2016 by Melinda K Lyons

Life In The Afterlife: Embrace Where We Go In Spirit On The Other Side And The Unbreakable Bond/ Melinda K Lyons

Cover and Interior Design: Melinda K Lyons

ISBN:1522878270

Anchorage, AK 99502

Melinda K. Lyons website: http://www.lastfrontiermedium.com

This book is dedicated in loving memory of

Chad Masanori Tohinaka
Returned Home November 17th 2012
&
Aaron T. McClain
Returned Home May 11th 2011

I know we will meet again in Heaven.
Thank you for loving and guiding me through my journey.

Contents

Introduction

It's a grand thing to embrace with an understanding that nothing is a coincidence, but Divine timing from the Higher Realms. Yes, I said it. Higher Realms, or commonly known as Heaven, Paradise or the Kingdom of God if you will. It is all the same to God and Spirit, for it doesn't really matter what you call it or Him; it's all the same to Creator. In this book you will be able to learn more about Spirit, the Other Side, and how we are all joined together in what is perfect, and in Divine unity. We cannot live without them and they cannot exist without us, for we are all in need of each other more than we may know. This book will help give you the set of tools, and wisdom of a deeper understanding, to actually communicate and listen to Spirit, more than you may even realize. Spirit plays a gigantic role in our lives, influencing us to make wise decisions vs. those that we may later regret. But that doesn't mean that our role here is to be perfect, or to live up to a certain expectation or agenda. Rather, the idea is to show you that God, and Spirit do not expect anything from you, except love.

AS THE WORLD CHANGES, SO DOES GOD'S APPROACH

Church terrified me growing up, for I was made to believe that you weren't good or worthy in the eyes of God, because you didn't follow

His "rules" or "commandments". I would cry almost every night, desperately wanting to be accepted, to feel that I would be worthy, or holy enough to be greeted at the gates of Heaven. But did you know that God actually doesn't expect perfection from you at all? From my own journey, including sending messages from Spirit to their loved ones here, I have been taught that God understands that you are human for He made us that way.

"We have been forgetting, that our true path in this life is to love, and to spread that love to every person we meet, no matter our differences, and this is the message I bring."

I will never forget one of the most influential moments I have ever experienced, which happened during a conversation with a good friend. She loves God, and she was the one who brought me closer to Him, when I was falling off my wagon of life.

We were having dinner together at a place that just opened up. She was intrigued, and like many religious folks I have met, she keeps an open mind, while asking how God would be accepting my work. I thought good and hard, but then quickly Spirit brought me the words that I never thought I would be able to say without hesitation, or disbelief. I said to her, "If God didn't want me to pursue this life, He wouldn't have allowed me the gift in the first place, or to anyone else." She became more intrigued as I continued, "When God brought forth Christ, He did this because it was the only way to make the people see, and feel His love for us. Back then, executions and prisons were horrific, and extremely barbaric. People were thrown into pits, torn to pieces by lions while still alive as punishment for just stealing, or betrayal. Back in those days there was no such thing as love, but more of honor, and obedience. I personally have no doubt that Jesus was crucified not just to show His love for us, but to give us a taste of our own medicine. His crucifixion was to help people see that love is the only answer to God."

The further I got into the depths of my reasoning with God, and about my Mediumship, my friend then asked, "But don't you think that God wants us to continue to follow His rules in the Bible?"

I replied, "I have a deep belief and feeling, that as crazy as this sounds... He has brought forth people like me, and many others to bring back His word in a different light. Not changing the light or His word, but expanding it in a more accepting, and less dramatic way. His approach centuries ago, was not only overwhelming to many, but also extremely impactful. However now, I believe that God has decided to adapt a new approach to the people of today. Not to say that God has changed, but because the world changes, so does God's approach for us to accept His love and mercy for us all."

I mentioned Christ, because I am a personal believer in Him, but that is not to say that is the only way to God. This is just part of my belief, and even God has shown me you don't have to only go to Christ, to be accepted into God's kingdom. We are all born in His image, for we are all created from the same Source. I spoke of the Bible reference to my friend, to help her see it in a way that she could better understand. That is how Spirit will relay the messages to us, and in her case it was about Christ.

I know you might be thinking, *"Since when does a Psychic Medium follow the messages of God?"* Well to enlighten that thought even more, this isn't about me, but about you understanding the concept of God, and why He has people like Mediums sending messages from the Other Side. Far too often we forget that our true path in life, is to love, and to spread that love to every person we meet, no matter our differences, and this is the message I bring.

I've been visited by Angels, taken to see Heaven, and have met some of the most holy, and this is something I believe the world deserves to know. This message isn't for me, but for everyone, since all of us were created in this world that was built from love.

God is not dead, but very much alive in all of us. He will forever remain our Creator, our teacher, and our true Source of love. Spirit has brought me the answers to the many questions we have, and for one reason only, because **God still loves us,** and even more than you may know. He isn't disappointed in us, He isn't full of shame; quite to the contrary, He is full of light, pride and love for us more than ever!

MY NEAR DEATH EXPERIENCE

At sixteen years old I underwent what is commonly known as a near death experience or (NDE). It started at a boyfriend's house where we were enjoying our summer weekend with a typical TV and food afternoon. He had few food options but luckily he and I had shared a hotdog that I'd never had before, with cheese bits within the dog. Little did I know that this would soon turn from lucky to unlucky.

Eating was normal, however within less than 24 hours I was engulfed in hives from head to toe. We didn't know what was going on. I had never heard of such an after effect from food that was being rejected by the body. Never heard of anaphylactic shock either but later I surely got the crash course. Within less than twenty minutes of calling 911, I began to feel funny. Have you ever seen someone's face go pale the instant they see something that's obviously not good? That "Oh $h!t" face? – That was the look of the EMTs the second they came through the front door of my boyfriend's house. Quickly they did what they could by hooking me up to what seemed like hundreds of Benadryl tubes while asking me questions about school to try to keep me focused. At first I thought everything was going to be okay yet there was something still not seeming right. About five minutes after their arrival my throat got too tight to the point where I said, "I can't breathe."

One of the EMTs that sat in front of me said to breathe through a paper bag, for a panic attack can feel like a heart attack. I did what he suggested but it was no good, my ability to breathe was diminishing by the second. Without notice, the last words I remember saying a second time, "I can't breathe…" Suddenly I collapsed. The instant I passed out I awoke, for that same EMT immediately shot my leg with an EpiPen (Epinephrine Autoinjector).

If you don't know what an EpiPen is, it's a device that is filled with Epinephrine that you shoot into the leg of someone who is suffering from Anaphylaxis.

Within a matter of seconds I found myself in an ambulance where the EMTs were pumping me with more Benadryl trying to keep me conscious. All the while the light distracting me overhead, blinding my sight was not your typical light in an ambulance vehicle but something supernatural. Although there was so much noise going on around me I couldn't help but find beauty in this light over me. Gazing deeper into its integrity surely I must've known what I was getting myself into considering how much of a "Bible thumper" I was. But no. I was too distracted. Too overtaken by this supernatural vertigo to notice the EMTs calling my name, to hear what soon sounded like unfamiliar soft blurs in the distance. Without warning the light consumed all of my *being-ness* and that's when it really got real.

I discovered myself floating out of my physical body and watching the struggling men who were dedicated to saving lives. But without delay, without doubt or worry I moved on to a nearby sidewalk where I sat down in peace as I watched the ambulance rush past me. "Oh, there it goes," I said out loud as I pointed in the direction of the moving vehicle where my body lay.

And that's when it hit me. That realizational moment, that stomach dropping moment when I knew something had happened that I felt could not be undone. As the fear crept within my consciousness that's when I eyed a pair of shoes that were a part of someone unfamiliar. The friendly unfamiliar kneeled down to my side, placed a comforting hand on my right shoulder then softly asked, "Do you know where you are, Melinda?"

Without thinking I said, "Yeah...the strawberry post office near my house."

Then the unfamiliar *he* smiled caringly in agreement. Then he followed with a second question. "Do you know what happened to you?"

I responded with, "Yeah, I was in the ambulance, and that's when I found myself in the white light *–wait. Does that mean??"*

The tranquility residing along his expression never steered but remained as it were. Placing his hand on mine, this mysterious guardian proceeded, "You will have enough time to get back to your body but first there is a very special someone that wants to speak with you. Don't worry Melinda, you are safe and everything will be okay. You will see your family again."

Without words we both stood, joined hands and ascended together to another dimension in what seemed like a matter of milliseconds. Flying like shooting stars we ascended to a place filled with an endless plethora of light, positivity and serenity. The transition from this world, this physical density is nothing compared to what I had the grace to witness next in this...*Other Side.* As I came to the reality of what was happening in the moment, I was soon greeted by the unthinkable. Each drape, each wrinkle to the rhythm of His robes were joined in harmony with speechless radiance. Never before had I ever witnessed such cleanliness from such a person. His voice was soft like something of a hymn. His shimmering skin brought warmth to your being, engaging all of your sense of self the moment one were to gaze upon this rarity. Each sparkle dancing from Him gleamed as if a billion stars from the galaxy were engraved throughout His entire form. His presence stole my attention, my heart and sight of anyone else. "I can't believe it's you..."

In silence Jesus took me into His loving arms.

Without much effort He gave me a rare opportunity. *"Melinda, I want to thank you for following me as your loyal service to me. Your love touches me. And I am thankful for your loyalty. I would like to give you a chance to go back to Earth and share this experience of me with the world. Tell them of me. Tell them of my love for them and how I am still very much alive."*

I listened as His Holiness spoke.

"But before you go back, I know you have many unanswered questions, so I am giving you this chance to ask me anything you want. But ask wisely, for your time is not long with me for now."

As I asked my long awaited questions His smile never left His face. His eyes rayed non-defiant nobility. It was indescribable. After what felt like hours of conversation in the glorious presence of Jesus, the Virgin Mother Mary and many others, including Angels, He had one last thing before I returned.

"Melinda, now that you have the answers that you needed and the visit of Heaven, there is one last thing. I will be granting you abilities likewise to mine. I know you prayed to me, asking for an opportunity to devote your life for your fellow brothers and sisters. I know that you asked to be as glorious as I. Although the world will not be as welcoming of this new approach, I have faith in your dedication and loyalty to me. Please take this gift and use it for the best of humanity. Please help them to remember my glory. It is time to bring back the witness period. —But know now, this will not be an easy road. You will be faced with many trials."

Without the need to speak, He could sense doubt rising. While giving me the seconds to gather the question I followed with, "How will they know I am truthful? What if no one believes me?"

He, the brightest of all that sat beside me in confidence answered, *"There will be those that will doubt but I am certain of your stamina, Melinda. You will know what to do for I will be near to guide you. Many will be with you guiding you to provide the truth that they will need."*

After a slight gap at the end of His spoken certainty, His holiness spoke, *"Do you have faith in me that I will provide for you what you need?"*

Without delay I said, "Yes."

His smile continued with, *"Then you have nothing to fear."*

After I took His gift for the good of mankind, I thanked His holiness for this rare greeting in Heaven. And without blinking, I woke up in Anchorage, Alaska's Providence Hospital where all of the females in my family were circled around my bed filled with tears and relief as I opened my heavy lids. Little did I know that I had completely forgotten all of my visit in Heaven. For over ten years I had no memory of my visit and my profound conversation with Jesus … 'til now.

God is not dead, but very much alive in all of us. He will remain to be our Creator, our teacher, and our true Source of love. Spirit has brought me the answers to the many questions we have, and for one reason only, because God still loves us, and even more than you may know. He isn't disappointed in us, He isn't full of shame, but of light, pride and love for us more than ever!

THE PURPOSE OF THIS BOOK

To remind you of your true calling in this world and why we are all joined together in the harmony of the Universe and how we can learn from each other without judgment. To enlighten the world with God's words by the gifts, the abilities I have been given is not some sort of simple "trickery" or "parlor trick" but it comes from the glorious gift of Jesus Himself that He Himself bestowed. I use these gifts such as healing, Mediumship, and highly sensitive Psychic Abilities to grant a higher level of awareness with a deeper concept of the consciousness.

Here you will discover and learn more about the process of crossing over to the Other Side of this physical illusion we call "reality". You will be guided by my expert Spirit Guides throughout while also reading writings by some of the most highly evolved Ascended Masters through me as the vessel.

I know this may all sound a bit crazy. Trust me, I never thought in a million years I would be doing any of this let alone taking the time to write a whole book about it. All I can say is this... Let me at least take the time to share with you the idea, the remote possibility, that if God, this galaxy, and other miracles are "possible" than why not life in the afterlife? I am sharing what I know and have experienced personally. While sharing countless experiences of my clients during sessions they had with me.

This book will also give you the opportunity to learn how you can hear from your departed loved ones without the use of a Medium for we are all a part of the same energy. Our departed loved ones are never actually "gone" but just in a different dimension of this vast Universe.

Crossing Over

Personally, I don't like to say that we die anymore. Not that I don't accept our fate, but that it isn't really true based upon our soul. Sure, our bodies die, but that doesn't mean that our soul and our love does. For when our last breath is taken, that is when our Spirit will be released into the true form we were created to uphold.

Our souls are made up of energy, and that energy is made from our Creator, God. We are all in union with each other based upon our souls being made together as one, while still in tune with individuality. When we cross over, there is no more pain, sorrow, fear, guilt, hatred, anger or any of the negative emotions we harbor here. During the transition from human to Spirit, we are first greeted by our loved ones from the Other Side with love and open arms.

Once we are in the acceptance of our passing, Spirit will give us an opportunity to make our first few visits to our loved ones on Earth. Once we are able to send our love in various ways, is when our *real life* begins in Heaven. As we ascend to the Realm at which we are placed in, depending on our life lessons, and wisdom, more will come into play.

This isn't to say that some Spirits are better than others, but that there are those that are higher in knowledge with greater wisdom, that are then teachers for those less experienced or knowledgeable. Just like when we are here learning life lessons, Spirits are taught on their lessons they have yet mastered. Each lesson is brought forth to each soul with love and guidance, treated as the most treasured. There is no judgement on the Other Side, for each soul only transfers love, and gratitude, shared with laughter.

THE TRANSITION

Crossing over is a beautiful process that occurs without hesitation of any kind. When a person takes their last breath, Spirit shows this individual that they will instantly be reunited with their loved ones. Some may find themselves with family, friends, fellow co-workers, Angels, and even higher deities such as Jesus Christ, Buddha or the Virgin Mother Mary. We all will experience a very special unification process during our lifting of the soul out of the body.

Spirit describes the soul's transition will immediately feel like an immense amount of freedom, that gives them a chance to remember the soul's brilliance. How it occurs is breathtaking (pun intended). Some souls will be shown God's brilliant light, showered by unconditional love. Or they will be gently guided out of their body by the blessing of sight, and see their already deceased loved ones standing before them. Giving the person comfort and reassurance, of not being alone during their crossing over process is essential to Spirit.

Because of the heart struck moments many souls will experience during their transition, especially if from a sudden passing, the soul will be gently guided. Each soul is always greeted, never left alone, no matter the faith, or lack thereof. Each soul will be treated with absolute pure love, and respect, in order for them to know they are safe and in good company. While there may be moments the soul will struggle with acceptance, the fellow souls guiding and comforting this new transitioned soul, will not only talk to him or her, but give them a chance at seeing how they passed if necessary. This can be a difficult process, especially if the newly transitioned soul doesn't want, or know how to accept their passing. However, the love of our Angels, loved ones, and Spirit Guides will do any and all things possible to give this new transitioned soul the gift of acceptance.

OUR TRUE FORM

The feeling of being a soul without a shell, like the physical body, is difficult to describe at first blush. But to do the best I can, what I have learned from Spirit is the feeling is very light, free and full. There is nothing missing when you or I transition into our Spirit form. We are made of energy that is connected to Source. The Source of Life never diminished when in the physical illusion that you are now while reading this book. It is the formlessness that once was never manifested that you return to once again in your transition from here to there. The soul is reminded of this wonderful energy feeling that is forever full of love, peace and security while regaining unlimited consciousness of the timeless intelligence that is forever connected with Source within the Universe.

The other sensation that Spirit shares, is what they look like. The soul is made up of energy, and energy is something that never was created, and can never be destroyed. For this, the soul is adaptable to limitless surroundings, situations and abilities. The soul is able to be any form it may choose or feel at the moment, thus enables the individual soul to feel complete every second of every minute. In order to be fully free, the soul must be fully capable of transitioning in any way they feel is who they are. So if a soul would prefer to be a male or female for example, then that is who/what they can become and remain if chooses.

This is apparent for the soul's growth within itself, to be closer to God, Creator.

In order to grant you a visual, imagine being underwater and you are waving your hand left to right, and as you do so, you are seeing the water move in slow motion. You can see with your naked eye the concept of the water transfer harmoniously without interfering with the rest of the ocean. It moves symmetrically for it's all the same molecule, while honing its individual drops. This is the same for our soul. When the soul moves from one location to another, it moves within the Universe, in union with the rest of the energy that surrounds it. The energy of the soul has a specific vibration, allowing the soul the unlimited ability to move within the Universe without trouble. What continually surprises me is how beautiful the Spirit form continues to become.

Throughout my journey with connecting with souls, Spirit brings me more impressions and creativity to the form they choose to represent. Our energy is divided into two categories: the *Masculine* and *Feminine* of creation that are distinctly different energy vibrations that are both equal halves of Creator. This would carefully explain why when each soul I come into contact with in connection with people's loved ones are identified through detecting and feeling the Male and Female energy distinctions.

Honestly I don't know how they are different –even as a Medium I don't have the best way to describe how I know they are different considering I can feel the energies in readings with clients. But the best way I can describe it if you really want to know, is most often they feel as they "sound". That's the BEST way I can tell you this. I know this may sound a bit cliché but when you picture a male you picture strength, leadership, loyalty, protection, security etc. With a female energy some may picture nurturing, mothering, emotionally empathetic, delicate, graceful, etc.

In the Spirit form, we hone our truest form we hold which would also go along with the gender that you are or that you feel you should have been born in. Which would explain 99% of most souls that I encounter, are the same gender that they were when physically alive. Each soul that feels they are meant to be a certain gender is the gender they will behold because that's the frequency vibration that you are.

In retrospect, I have been told we are endless in our form, and can be whatever we feel comfortable, for we are no longer bound by our human body. Truth be told, Spirit describes that we are surrounded by energy, because we are energy. And with this the body or form we choose, is only the bystander of the soul's true nature. The energy of a soul is Universal, which means in short, boundless in form, endless in length. There is nothing we cannot do or become in Spirit.

Entertain my creative thought, and picture a television that is doing that annoying static chaos. This is what happens when you aren't getting the reception of the channel you are trying to get, but have you ever wondered what that static could represent? Now picture your loved one in Spirit, and try to imagine this static running through them, and within them millions of miles per second. This is the energy of Spirit that permits them the unsurpassed ability of being everything for everyone. Now add color, like from a mood ring. This is how they express their level of progress during their lessons, and how they essentially feel. The soul is all energy, which is also based upon love, and feelings. So instead of feeling the energy inside of them like they did as a human, they become that feeling, and the color. Their color dances to their mood in the moment at which they are feeling. They don't have to if they don't want to but it's a choice of course.

The soulful being of oneself is truly wondrous. This is the picture Spirit wants you to truly accept. This is their true form on the Other Side in Spirit. Your true form now and for all eternity.

As the soul begins to regain memory of what it is to be *soulful*, the next step is understanding where they will be going, and how long it may take.

Understand, Spirit never forces another soul to do or go anywhere they don't want to. All of Spirit in Heaven, will only do their part in sharing, and showing this soul what to expect, and accept in their new, or old reality.

PREVIOUS LIFE REVIEW

Next step in Spirit, is honing the things they cannot change, and the things that they could have. A *Life Review* is where the newly transitioned soul will be spoken over with their Spirit Guides, and God about their previous life. They will discuss the instances they excelled in, and how they could've handled other situations better. There is no grading scale in our Life Review, but more of showing how the individual soul could have loved better unconditionally, without judgment of themselves and others. We are all imperfect. No soul can be perfect in their Life Review, for we're placed on Earth in order to learn on how to love in all instances, no matter the gravity. There may be a place, and time where the soul may not understand what it is they didn't do their best on, and that is where the soul can have a chance at reliving the experience through the other person's eyes. If they had a fight with their spouse for example, then that soul will be able to see, and feel the impact of the experience through their spouse's eyes. They will feel the emotions as if they were their own, along with hearing and thinking the thoughts, whatever they may have been as if those thoughts were their own. Basically, the soul will become this person for a brief moment, in order to fully embrace all of the hardship they may have caused the other person.

But again, no soul is graded. So you can't fail at life necessarily, it's not like your Spirit Guide is going to give you an F for failure. Instead, the point is to allow you the opportunity to understand the changes that you could've made, if you responded differently. No matter the cause, Spirit doesn't look at fault. There is no room for faults, what matters is how we essentially feel during the experiences, and how to love each other without judgment.

All the while the soul is taking in the experiences, and understanding the value in their lessons learned and yet to learn. They will be in a grieving period where the soul can let go of any of the negative emotions like guilt, resentment, anger, grief, regrets and any other pains or hardships this soul is enduring.

After they have forgiven themselves, and the others in their previous life, then the soul is able to ascend to the next few steps in their new soulful life. A Life Review is a healing method for the soul to continue their growth in Spirit. Without this step, the soul would continue harboring all of their negative, unhappy emotions that could prevent the soul's spiritual growth. Every soul must go through this step, whether it's emotionally unbearable or exhilarating, it allows every part of their existence to be cleansed and free, to move forward positively. I also call this the *Soul Cleansing Period*, but whatever you call it, it's evident for our soul growth.

SOUL CONTRACT

We have what I like to call a ***Soul Contract***, and this contract is between God and you, of what your obligations are when you're born in your human life. We all have this agreement, and all of us have signed up for something different. No contract is the same as the next, not even a little. The reason behind this, is because you agreed that you wanted to learn certain life lessons faster, thus bringing you to Earth. In my experiences so far, Spirit has informed me that once your lessons are up, and you have done all that you could do here on Earth, including fulfilling your true life's purpose that is when God will cross you over the to the Other Side.

Does this mean that your death is set in stone, and is predetermined? Yes and no. Do you know that joke about how the person drowning in the ocean needs a boat to be rescued, and three fishermen arrive, asking the man to hop on their boats? But ultimately the man drowns because he said to the three fishermen, "No thanks, God will save me." And when the man drowns, arrives back to God and asks Him, "Where were you?" God looks at the man and says, "I sent you three boats you dummy!" It's a lot like that, but without the dummy part.

The man could've easily survived, but instead of using his survival instincts by jumping onto one of the other boats, he drowned from his own stubborn mindset. This isn't to sound negative to those that have lost a loved one at all! In fact, when a loved one departs, Spirit most of all wants you to embrace the reality that comes with what we are in control of, and what we are not. So could this drowning have been prevented? Yes. But there are going to be moments where a soul is ready to go back Home, and when the soul has made that decision, the process then goes into action indefinitely.

There is such a thing as free will on the Other Side, and so your soul can either choose to learn those lessons, or not. But if you have yet to learn those lessons, then you still have a chance to continue learning them on the Other Side. So this isn't to say that you only have one chance at learning, and at mastering your soul, for it's provided to me that you can still continue learning, and living very much in Paradise.

BEYOND THE GATES

Crossing over is probably one of the most talked about wonders that most want to know is real. Just like many other topics, this too should be handled with great care, for this is something many would disagree with a large dose of animosity. However, this is also probably one of the more fun topics, and I feel it should be explored with curiosity like that of a child in a chocolate factory.

Being on the Other Side is something that was just as crazy talk to me, as anyone else would figure, but I can admit today that I have been there. Not only was I introduced to this miraculous wonder with my best friend Chad, who tragically departed in November of 2012, but I also learned more about how much it is beyond our own imagination!

I was greeted with the open arms of many good souls, and they all were gleaming with an enchantingly colorful glow about them. Each Spirit had their own unique color, and tone of energy flow, that is nothing short of remarkable. They smiled and gleamed with joy, and would spread their love with their own special talents all around.

There were children running and giggling as they played with their own pets from kittens, puppies, lions, to tigers and even bears, oh my! Let's just say, they made it like a giant circus, and it was spectacular! I remember that there were colorful lights within the air, and within us. Colors that even Earth can't even create, because it goes beyond the color wheel.

Never once, did my friend let go of my hand while he took me on this grand tour of Heaven. I was surprised during this adventure, for it was nothing like what so many people actually believe. IT'S SO MUCH MORE!

Believing there are these pearly white gates, or golden gates, I don't know this personally for sure. I think that what God and Spirit had shown me, was just a mere taste of what it is like on the Other Side. Spirit didn't take me to the great gates, because that wasn't the more important part, but to show that they are living beyond our physical forms when they pass. That's the most important message here. They wanted me to see firsthand, to be able to tell you that they are living happy, and very much alive on the Other Side.

I can still recall the sky. It wasn't just blues and pinks, but every color you could possibly imagine, and then multiply that by a million! The ocean wasn't just one solid force, but a force that blended within all, and everything, and everyone. It wasn't some molecule we have come to know here, for it is all energy, thus without boundaries.

Music played throughout the entire Realm. This was not music that you could hear with your ears, but within your energy. The melody didn't have a limitation of sound, but an endless course of streams, that echoed beyond the distance of all. You could feel the music being played within yourself, while witnessing the sound play a rhythmic motion unto every creation, and soul that exists.

HOME SWEET HOME

There are no boundaries in the Realm of Heaven, but an unlimited fantasy beyond our wildest dreams. Even now it's hard to really recall the visit I had the privilege to tour, but the moment that I stepped in this Realm, all I could feel was enormous amounts of love, safety and peace.

This portion is quite important to Spirit that you learn to know. When we cross over, we are not only in the forever bliss of love, and peace, but we also have a Home of our own shared with our own Spirit family. This Home is a place where you and other souls, are to share in abundance, and acceptance of one another. This place you live, is where you will not only have the freedom to do as you please, but to be able to have the support, and continual guidance in your spiritual lessons. The major role that is to be accepted and understood, is you will be able to have unlimited love and security in this Home forever.

As you grow, so will you and your Spirit family. The union with our Spirit family allows you to learn about how companionship truly is, and what it all means to love unconditionally. The family will guide you to hone yourself in your own abilities, and as you grow, so will they. When they grow, so will you. The purpose of the Spirit family, is to fully embrace the true meaning of companionship, loyalty, respect, unconditional love, responsibility, trust, honesty, and accountability.

It is something that most people wonder about when reaching to the Other Side. A loving home, filled with safety, without fear, with a loving family. God makes sure you will have that and *more*, the moment you come back Home to Him, and to your loved ones on the Other Side. God knows how much you hold in your heart, your deepest fears, and what your hopes are, and this book is to help you understand that *He hears you, and more.* There is no fear, or anything uncomfortable on the Other Side, but love, safety and peace.

WAVE YOUR HANDS IN THE AIR

They even know how to have a good time on the Other Side. When our souls cross over, we don't lose our true humor, and our love for laughter, but all of that is actually enhanced a great deal! I can't tell you how many times I have had such wild, and wacky, funny stories told and even shown to me from Spirit during my sessions. They'll stop at nothing to remind us that they're continually laughing, and are full of life on the Other Side. Just because they may be more wise, doesn't mean they don't know how to have a good time. In fact, that is what they celebrate the most on the Other Side, is how to love and to laugh.

One visit from Spirit I will never forget, was when I was being introduced to my Spirit Guides, and some of my Spirit family in a dream. And during this time of being introduced to my Spirit Home, one particular soul I felt was the leader of the family, who stood out the most. He assists the family together, by being the higher role of influence, and guidance. But while he was taking me to the kitchen, and showing me this mountainous amount of food that was beyond glorious, one Spirit came after me saying, "Hey Melinda, you won't believe what I learned! Watch this!" The next thing I see, was this soul forming himself into different shapes and sizes! It was wild, because he then gave himself huge arms, and pecs like he was the Hulk. Even in Spirit, they know how to have a good laugh every now and then. But telling from my face of total confusion at the time, the leader of the family said, "Hey, dude you're creeping her out." When I look back on that now, it's only too funny, and such an awesome memory to hold.

To be clear, these steps I have listed above, and the ones I will be listing later are not necessarily in the exact order. To be honest with you, I don't know for sure, which step is first or last. But again, Spirit never wants us to focus so much on those little details. Spirit's focus is for us to remain on the bigger picture, that they are forever loving, and guiding us from the Other Side. I will never be the type of Medium to say that I have all of the answers. But what I do know is that our departed loved ones are always with us, every step of the way, no matter the Realm.

When our body dies, the soul remains very much alive and well. Spirit never wants you to hold fear of the Other Side, and of crossing over. We all want to have the comfort of knowing that there is nothing to worry about, and that we are never alone or forgotten. Their message here, is to always keep them in your heart, and as long as you do, they will forever help and guide you to hear their voice in endless ways.

Spirit's message is…

"Let not your heart be troubled, for we are a thought away. Your love is ours, and our love is yours forever and always. Keep faith in us, and you will hold faith in Him. You are His love, never forgotten, never left behind."

The Other Side

The concept of the Other Side is complex, not to mention a bit overwhelming. But Spirit wants you to understand that the Other Side coexists with Earth, you and I here, and now. To be factual, there is no such thing as another side or afterlife but instead, a releasing of one's higher self or consciousness from the physical limitations that are in fact illusions. When a person, or to say their physical illusion ceases to function: the consciousness that is connected to Source, to the highest level of intelligence gives way for the soul to embrace their true identity which is energy once again.

So to be clear, there is no such thing as an afterlife for the life that exists is within you. *You are life.* Life is not what happens to you, but *is* you. That being said, when our body dies, the physical illusion is no longer one's "reality" which thus enables the soul to move forward towards a higher level of consciousness. However, for a better understanding of the concepts of "life after death" I will use the phrase the "Other Side" throughout the duration of this book.

THE SCIENCE OF US

The Universe we exist within, not in but within, is massive. We don't live on Earth, but within it, and within all there is, and ever was. The moon, the millions of stars, planets, even a comet to picture are just the small sum of objects floating around within the one hundred billion galaxies of the Universe. According to the amazing astronomers and their best estimates there are at least one hundred billion galaxies in the observable Universe.

Notice the word *observable.* The underlining hint there is more than what the eyes of our experts can see. They were able to count the galaxies in a particular region then multiplied this up to get an estimation of the number of the whole Universe. So even then, they were also able to detect the galaxies also change over time. Such as the Milky Way is on a collision course with its neighbor, the Andromeda Galaxy and both will merge in an estimated four billion years.

Speaking of the galaxies, have you ever wondered what stars are made of? They're made of exceptionally hot gas. The gas is primarily hydrogen and helium, which are the two lightest elements. Stars get their shine by burning hydrogen into helium in their cores then later in their lives create heavier elements.

If you don't think that's impressive then try to imagine the extraordinary findings from successful physicists determining the exact percentage of star mass in our body. That's right, you're made up of stardust. Trying to skip the immense details in their findings, I'll sum it up by saying the human body is about 60% water whereas hydrogen only counts for 11% of that water mass. Even though water consists of two hydrogen atoms for every oxygen, hydrogen has much less mass. They have concluded that 93% of the mass in our body is stardust. With that, physicists have discovered that the apparent density of matter is an illusion created by our human senses. This includes the physical body, which we see and think of as a form. When in truth it's actually 99.99% empty space. The physical body is a misperception of who we are. Which only expresses just how massive space is between atoms compared to their size, while there is as much space again within each atom. How difficult it may be to comprehend this vastness of space in our own bodies not to mention the entire Universe. But the further in depth you go into learning about your physical form you will only learn that you were never a solid form at all but only the illusion of such that is created by the mass, the elements, the energy bundled together. So to say again, your body is essentially formless, that is life founded by the Source of consciousness that exists within the Universe.

This is to suggest that one's ignorance to believe that human existence is the only life form in the Universe is questionable to say the least. I have no doubt that if we can be made up so easily by stars and other elements, there is no reason to think that other lifeforms wouldn't become a likely factor.

You aren't just a person that is sipping a cup of coffee, but exist within that coffee, and all that makes up that cup, and you solid. It's the same with driving your car, riding your bike, walking your dog or reading this book. All that is here and now was created by energy, and that energy coincides with each other, within everything harmoniously.

With these scientific discoveries you can also say it may explain why people that experience visits from souls that have crossed over say they are shimmering beings like that of star like entities. This would also support the common sightings of Angels that is most often described as seeing stars in your midst.

The Other Side is not another "world" necessarily. What Spirit shares, is that it is another Realm within other Realms. To say: *the Other Side is another level of perception and that each dimension is a different level of consciousness of oneself.* Because energy is all that there is, the Realms coexist within each other, including Earth. There is no up or down when it comes to even Heaven or Hell, because every dimension is within other dimensions, coexisting harmoniously without fail. So while one Realm will be functioning in its own energy wave, so can the rest without ever disturbing others within this vast Universe.

TIME IS AN ILLUSION

In the Spirit Realm, there is no concept of time. So with that, there is no past or future. More of, they all coexist within one another in harmony, allowing limitation to be non-existent. That's another reason why some people will say that their near death experiences were quick and slow at the same time. Some have even experienced a sensation on the Other Side during a deep meditative state, that will cause them to feel as if they are moving fast and slow at the same time. This too I have experienced, and to tell you the truth, it almost drove me crazy! I would end up confusing the concept between Earth time, and with the Other Side. The truth that I have come to know with Spirit, is the speed here is not the same there.

To entice your thoughts even more, in the year 1905 Albert Einstein proclaimed a theory stating that the speed of light is constant and absolute – it's always going the same speed, and nothing can go faster than that. In fact, as things travel at speeds approaching the speed of light, strange things would happen to them. They become shorter in the direction of travel, their mass increases, and time passes more slowly for them. Even though space has three dimensions, time only has one. Einstein put them together in one four-dimensional system where space and time cannot be separated, or viewed independently. In his system, energy and mass are actually the same. That is the fundamental point of $E=mc^2$: Energy equals matter times the speed of light squared. You only need a minute amount of matter, say, an atom, to create a tremendous amount of energy. Because Einstein's theory was so strange, to prove this true mathematically, experimenters would carry extremely accurate atomic clocks on high-speed jets while undergoing around-the-world journeys. When they had compared these clocks to the accurate clocks they left at home, the traveling clock would indeed go slower, losing time.

"Everything is energy and that's all there is to it. Match the frequency of the reality you want and you cannot help but get that reality. It can be no other way. This not philosophy. This is physics."

-Albert Einstein

Even though honestly more than half of what Einstein discusses I barely can comprehend, in this theory however, his points made too much sense towards the concept of time on the Other side.

The process of thinking and doing are in the same frequency, occurring at the same moment. The act of doing and thinking are alike, allowing the cause of creation to take place without hesitation. With that, speed is not a factor on the Other Side, but more of a cause of being.

Remaining in the present moment. The present moment is the course of "what happens", the essence of what is in existence now, that is to say the illusion of time is based on what "good" or "bad" moments happen in our lives. And with the course of these moments being the essence that established time itself, would suggest that time is another illusion, only a matter of a false sense of one's perception on the surface. But without those "life moments", experiencing the "good" or "bad" on the Other Side, than how would we know that time is really in play ever? Simply put, it's not.

In fact, to entice this theory further, let's imagine that there was no such thing as the "Other Side." In truth, if you were to stand in your living room with your eyes closed and slowly imagine that there was no couch. There was no coffee table, no TV, no rug, no lights, no fireplace perhaps and whatever else that you can "physically" see in your living room. Then imagine all of that vanishing into thin air along with the floor, the roof, the walls and everything that is "surrounding" you. Including the sun and the moon that gives way for all to rise at dawn and lay at dusk. They all diminish. The items that are "physically limiting" are no longer a factor and without the physical illusions that are limited based on the matter of the "life" expectancy, you wouldn't have anything but the here and now. Can you imagine that? Not yet? Okay what about this…now picture your physical body that you are in –by the way, what does that mean to be *in your body?* How would one *know* they're *in* a body, if they weren't made aware they are made of stardust while possessing the very Universe within themselves? Interesting concept indeed.

How would one know such a thing like this if they were never taught but perhaps just always knew the truth from within their *beingness*?

Now we obviously know that our physical illusion has a time limit expectancy –that is to say, depending on the individual's physical willingness or ability to survive, to live. But then let's say that your body, your physical illusion didn't "die" but just stayed the way it was forever. If our physical illusions didn't "die" then how would we know that time was passing by? If everything was always the same, nothing changed, never facing the gruesome reality of age and everything, literally *everything* remained in the same stream of existence... then all that would be was the presence of *now*.

There would be no past or future but just the now that is in our presence, the existence of life as we know it. The time I am referring to is clock time. The course of the Universe does not rely or function on the Earth's clock but on the existence of presence. With this, there is no restriction such a time or "time limit" but only the course of existence.

ALL TALK NO WORDS

When in our true form on the Other Side, the act of speech is not done in a physical sense, but done by our thoughts and feelings. Telepathy is the dialog that is taking place on the Other Side, and is forever a piece of you even on Earth. If you're not aware of the nature of **Telepathy**, it *is the act of talking without the need of your tongue. It is a communication on the Other Side that is the truest form of dialog done through one's consciousness. A transfer of thoughts, ideas to one or more levels of consciousness beings through the course of energy. Communication* *from one mind to another, by extrasensory means – Te-lep-a-thy.* Telepathy is not hearing others with force but through the natural form of energy that connects everyone in existence together as one.

Imagine your deceased loved one appearing before you in a dream, but you don't hear them in your ears, but rather inside of your core. Communication in Spirit form is done by the course of our feelings which enables each soul the privilege of freedom of speech. The dialog is within the source of your feelings, and with those feelings, relays to other souls where you are emotionally, and even intellectually.

Because Telepathy is based on our thoughts, some people have asked if this means you're not allowed time to your own private thoughts. That is, "Can you have privacy to yourself, without another soul prying into your private thoughts or emotions?" Yes. Reason being is because all souls in Paradise have the absolute dignity, and respect for you, and others when it comes to your privacy. There is no judgment when in Paradise, with that, they give you the leverage of your own thoughts and feelings freely and privately if needed.

Just like how the Earth has its own communication with itself, like flowers, trees, water and other organisms and molecules on the planet, the Other Side has something similar. The Other Side is much more advanced in levels of communication that correspond to all that exists. Telepathy is the only language that exists on the Other Side which is another major reason why many Psychic Mediums, including myself can understand, and communicate with souls that spoke different languages. They don't speak out in the Universe, but inside all that is.

Have you ever thought of someone suddenly, and then get a text from that person? Have you had a song pop in your head, and it keeps repeating over, and over, then sure enough that song is playing on the radio the next time you turn it on? This is no accident, and is a strong indication of your inner ears, listening, and giving you the messages to your human self. This used to drive me insane, because I would recognize this, and then wonder how that was happening so often. Little did I know at the time, that it was all from Telepathy. To say, it was Spirit letting me know ahead of time what it was I would be either hearing or listening to.

We are Spiritual, unlimited beings with potential greater than that of any other physical thing on the Earth Realm. Alive on Earth, we all possess our abilities including Telepathy, without being consciously aware that we're using it. It is the only way our Spirit Guides, Angels, loved ones and God will speak to us on the Other Side when we leave this Realm.

If you wake up from dreaming of a departed loved one, take the time to remember how you communicated with them. I have experienced countless times with Spirit, Angels, and God through the means of dream visitations. The way of hearing is also a process of feeling, along with a strong sense of knowing. You won't have to think or process, or understand what they are saying, you will already hone them in that moment, without confusion or delay. When you are able to accept more of yourself in your spiritual sense, you will be able to have many of these kinds of experiences that will continue to blow your human mind.

Of course many dream visits from our departed loved ones will communicate in the act of speech through human form, but this is only done in order to not confuse you during their visit. Unless you're used to this reality, and have already accepted it, they will continue to visit and speak with you as the human they once were.

There are many people that think they have to learn Telepathy, but I am here to tell you that is completely false. This isn't something you learn, but that you have already acquired the instant you were created in Spirit. It is a part of your higher being on the Other Side, in your true form. The further you accept yourself spiritually, the higher you will notice your Telepathy expands naturally. It will be almost impossible to ignore when you experience this spiritual wonder.

During dream visitations, many have also experienced Angels, their Spirit Guides, and even their loved ones from the Other Side speak to them without opening their physical mouth. Their tongue of Telepathy is that of a spiritual one, that is something you don't learn, but is a part of you. You already have the ability the second you cross over, for it is part of you, and forever will be.

THE SEVEN REALMS

There are different levels of Realms, or Planes of the dimensions on the Other Side. Each level is higher (more energy) than the last, which allows Spirit (human souls) to grow closer to our Source, Creator. Each Plane is different from the next based upon the different amounts of energy, and lessons/ wisdom honed.

Below is a list of each Plane to show you the course at which we ascend to after we master a set of lessons, and a certain amount of wisdom. With each Realm, I will describe each and how they coexist within the Universe. Each Realm is its own specific energy frequency, and with that, so are the souls that reside on those Realms. Each soul has an opportunity to always ascend higher to each Realm as they continue to grow with the help of Angels, Spirit Guides, Ascended Masters and fellow human souls.

To make this clear, to say that these are the only Realms in the immeasurable Universe would be confining the incomprehensible potential. Truth be told we cannot essentially determine for sure just how many dimensions there actually are. So here I share what I know that exist with certainty but to express I have no doubt the high probability that there are many more we humans do not know nor could comprehend.

~ **REALM ONE:** *The Earth Realm (The Material Realm)*

~ **REALM TWO:** *The Astral Realm (A World Between Worlds)*

~ **REALM THREE:** *The Realm Of The Spiritual Concept*

~ **REALM FOUR:** *The Realm Of True Beauty*

~ **REALM FIVE:** *The Realm Of Illumination*

~ **REALM SIX:** *The Realm Of Ascended Masters*

~ **REALM SEVEN:** *Source, Creator And All That Is True*

REALM ONE: *The Earth Realm (The Material Realm)*

This Plane is the lowest of all of the other Planes due to the excessive amounts of dark and negative energies that reside on Earth. Due to the high population of humanity on the Earth Realm, there are more and more souls that become Earth Bound, due to refusing to leave the material world. Earth is meant to be the board game of learning, mastering, and achieving our karmic success by allowing Earthly experiences to be our spiritual teacher. Earth Realm is made up of the physical/ material energy frequency that is very dense, and heavy within the Universe. Souls that discontinue their spiritual journey towards the other Realms, will be extremely limited, and bound to only what is possible on the Earth Realm, which is not our Source, Creator's desire.

REALM TWO: *The Astral Realm (A World Between Worlds)*

Within this Plane, there is a close connection between the Earth Realm, and this one. The Astral Realm is next in line of the Other Side, and is where many will go when crossing over depending on their spiritual lessons, and wisdom attained. Here, souls can easily connect with the Earth Realm, as Earth Bound souls can connect just as easily with the Astral Realm.

During sleep, many people describe an out of body experience (OBE) by doing what is commonly called, *Astral Travel* or *Astral Projection,* where they are able to communicate with Spirit, and the Other Side while still here on the Earth Realm. Most often Astral Travel is described as the soul leaving the body for a temporary moment, to explore the Other Side for very specific reasons. The Astral Realm is a place where most often a departed loved one will visit us during our sleep, while still giving off the feel of the Other Side, as well as the Earth Realm. It will feel light and loving. Many that cross over may remain here for a short time to even decades in order to process, and accept their passing. Other souls from higher Realms may come down to the Astral Realm to greet, and comfort the souls that are newly departed.

REALM THREE: *The Realm Of The Spiritual Concept*

The Third Realm of the Other Side is where the soul has accepted the spiritual concept of themselves, moving on from the material world. Here the soul can choose two paths of their journey to oneness with Creator. One path, they can choose to remain here on the third Realm by acting as a Spirit Guide for another soul that is still on Earth. Or, this soul can choose to reincarnate, and act as a *Lightworker*, to aid humanity by bringing light, love, awareness, achieving a higher level of consciousness amongst all it comes into contact with. Either choice is highly beneficial to the soul's growth. This is considered a placement of higher achievement of awareness and energy. More light, and love reside here, which is what the soul has attained during their spiritual journey.

REALM FOUR: *The Realm Of True Beauty*

The fourth Realm is something no human can experience without mastering the three previous Planes. In this Realm, there is beauty beyond sight, and sound beyond hearing, more than the human body can, or may be able to comprehend. There are no words in order to truly describe, or bring justice to the pure magnificence of this Realm. There is only pure light, and love that reside here. Light that is almost incomprehensible, along with sound, and images that are almost impossible to describe. Sound doesn't echo outward, but *inward*, within all that coexists in all that is energy. The beauty of this place is glorified in ways that will only leave you breathless. The colors are more than just colors, and movements are more than just a physical reference. Everything that is, and will be, is bolder, lighter, purely vibrant coinciding with all that is energy.

REALM FIVE: *The Realm Of Illumination*

Here on the fifth Realm is where all of the highest levels of wisdom, and understanding exist. The highest level of knowledge is obtained, and creation is born. Souls, including Angels of this Realm aid humanity on Earth by bringing new inventions of technology, and ways of healing through reincarnation from this Realm. Souls on this Realm work closely with humanity as either Spirit Guides, to bring the highest levels of enlightenment through humans, or as a reincarnated soul themselves. The highest levels of love and light reside on this Plane in order to establish more cures, ideas and ways of living for the highest good of all concerned.

REALM SIX: *The Realm Of Ascended Masters*

This sixth Realm is the next in line under our Source, Creator. Those that coexist on this Realm are of the highest levels of wisdom, knowledge and an all-knowing Master on all levels. Souls such as Ascended Masters, and Archangels reside on this Plane, and are in direct contact, and communication with God. Ascended Masters include, Buddha, Jesus Christ, the blessed Virgin Mother Mary, and Mother Theresa to name a few.

Archangels that reside on this Plane include, Archangel Michael, Archangel Raphael, Archangel Gabriel and many others. Those that choose to reincarnate from this Plane, do so to serve as teachers for humanity. Souls from this Realm have the Divine ability to come and go from the Earth Realm if decided in order to benefit, and aid humanity. In doing so, their light and energy will be an ever advancing pull, that you will have no choice but to be drawn to their teachings without delay. The purpose of this Realm is to establish an advanced level of consciousness for humanity with our Source, Creator.

REALM SEVEN: *Source, Creator And All That Is True*

This is where the soul reunites with our Source, Creator and obtains the highest levels of knowledge, intelligence, wisdom and an all-knowing. Here the soul has completed their journey. While becoming one with God, the soul retains their individuality as which they were created. When a soul claims their place on this Realm, they are greeted with glory, and a humble gratitude for their accomplishments. Only pure Divine and absolute love coexists here. The souls that reach to this level become one with Source, our Creator, becoming an all evolving powerful force of light, and love.

THE PURPOSE OF EACH REALM

We are born again in order to learn the lessons that which we are meant to master, in order to obtain our birthright, which is to be with our Source, Creator. God doesn't want you, or anyone to think that you have to earn your way to Him in order to be unconditionally loved, or valued. Here, we're shown our reasons for our mistakes, and how to learn from them in order to understand all that there is, and forever will be. The process of growth within each Realm is essential in being able to attain the highest levels of wisdom, intelligence and knowledge possible.

It is no different than going through your life here, and having to attend school. You can't go from elementary school, and jump to high school, skipping middle school. In order to obtain, and attain more knowledge, you have to go through a vast number of experiences. With these experiences, you are then allowed to teach what you have learned, and with that, you will further grow into your higher self, learning how to guide and teach other souls. Counsel is a large reason why Spirit Guides are available to us here, and on the Other Side, for they grow too as we do.

THE HIGHER THE BETTER

The benefits of each Realm are affirmative, for each Plane provides more opportunities of lessons, abilities for the human soul, and knowledge. Each Realm provides more chances for the human soul to ascend to our Creator, which is the ultimate goal. We are not bound by just the physical Realm, but granted more beyond words! As you grow in knowledge and wisdom, so do your levels of energy, which allows you to be more limitless in your capabilities in the Spirit Realm. Many also believe that the higher you ascend, the more God-like you become, which is true! No, you aren't a God to say, but you're limitless with ultimate power that is granted from Source, Creator and the Universe. The more you hone yourself, the far greater your talents, and skills ascend.

Why wouldn't one want to grow? I don't know about you, but if I was told I'm not allowed to grow anymore, I would probably go out of my mind. The idea of never growing further is such a tragedy, not only to the human mind, but to our spiritual selves. The human soul was created to enhance the Universe in billions of ways, and the more you grow, the more you are aiding, and building a more beautiful Universe.

Let's see…what are the benefits of this kind of growth you may ask?

Loads.

Not only do you attain more awareness, but so does your energy. Here are a few of the many benefits to spiritual growth to oneness with Source, Creator, and the Universe…

- *Become Ultimate Awareness of Being*

- *Become A Supreme Vessel of Intelligence*

- *Become An Ultimate Source Of Universal Supreme Love*

- *Become A Supreme Vessel Of Knowledge*

- *Obtain Absolute Wisdom*

- *Become Ultimate Energy Through Source, Creator*

- *Limitless Power From Our Source, Creator The Universe*

Not only are these possible, but they are our birthright and privilege. The benefits are so vast, that it would be impossible to understand all of them at once, which is why we are granted the blessing of lessons. Lessons are a wonderful teacher, and with that, we are able to hone our benefits on the Other Side and on Earth, during and after our experiences. Thanks to the mercy, love, and blessing from God, we are able to receive our gifts through lessons. The benefits are grand, and the way to obtain these blessed benefits is by experiences, and expanding yourself with others. Here are some of the many lessons we are to learn, and understand in order to hone our benefits…

- *Unconditional Love Of Others*

- *Unconditional Love Of Thyself*

- *Worthiness Of Others*

- *Worthiness Of Thyself*

- *Mastering The Concept Of Patience*

- *Mastering The Concept Of Accountability*

- *Mastering The Concept Of Responsibility*

- *Understanding Of Others*

- *Understanding Of Thyself*

- *Forgiveness Of Others*

- *Forgiveness Of Thyself*

- *View Others Without Judgement*
- *View Thyself Without Judgement*
- *Understanding The Act Of Selflessness Through Others*
- *Understanding The Act Of Selflessness Through Thyself*
- *Understanding The Concept Of Self-Sacrifice Through Others*
- *Understanding The Concept Of Self-Sacrifice Through Thyself*
- *Mastering The Act Of Loyalty*
- *Embracing All Emotions Of Existence Without Shame Or Guilt*
- *Mastering The Illusion Of Finding Fault In Others And Thyself*
- *Coming Into Complete Circle With Creator, The Universe And All That Is Energy Through The Course Of Mastering All Karmic Action And Reactions*

Each lesson can take a human soul centuries to master in their course of lifetimes, either on Earth or the Other Side. The more you are able to accept all that is love, the more you will grow closer to your true self, that is an all-knowing being, that is a part of God, who is our Source of all of the Universe.

THE ULTIMATE BLESSING

It is our choice of what we choose to live by. I cannot tell you how much it saddens me when someone chooses hatred over love, simply because I used to be one of them. Not because I didn't want to love, but because I truly didn't understand it. It was out of fear, out of lack of acceptance of myself. But with love, I have been able to grow closer to Source our Creator, and with this knowledge I have been blessed in sharing this with you. We are here to expand, not shrink. We are here to become brighter, not darker. Source wants you to shine your light as brightly as ever possible, and with this information I truly believe that not only will you be able to accept more of who you are, but also in others. Even in our worst of enemies, we are being tested to love others no matter the hardships. Love them, even if they cannot find their love for you. Pray for others that cannot pray for themselves. And find beauty in the darker moments for all you know, you're being shown the true lesson that is meant for you to hone.

Connecting
With The Departed

To communicate with my loved ones, I do nothing different than most others, I pray or talk to them. Now this may come as a shock to some, but you don't have to only pray to God to wish your departed loved ones well, and love on the Other Side. Creator wants you to understand that this is the real deal, and is so passionate to teach us that love on the Other Side doesn't just go to Him, it goes to ALL in Heaven on the Other Side. He is an unselfish being as we have been taught.

I remember doing a reading for a gentleman, and he was such a trooper for he had a difficult time understanding the way I work. He was so set on one way of communicating, and praying, which he thought was to only God. But I shared with him that you can also pray to your departed loved ones, by wishing them love and harmony on the Other Side. He was confused. Then I heard Spirit say, *"Praying to your loved ones is not a way of worship."* When you can separate the difference, then you will be able to no longer feel guilty for praying to your loved ones on the Other Side. So I said to him what I had heard, then added, "God and Spirit know in your heart that you love and honor them no matter what. They know us more than we know ourselves." This is no mistake that we are held by our actions and thoughts, and many of us are raised to believe that if you don't worship God, then you are damning yourself.

NOT TRUE! Don't get me wrong, God is not a force to be reckoned with, however He knows when you pray to your loved ones that you are expressing your love for them. He is not a selfish force that is going to say or think... "What?! You're not talking to me!?" That's not His response, but in fact Source is the exact opposite.

After a few years of my own experiences, I was confused myself. Growing up, I was taught to believe that if you didn't only pray to God, then you were dishonoring Him in some way, but that is far from the truth. He wants you to love and to continue sending your love to your loved ones on the Other Side. Whether it is through prayer, talking, thinking, drawing, painting, singing, dancing, writing or however you send your love out to them in the Universe. God sees that purity in your heart and soul, and is proud of it. His purpose is to teach us love, love in the worst and most difficult circumstances, even if that means being worlds apart. That is our test, and as long as we remain to have love in our hearts, He will never stop you from expressing that passion that He Himself gave you.

This is to help you continue your relationships on the Other Side, and what a better way than to connect with your departed spouse, brother, cousin, friend, or mother in the comfort of your own home? There you are able to find a nice quiet space, where you can **Connect** and wait for a **Response** from them.

Connect and Response, is a term I like to use when you are trying to reconnect with your departed loved ones on the Other Side.

Here you can take what steps I have provided, on how you can easily connect with your loved ones on the Other Side without the use of a Medium. Doing these steps isn't so much of a guarantee. Please keep in mind when trying to connect with loved ones, some souls may have already been reborn here in the physical world, for another chance at life lessons. So if you are not receiving your response, this may very well be the reason.

-Connect: By bringing the memory of your loved one to the surface of your mind and heart to establish an energy connection. This is a simple step, and doesn't require candles or any kind of ritual. If candles suit you better, then by all means go for it. I do like to suggest that if you want to use candles, *only* use white candles when connecting with souls on the Other Side, or when preforming any kind of ritual or a spiritual activity. This brings a sense of peace, tranquility, and holiness to your home and a great ease of positivity. You connect what you attract is what I believe, thus what you focus on is what you will bring about into your life, giving it a way to manifest.

The most effective way in establishing a connection with your departed loved one, is by your feelings. Spirit best responds to our level of compassion, love and even pleas from the deep desire to be reunited with them again. When you are focused on that love, they will hear you the most. Below are a few ways of establishing this connection with your departed loved ones, without delay…

LOVE LETTERS: are a great way in giving your loved ones more of your love to them in different ways. When you write these letters, you can ask them to be present with you, so as to give you the peace and reassurance you need, that they have heard your words.

They may even read, or hear what you are saying inside your head and heart while you're writing the words on paper, or even on your computer. Spirit also says they love it when they are read the lovely letters out loud. They encourage this process for it allows both you and them another chance at closure, healing and a release of any negative emotions they/you could be harboring. You are not responsible for healing your loved ones, but they share this will help you more so, and they always enjoy a moment to have quality time with you in Spirit. If you plan on reading to them out loud, ask them to be present during your reading of the letter. They assure you they will hear each and every word with such appreciation.

PRAYER/SHARING FEELINGS: is a very old, yet powerful way of establishing the connection with your departed loved ones. They don't need a bunch of mumbo jumbo that you are told to buy online in a kit. No, they only need your heart. Their response to hearing our love is so true and pure. When you take the time to include them in your day or in your thoughts, they are always there to listen with unconditional love and genuine appreciation.

PICTURES: are a wonderful and easy route in reconnecting to the memory of your departed loved one. The memories will simply flash back into your mind, uncovering the strong, loving bond you once had with this person. Without much effort, the soul of your loved one, will take heed on knowing you're thinking strongly of them, and if asked, they'll be there to comfort your grief.

ITEMS: that your loved one used to own or cherish, is another wonderful and simple way of connecting with their soul. Their love for you is stronger than ever before, thus when you hold an item that resonates with you of who they were here, they will instantly feel the feelings you're forming in that exact moment. Please understand, our loved ones are not bound, nor connected or attached to any of the items they once owned, or used. The only reason they will connect with you when holding or being near this item, is based off of how it makes you feel.

LOCATIONS: that hold a certain memory whether good or bad in your heart, they will be with you when, and if you return to this space. They do not remain in any particular location such as where they died, simply because they are not bound by this location. Instead, when you take the time to visit locations like their resting place, home, place of work, or even their former bedroom, they will be there the moment you arrive, to help you feel their presence during this thoughtful visit. They do not harbor faults, or resentment if you are not able or haven't visited these locations even if years have passed. Their only focused on what your heart speaks within your soulful being that is eternally connected with them in the massive Universe.

-Spiritual Note: I highly suggest when connecting with a departed loved one, to only do so during the day. This avoids the highly negative hours during the night which some call the, "Witching Hour" or the

"Psychic Hour." *The hours to avoid unnecessary entities when connecting with any souls on the Other Side, is between the hours of 1AM through 5AM. This ensures your safety from negative Spirits that like to trick humans. This is based off of my own spiritual and paranormal experiences, and through my clients' experiences. If you choose to connect with a departed loved one on the Other Side during these hours, you are doing so at your own discretion.*

In order to know if you have established a connection with your departed loved one, I request you look beyond sight. It may sound a bit cliché, the truth is however, Spirit establishes connections best, based upon how you may be feeling.

Some say, they will immediately start feeling happy when they start talking with their loved one. Some have shared they will begin to feel a slight touch on their cheek, because they gave their loved one permission –But touches from Spirit are not for everybody. For it does require a bit of tolerance to accept this spiritual nature.

*-**Spiritual Note:** Our departed loved ones will never touch you without your said permission. If you are being touched by an unseen force, and it doesn't make you feel comfortable, then this is NOT your loved one. It would be foolish to not give you fair warning in the Universal truths on the Realms beyond this that not all entities are good nor trustworthy. Take your intuition into account. Beware that some entities are devious by originality, veiling you into believing they're your loved one, so please remain cautious.*

-Response: where you begin to see a response of that love you give to your departed loved one coming back to you in the same, or greater harmonious intention. After you have established a connection, the next step is to wait for their response to reflect back to you. The response from our departed loved ones will happen in various ways, so be sure to keep your heart and mind open during this time. Their response usually isn't right away as one would expect. In fact, they will send you their love in the time at which they have determined will be the most effective way, for you to receive and recognize their loving messages. Some may have to wait for a response back in a few hours, or in a course of a few weeks, to months. It all depends on whether or not you are emotionally able to receive their messages, without hindering your heart more. Once we are in alignment with what we are asking, that is when the messages will begin to flow because we are more receptive to receiving them with appreciation.

The further you read throughout this book, you will see almost countless ways Spirit will send messages back to us. Just keep an open mind to what they may be sending you. Think out of the box, looking into the possible, in- depth underlying messages you may be receiving and just haven't noticed yet. There are so many countless ways Spirit communicates back to us, that I've decided to incorporate that throughout the majority of this book. There's just too much detail to only put it in a list, a list simply wouldn't suffice for the idea I want you to picture when it comes to Spirit's dialog.

THE POWER OF THOUGHTS

I had a reading experience with a woman, and I could sense in her email the urgency that she held for guidance from Spirit. Although she didn't tell me who she was wishing to connect with, I kept hearing over and over the word, "husband." That broke my heart, and I had hoped it wasn't true, for the passion I had felt was strong towards her from Spirit. Later on however, she had indeed confirmed, that it was her husband that had passed away.

While I was sending her validations and conformational messages from her beloved, I felt a need to ask her if she had many unanswered questions.

After I feel all the important needed messages are sent, then I will ask my client what questions they may have in return to give them anymore clarity that they may need to move forward.

She did, and the most common question I get from my clients including her was, "Can you tell him I love him, and miss him?" Without hesitation I told her, "You don't need me to tell him that. You have the ability to tell him yourself by just saying, thinking or feeling it. Our messages are fueled by strong emotions, and those emotions then create an energy frequency out to the Universe, which then connects to your loved ones. He hears you now as you ask me."

Spirit says, *"You don't need a Medium for us to hear your love."* All they need is you and you alone. Of course, it doesn't hurt to ask for a Medium's help to give you specific messages or validations that you may be in search of, but ultimately, the use of a Medium for you to send your love is not required nor necessary. Spirit works solely on love. The love we hold for them is harvested from energy and when that love (that is energy) is transferred to them through our thoughts, they hear and feel those feelings. They are not long gone to hear your love or your messages at all, in fact they can hear and feel you more than you can hear and feel them. Did you know that? The reason is because they are on a Plane that is cleared from the chaos of the world. Their way of hearing, seeing and understanding is not used by a body that they once borrowed here, but of their soul which is a strong spiritual being that was and will remain to be eternal.

If you are ever in the need to send your love, you can do so either through the act of spoken words or your thoughts. Our departed loved ones hear us indefinitely. Literally the instance you are either thinking, remembering or imaging your loved one, they are receiving that frequency that is charged by your thoughts and emotions. In fact, did you know that whenever you find a memory or thought arise in your mind randomly of your departed loved one, it's happening because of them thinking of you too? It's true! Because we are all interconnected by the indestructible bond tied by the energy that is Source, all souls including the ones on the Other Side are able to send their love to you through their thoughts. So the next time you suddenly, without explanation start thinking of your departed loved one, remember this Universal truth.

RETHINK OUIJA

I know there are numerous other methods when contacting the dead, like so many have said they have used a *Ouija board*. Ouija is a board also known as a *Talking Board* or *Spirit Board* that allows people to communicate with the dead. This device was created originally back in the year 1894. It is a flat board marked, or even the oldest of boards are engraved with the alphabet, the numbers 0-9, the words "yes", "no", and even "hello". Not all, but most boards will have "goodbye", along with various symbols and designs to enhance its mysticism. To use such a board, you would introduce yourself, while calling attention to the souls on the Other Side and then proceed with your questions. In order for a soul that is using the board to answer back, the person(s) using the board must have their hands placed very lightly on the Planchette, (a heart-shaped piece of wood or plastic with a circular glass seeing through the center). This moveable indicator allows the Spirits to relay their messages back, by spelling it out on the board during the séance, or session. It would have to move while the fingertips of the participants are placed ever so gently on the top of the Planchette. However, I must ask that you rethink this method, for it is ***not the way*** you may want to go about connecting with your departed loved ones.

You may be wondering, *"Well what's the difference between using a Ouija Board vs a Medium?"* The difference here is vast due to the amounts of caution that Mediums are usually aware of. See, when a Medium connects with Spirit, they only do it with a limited amount of connection for we have overall control of what information we receive, and how we receive it. Whereas with a Ouija Board, there are *no limits* to how Spirit will come through. Spirit can manipulate the board because one, you gave it the power to, you granted the Spirit permission to infest in your life and in that board to communicate with you.

Then some people ask, "But what if I am only asking for one soul, like a family member or a friend? Doesn't that then limit who comes through the board?" Unfortunately, no. The reason is because a Ouija Board is an empty device, that you and other people give the Spirits permission to manipulate the board. However, what a lot of people also forget to realize, is when you speak to Spirits to come through the board, you are essentially inviting ALL Spirits. Whether "good" or "bad", they WILL hear your call, and come through whether you wanted them to or not. Now can you limit that by saying something specific to make sure that only certain souls come forward? I believe so –but that is still NOT a guarantee that only those that you call forth will come through. When you use those devices, you are using them at your own risk, no matter how safe you try to be.

A Medium works with the help of Angels, Spirit Guides and God. Not all Mediums use their gifts for this, but most do, and very rarely have I ever met another Medium that would talk of being possessed, without the permission of that Medium. For example, I prefer to only connect with a client's loved one and with the protection and guidance from my Spirit Guides, God, and Angels. I do not ever allow a Spirit that either I don't know personally or that my client doesn't know on a personal level, for the risk of attacks is highly probable.

With that, when a person uses a Ouija Board, most are people that don't have any experiences with the paranormal or supernatural at all, and are doing it usually out of curiosity. However that is how you can get into large amounts of trouble if you're not aware of the possibilities, and the potential dangers. Especially if the person(s) are not aware of how to shield themselves properly, with the Spirit Guide's or Angel's assistance.

Another question I have heard is, "What if there is a Medium using the Ouija Board? Does that make it safe?" No, and actually it can become even more risky, especially if that Medium is going to use possession during the séance by choice. Personally, I don't do séances, due to experiencing Spirits that refuse to listen to your requirements during the sessions, for they still do what they choose anyway because of the Universal Law of Free Will. We must also remember, that not all Spirits that come through those boards are going to do what you tell them, or ask them. More than half of them that come through are usually Earth Bound souls that are rebellious and refuse to move to the Light, to Heaven.

If you're ever thinking of communicating with your departed loved ones, I would please urge you to **rethink using a Ouija Board.** This is just my own personal opinion, and you are able to take it or leave it. I will never say the board itself is evil, but I will say this…

"It's not the gun I would be worried so much about, but the person that is holding the gun."

That being said, you're still able to connect with your loved ones on many levels and with many ways without the use of tools or equipment at all. There is no need for any of those things, and to tell you the truth, I have seen people receive more validating messages from Spirit, without them ever having to use a device at all. More than half of the time, Spirit doesn't need you to use those things…you just need to keep your heart and mind open to the endless possibilities. Spirit is endless in surprising us, and it's up to you how you choose to handle and accept those messages.

ASK FOR A SIGN

Asking departed loved ones for you to receive some kind of a sign or a message from them can be very effective. It would be fair for your loved ones if you give them the freedom to send you messages of their love more openly. If you ask for an eagle on Monday at 4 o'clock, it's not giving your loved ones enough leverage for their message to be the most healing for you.

They encourage you to ask for signs of love, healing or encouragement, but try to remain open to their message with patience and understanding. Spirit's ability to communicate with us is incredible, and only can be even more incredible, if we allow them the freedom to be creative on their own terms. The purpose of their messages is to send you love in their unique way so you know it's from them specifically. Limiting how they do so, wouldn't be the most beneficial for you in knowing that this is from your loved one.

Not always are they going to be moving objects, or messing with your electronics. Sometimes it can be as simple as putting a song on the next few times you hear the radio that will remind you of them.

Personally I like to write letters in my journals to my departed loved ones, and in doing so, I am establishing the *connection* while writing because of the feelings, and the visualizations my heart is creating in the Universe. Thus, with the connection, I then am able to start receiving that same *response* back from Spirit. This is a wonderful way of expressing how you feel, without having to say anything, but by visualizing.

If you're able to stomach this next option then I would also like to suggest another way of connecting with your departed loved ones. The reason why I say "stomach" is due to the amount of awareness and tolerance it takes to handle this because a lot of people seem to have a hard time accepting that it's okay, and very common. You can also ask your loved ones to touch your shoulder, or hand, or wherever you feel comfortable to receive a confirmation that they're with you. Most folks I have noticed are terrified of being touched and would rather not, which is why I don't suggest this to just anyone. But only to those that feel they can handle it without fear.

Once you can eliminate the fact of being touched by an unseen force, and focus on the fact that it's your loved one, and not some random Spirit, then the fear is no longer a factor.

The first few times I got touched by my friend Chad, it was wild! But then after a while, it wasn't so hard to maintain my composure when receiving those messages. In fact, there was an instance I was in a local store in Anchorage with my daughter, Josslyn, twin sister Carolyn, and my baby nephew Dominic. I had just stepped away, feeling an energy *pull* to a certain aisle.

And while I was looking at various lipstick options, the next thing I know, I felt a tug on my shoulder. It caused me to look behind me, but to my surprise no one was there. I literally had to keep staring around me, hoping if someone would just acknowledge that look of, "Oh sorry, didn't mean to tug you." But no one did. It was just so unexpected, that I immediately went back and told my sister.

Your loved ones don't want to scare you, but only give you the message that will build you up, and help you move forward in this life. It took me a few months to get used to it, but over time it came to the point where if I didn't feel Spirit's touch, literally daily, I'd begin to feel as if I had lost a limb or a part of my norm.

If you have experienced touches from Spirit, you are not alone. There are countless people that have witnessed/experienced the same phenomenon. The only caution is to remain very specific, and ask only your loved one that is departed to give you this kind of sign. As there are many possible souls that may also try to touch you, and pretend they are who you think, or hope they are. This is also something that you would be doing at your own risk if decided. Again, there are NO guarantees that it could be your loved one, but maybe with the help of a Medium or another spiritual source, they can assist you in knowing for sure. You can also ask Angels to be present and to give you the reassurance that it is your loved one that is either around or touching you through a dream visitation by simply requesting.

Not always will our departed loved ones give us this kind of sign, for it also depends on their energy vibrational level and the reason behind why you are asking. If you are only asking because you want it for entertainment, or to see what happens, nine times out of ten, they won't bother. But if it comes from the heart, they will hear your plea, and usually will be able to give you that small touch to give you a sign.

REINCARNATION

During my sessions if a soul is not able to come through during a spiritual connection, this is usually based on the Universal understanding that all souls have to go through what is known as a *Reincarnation Process*, in order to continue their spiritual growth. All souls will reincarnate at least once in order to fully embrace their understanding of certain lessons they have yet mastered. Reincarnation is *where a soul is reborn on the Earth Realm during the present moment of Earth.* So for example, if a woman named Susan had died in a car accident in the year 2015 and she and Spirit decided it'd be best if she reincarnate in the year 3000, then Susan would have to wait during the present moment for the year 3000 to arrive to Earth *presently*. She would not be able to zoom to the future to be reincarnated for there is no future in Spirit but only the present moment that is currently the Earth time that it would be. As I have stated before, there is only the present moment that is in existence of Spirit's nature of one's being. If Susan chooses to reincarnate she would have to wait for the time at which she chose to arrive on the Earth Realm. Essentially she would patiently wait for the specific Earth year to arrive in order for her to be reborn in a new life as a new physical form.

Now to challenge this concept a little more, let's say Susan wanted to visit a past life –let's say around the 1800s. Then Susan would have to travel back in time, that is, Earth's timeline in order to relive (re-experience) her previous life in the 1800s. She would not be able to reincarnate in the 1800s because the 1800s no longer exist on the Earth Realm *presently*. Instead she would only re-experience a past memory which many would most commonly call **Time Travel**. You cannot relive your past but only re-experience it. One cannot simply go back into time to redo something that is already done. This is most commonly known throughout other spiritual and religious beliefs, based on the deep knowing that we cannot learn everything by perfection but through the acceptance of life and love through much experience.

Reincarnation is simply to allow the soul to be reborn to extend one's vibration by expanding knowledge through further Earth experiences. When the soul chooses to reincarnate, the soul connection will not be established during a session, due to no longer holding any memory of their previous life. However, do not be discouraged, for this is a joyous moment for the soul to continue their journey at being one with Source, Creator.

So, if you are doing the best you can, and cannot seem to find any response back from a departed loved one, Spirit would like you to keep this in mind.

A REASSURING KNOWING

Spirit knows more about our hearts than we may think. They know when you visit their resting place, look at their photos, or read a poem they once wrote. They never stop visiting and loving us more than we could ever imagine that was ever possible. It may be a bold statement, but the truth is the Other Side is real and the myth, is that it doesn't exist. Spirit knows when you think, and miss them as hard as you may do. They ask you to never, for one second, ever doubt their eternal existence, for they do hear and feel your love just as much as you do.

Spirit Communication

Once Spirit knows that they are filled with freedom on the Other Side, that is when Spirit will try to communicate with us on every level possible. Our loved ones know how much we miss them. They know how much we think about them, how much we pray for them, and they do the same for us just as much. During the times where you may feel more alone without them, that is the time they will be with you the most. Our loved ones never left, but are just in a different form, that allows them to be there for all of their loved ones more than ever before.

In order for me to give you plenty of examples to show you just how much they are with us in every part of our lives, I am going to give you a list of the most influential ways they can communicate with us personally. Each topic will consist of examples to relay to you different levels at which Spirit can communicate by the power of influence.

⟋ **THE INFLUENCE OF ANIMALS**

⟋ **THE INFLUENCE OF CHILDREN**

⟋ **NUMBER SEQUENCES**

⟋ **DREAM VISITATIONS**

~~~ **APPARITIONS**

~~~ **PARANORMAL ACTIVITY**

~~~ **THROUGH MUSIC OR MOVIES**

~~~ **THROUGH OTHER PEOPLE**

~~~ **THROUGH THE GIFT OF SMELL**

These are the most influential ways that I have found Spirit to bring their messages forward, in order for us to hear and feel them. I have witnessed so many ways Spirit brings their messages for their loved ones, that it continually surprises me.

When I first started learning about my Mediumship, one of the first things that I had to accept, was that nothing is as it seems. To explain, something may seem like a "coincidence" at first, but once you start to open up your mind and your heart to the unlimited possibilities, that is when you begin to solve the mysteries that are being laid out before you.

~~~ **THE INFLUENCE OF ANIMALS**
PAW PRINTS

That exact similar message happened to a friend of mine back in the year 2013. He was put in an unfortunate place where he had to put his beloved dog down. Sometime after, something happened to him that he wanted a bit of clarity on. He said, "I had to put my dog down as you know, but something strange happened the next morning after, and I want to know your thoughts about it. I woke up and as I opened my front door of my house, there were fresh dog tracks from my door, leading all the way down the street in the snow. But then I debunked it because I saw it was a stray dog walking around the neighborhood."

This is a profound example of how much people forget to stop looking with their eyes and look with their hearts. Of course my heart goes out to my friend, because he was absolutely devastated when he lost his pup, but I almost wanted to shake him awake! After a few minutes of letting him vent off his frustration, I then told him, "You need to look at the bigger picture. Just for a minute, think about this possibility. Did it ever occur to you that Spirit brought this dog to your door, leading those tracks, so that way you could have a larger sense of hope and love in your heart? Spirit is a very influential being and they will ask other people, and even animals, to do their work in being able to send their messages to you."

He thought about this, but quickly argued that it was nothing but coincidence. And that's okay. This is a very illustrative example that until you can allow your heart to open to that kind of love, you will only look at it as nothing but a "coincidence" on the surface.

WHAT THE QUACK!

A few months after I had learned of my dear friend Chad's passing, I was invited to be a maid of honor to another longtime friend's wedding. It was indeed an honor, and it was a gift that I will forever treasure. However during this trip and being involved in the wedding, I couldn't help but feel even more depressed.

Because I was trying with all of my might to be supportive for my friends, I would do what I could to shake this pain I was continually enduring. Then one day, after having a conversation that made me remember even more about Chad, I decided to go out on their porch, in their backyard. Tears were being held back as I asked Chad to give me a sign, anything to help me feel that he was present. While gazing at the river that was located directly behind their backyard, something remarkable happened. Standing there, feeling even more alone than ever, I all of a sudden was struck with this beautiful, graceful sight. Three ducks soared from the river, flew towards my direction, making a complete circle in the yard, then quickly made way out of sight down the river. It was such an incredible moment, for I can still remember the sound their wings made when they soared. Joy consumed my heart and a huge smile rang through my whole body. I couldn't believe what I had just witnessed, and the message I had gotten was even more overwhelming. For then one of my friends told me that one duck was female, while the other two were male. It told me then that they were symbolic. The female duck represented me, and the two males are my friends Aaron and Chad watching over me.

Even now it blows my mind just how incredible Spirit is when they really want to be. The influence of animals from Spirit, is a wonderful and beneficial route when giving you loving messages. Spirit can use the gift of any animal, or insect, to come across our path in order for us to receive the answers to our pleas. Spirit can ask the animals, influence animals or even influence us to a certain degree, in order to give us the messages that we need with love and validation. And because Spirit is a part of the Universe, it ensures that you're able to see these animals in the exact moment when you need to. Their timing is absolutely epic.

THE INFLUENCE OF CHILDREN

Do you remember the movie The Sixth Sense? Not only do I love Bruce Willis, but this film has a lot of truth when it comes to the nature of spiritual influence on our children. Now I don't believe that our loved ones will show your child something scary, but this does help us to see what your child may be experiencing.

Why do you think Spirit would influence children more than adults? Well, what does a child possess naturally more than that of an adult? Imagination, hope in a fantasy land, or their inner child. They dream of flying with Peter Pan and Tinker Bell. They visualize the possibility of being able to see Santa Claus in his big red suit after he slides down the chimney, and hopefully doesn't get stuck.

Our children are the most susceptible in being able to hear and see Spirit more than an adult, primarily due to them being closer to the time at which they were born. This is a large factor, for the younger the child is, the closer to the time at which they spent with Spirit on the Other Side before coming here. From the time of birth, each child is considerably close to their core of their spiritual self, which enables them to hear, and connect with Spirit easier. As they grow into adulthood, the connection for most adults begins to fade, that is, depending on their life mission and purpose and most of their state of awareness.

TO THE CORNER AND BACK AGAIN

Spirit will influence our children in order to give us the sign that we won't be able to debunk. When your child says something, or does something that you know isn't explainable, that is when you can keep your mind, and heart open to the major possibility of Spirit at work.

When my friend Aaron passed away from pneumonia, I was completely devastated, and held a lot of passion hoping he would come forward somehow. But nothing happened for months that I would be able to say, "Now that's him for sure." But then one morning, just as I had slept for what felt like weeks, I saw my daughter sitting on my bed with me. She was only three years old at the time, and she pointed up to a corner of the roof of my bedroom, while saying, "Guy." That's all she kept saying. I asked her, "You see a guy, honey?" She then looked back up at the same corner and repeated, "Guy."

For a long time I thought this was just a mere "coincidence", but then once my friend Chad died a year later, I woke up to the same thing! However, now she did it *twice*, pointing at two corners of the roof this time. "Guy, guy." She said, "Guy" in both directions of both corners, and it was one of the most shocking "coincidences" I'd had then. It struck me for she'd never done this before. It was a convincing moment that there's so much more than what most adults may see and feel compared to a child.

MY "FRIENDS"

Have you ever watched your child play by themselves, but then quickly realize they're talking to someone else? Sure, many would consider this to be just imaginary friends, but…*are they really?* Imaginary friends are great for the structure of a child to be able to build upon their own unique imagination and fantasies. But when you start to notice they include them more in their life, as if a person is really there, that is when you can really start to wonder.

Now I'm sure you may be wondering, *"But how can you tell the difference between them making up these characters, or if they're real?"* There are a few ways to tell the difference when investigating this. Below is a list I think will help in being able to tell the difference between your child's imaginary friends, from a possible Spirit influence...

- *Has your child said a name of someone that is deceased, even though you never told them about this person?*

- *Does your child draw pictures of characters, symbols, shapes, letters or names of the person that you know is departed?*

- *Do you catch your child talking to someone that isn't physically there on a regular basis, especially at night before bedtime?*

- *Have you seen your child do, or say something that you never taught, or said to them and* **know** *no one else has?*

- *Has your child talked about dreams they have about someone talking to them? Does this person in their dream relate to someone that you know is departed?*

- *Have you heard your child say a phrase, or a specific word that you know a departed loved one would say, or use frequently?*

- *Out of a very random moment, does your child come up to you and give you a hug for no reason at all?*

Does another person's child come up to you and hug you for no reason at all?

Has either your child, or another person's child come up and given you something, that is special to them for no reason at all?

Does your child, or another person's child, say something that sounds as if God, or Spirit was speaking through them to you? A word, or a phrase that sounds like something you needed to hear, exactly at that moment?

If you answered "yes" to any of these, you may very well be getting messages from Spirit through either your child, or through other children. Spirit won't always go up to your child and ask them to do those things. Most likely, the child will hear Spirit in their own intuitive way from God, and give the message without even realizing it.

Children are extremely susceptible to Spirit, and with the Other Side. They don't have to be aware that it is happening for the connection to be there.

More than half of the occurrences that take place, is a child thinking they are talking to another live person. Or if you ask them why they did or said something, you will find they may simply say, "I just felt like doing it." Children are an accessible vessel to the Other Side, due to their natural ability to keep imagination and a strong sense of an open mind. It is very important to realize that the moment Spirit is connecting with our children, we have to take the time to look at why. Then point to when it happened, and what you were thinking at that moment, before, during and after. Reason being, more often than not, Spirit takes the time to communicate with our offspring in order to help us see what we may not notice. I like to say, "When it's out of the mouths of babes, then it's gotta be something important."

NUMBER SEQUENCES

When the topic of Number Sequences comes up, I get a lot of quizzical looks. This is not something to be intimidated about, and I am certainly not about to tell you it's mathematics either. Lord knows I suck at math *terribly,* even with the help of a calculator.

What this is, is *an arrangement of numbers that bring you messages from the trigger of the placement of the numbers.* When you lose a loved one, it can be especially difficult at times to really pay attention to anything around you. However, because Spirit knows this about us, they will take the time to give us the sight of certain numbers that relate to the loved one that is departed.

For example, Chad died on November 17, 2012. Everywhere I go, I will see the number 11/17, as the expiration date, or let's say, on a product I am about to buy. Or I will look at the clock, and the time will be 11:17 and I will automatically be brought back to the memory of my friend.

What is even more interesting about Spirit, is when I was just about to start this topic, I had received a sign from Chad that just made me laugh out loud. I had noticed there was a bottle of sauce sitting on the counter in the kitchen. I thought this was odd, due to the fact that I knew I didn't take it out of the refrigerator, and not to mention, I hadn't used this sauce in weeks. I was even more taken aback at this idea, for then I heard Spirit say for me to look at the bottle cap. To my surprise the date revealed the meaning. The expiration date of this bottle of sauce was no joke, November 17, 2014. How wild is that?! I laughed and smiled my usual smirk, and just said, "…Thank you, love you too."

This is no accident and never a coincidence. We are being shown signs by the Heavens and it is my mission to help you recognize when the messages are being placed right in front of your nose.

It can be a challenge however, to really understand which numbers mean what situation, or person. This is when I like to urge my clients, that whenever you see the same number repeatedly, then it's time to analyze what it is you have been thinking at those moments, when the numbers appeared. Then clarify the meaning to yourself, by trusting the first thought that comes to mind. Doesn't matter whether it makes sense to someone else, what matters is that it makes sense to you, because they're messages specifically designed for you.

Some of the more prominent signs from Spirit with numbers are when you look at the clock, or anywhere and regularly see the numbers synchronized. Like 222, 333, 4444, 1111, 1717, 1212, 1010, 4747, and so on. Or if you see numbers that make you remember your loved one. Like the number from their work uniform, or the date, or age of when they passed, anniversary, birthdate or even an address. The possibilities are absolutely endless when it comes to Spirit and numbers.

The moment you see these numbers, is when Spirit is trying to catch your attention to heighten your state of awareness, that they're indeed with you, and are guiding you on your journey in your life.

DREAM VISITATIONS

In our sleep we become naturally in tune with the Spirit Realm, thus allowing Spirit and our departed loved ones an opportunity to connect with us on a very deep level. Being consciously aware of the idea of what may be happening supports the insight to the potential messages you are receiving. More so, recognize the feelings we get when we see our loved ones in our dreams.

DREAM SIGNS

Regularly I will see ducks in my dreams, and they will surround me with love and warmth that is overwhelming. Laughter, with a deep sense of peacefulness will intercept into my soul and I will wake up feeling incredible. Ducks are a personal message that my friend Chad is forever with me, in his own unique way. Reason for ducks is because duck hunting was one of his favorite hobbies when physically alive. Or I will hear his voice call out to me in my dreams, and then I will wake up with tears, feeling so much love, that all I want to do is dance and smile. What's even more intriguing is due to his unmistakable humor I will even go into a deep sleep state which takes me to a trance and during this trance I will almost immediately be interrupted from a loud "quack" echoing in my ears that sounds as if it came from an actual duck. *No kidding* –he actually does that and it always makes me laugh. But this I believe has much to do with my Psychic Abilities such as Clairaudience where I have the ability to hear Spirit voices and sounds etc.

Spirit will bring about into your dreams something that will help remind you of them instantly, without question. If you cannot feel it right away, then it usually isn't a visitation, but more of yourself manifesting them into your sleep because you thought of them often. It can be difficult at first to know which dreams are visitations, and which dreams are just from your subconscious. But the more often you take the time to notice the signs, the easier it can be to tell the difference.

When you receive a message from your loved ones, you will know the supreme difference between a dream created from your subconscious and a visitation from Heaven. Most often those that are in their dream state will recite the level of undoubtedly exceptional vividness of the occurrences. The dreams will be so real you will almost be mistaking yourself for being physically awake due to the supernatural sharpness throughout one's experience. From sounds, touch, to color it will all feel so true that most often one is unable to deny this miraculous intention/ visit from Spirit. Another major sign is by the energy you have when you wake up. Most often, our loved one's loving presence will grant us enormous amounts of energy that we will feel on top of the world. You will almost feel like your biggest crush just gave you a hug, or a kiss. It will feel as if you just fell in love for the very first time, by the man or woman of your dreams.

Others have also shared that when they receive visits from a departed loved one, they will remember their loved ones *glowing*. This is most common due to their level of Godlikeness when reaching more to oneness with Source in Heaven. I too have witnessed my departed loved ones in this similar impression. There was one very particular dream I had, where I had found myself standing before my friend Chad. He was the most glorious sight I had ever seen, and in the moment I didn't realize where I was, but as I looked into his eyes longer, it dawned on me. I was standing before a person who was once alive, but now technically deceased. Even more remarkable, his aura was something magnificent. He was *golden...glowing* and *shimmering* like nothing I had ever seen before. His eyes, his clothes, his energy was something so pure, so... brilliant, I was almost dumbfounded. He obviously noticed my apprehension from my face, and said, *"It's still me, Melinda..."* His smile, everything about him was so,... *Angelic.*

As written in the King James Bible, Jesus appears before James and Peter up on a high mountain alone, where Jesus shows His glory before them. They described His face as glowing like the sun, and His garments became white as light. The text reads, *"And was transfigured before them: and His face did shine as the sun, and His raiment was white as the light."*

(Matthew 17:2) Now, as I have mentioned before, I don't believe you have to go only to Christ to be accepted in God's kingdom. However, this text greatly supports these modern day experiences my clients and countless people all over the globe are witnessing every single day.

APPARITIONS

I'm sure you've heard someone talk about how they saw someone at the corner of their eye, but then they express that the unknown figure would be gone the second they looked at it directly. This is a pretty common experience that I have learned over the years that a lot of people tend to be shy to share, but you really needn't be. Have you yourself witnessed your own glimpse of an apparition, but you too couldn't debunk, or explain it? For sure it's no shock that people are coming out of their fear of judgment, and are sharing their own paranormal experiences. It's a taboo that is quickly becoming the norm. Sure, it can be scary, heck they still freak me out especially when they walk through my hallways in the middle of the night. Although, the only reason why it would startle me, is because I don't expect it a lot of the times. Not so much that the Spirit is there.

I'LL HAVE A SPIRIT STRAIGHT UP

My mother, Kathleen has always been the easily conversational type, which made it natural in her past years as a bartender to have people open up to her. However, it didn't take long until weird unexplained things would occur at this one particular bar where she worked.

During her work hours, when she was preparing to switch off the "Open" light, that lay in exposure of one of the bar windows, she then spotted a man sitting at the bar. Not thinking anything of it, she quickly went behind the bar to fetch his drink of choice. As she slid him his drink, he calmly sat at the bar with minimal eye contact. Normally she will keep people's mystery to themselves let alone their own problems but she couldn't help but feel this man was sobbing in silence.

She looked at him in compassion and asked, "Are you okay?" He looked at her with grief in his eyes, not saying much. There she knew something wasn't right, so told him the drink was on her. He sat there in front of her, paused, his body motionless as the words of the unspeakable fell from his quivering lips asking… "Does God forgive murderers?"

Being as this isn't your typical bar conversation, she remained calm for she could see his eyes were filled with guilt. Very calmly she listened to this stranger's words, but not too long after he waited for her response. She looked at him, and told him with love, "As long as you know in your heart that what you did was wrong, and want to take it all back...then yes." He gazed up at her as tears swarmed from his eyelids. Breathless, he responded, "Thank you. You are one of the nicest people I have ever met..." He then gave her his glass and asked for another round. But as she turned around to put the soiled glass behind the bar, she soon discovered that this mystery man was gone without a trace.

Spirit doesn't come to us without a greater cause in their soul. In this example, the soul of this man came to my mother because he felt in his being that my mom could assist him with forgiveness in himself. Some souls will appear to us in need of assistance, guidance, or even to deliver a message. Spirit is not without love, regardless of who they were in their lives here. They are just as loved as anyone else, no matter the mistakes they had made, and regardless of the choices or path they chose. When an apparition of a soul is presented before us, we must take time to ask ourselves, *why*.

There is this horrible stereotype, and misconception, that if you see an apparition then it must be because of a haunting. But I can tell you flatly, that is not always the case. It depends on the behavior of the soul, intentions of that soul and the level of their own energy vibration from lessons mastered.

-Spiritual Note: Not all souls that come forward are "good" natured. So please pay close attention to the feelings you have when you come into contact with a soul. If you have chills, with the inability to stop

shaking, then chances are you may be in contact with something negative. If you have a warm feeling of happiness, love, and security from a soul, then this is a sign of one being positive.

PARANORMAL ACTIVITY

Oh my, where do I start?! There are *way* too many instances to give about the impressions of paranormal activity. Paranormal activity occurs when Spirit wants us to hear their messages, no matter how minor that message may seem. I won't lie, many of my experiences of paranormal activity have been nothing short of mind boggling. But it doesn't go without saying, that no matter the kind of activity that occurs, they are doing their best at giving you the answers or message that either they need to share for closure, or that you need to hear for your own closure. The fact is...mainly most often it's about giving, or getting closure.

"WHAT THE...?!"

After Aaron passed away from pneumonia, I was as I said, devastated but not so much for me, but for him. Not too long after his passing, there were weeks of crazy, unexplained things happening. Simple things like, the radio turning on by itself, having no way of being able to debunk it. I still remember my reaction and how freaked out I was, and what's more...this was during the day. It wasn't at night like you would see in the movies. Of course I was freaked out, but to be fully honest with you –this only intrigued me more. But then, it got even more interesting to the point where I finally had to argue with Spirit to stop messing with my belongings. Little did I know, later I would discover that it was

Aaron, who was only trying to say he was okay, and in his case…it was to screw with my sanity.

Once I learned that Aaron was the culprit, I started witnessing even more unexplainable things occurring right in front of me. One instance I'll never forget was a bright, sunny summer day, and I was cleaning the kitchen to clear my head as I usually do. My daughter, Josslyn was in her room watching a movie. As I was cleaning, something happened after I had just got done wiping down the countertops. A little after I walked to the dining table and started rearranging items to bring a bit more organization to the surface, I began to hear a drizzling sound. I looked over my shoulder in the direction of the sink, but it wasn't on. I brushed it off, then went back to organizing the mail. But then I heard it again. After I placed the mail on the table, I walked to the kitchen that is open to the house, and then realized that the salt shaker had been moved. But not just moved, but had led a straight line of salt across the entire countertop, leading to the end, all the way to floor. So perfectly, that there was even a small pile of salt on the floor just under the end of the edge of the counter. Even crazier, my daughter didn't do it, for she was in her room the entire time. After I had realized this, I freaked out yelling, "I JUST CLEANED THIS COUNTER!" I was in such bewilderment that that's all I could say. Once I realized what I had said, I just laughed afterward. What was more startling to me, was the fact of what I was hunching before this instance occurred. I had been eyeballing the salt shaker for the last ten minutes before this happened. I kept cleaning the counter saying to myself out loud, *"…Why do I feel drawn to that salt shaker?"* I knew from my abilities that Spirit had something planned, and it just so happened to be connected to the salt shaker.

I have *no doubt Aaron got a good kick outta that!*

Of course, not all experiences of the paranormal are going to be funny, or be a good feeling. There are many moments where there are Spirits that will try to scare you, or even harm you physically, emotionally, mentally, and even spiritually. But that is where you have to recognize which ones are trying to send you messages in a fair manner vs the souls that are just trying to be the prankster.

-Spiritual Note: I will not be the type to not express this without full warning that you should ALWAYS remain aware of the different feelings from the messages that you're receiving. All entities will have different levels of abilities, and sources of energy to communicate, which can give off various feelings based on their true intentions.

When paranormal activity occurs and you find yourself frightened, it doesn't necessarily mean that the Spirit that is creating the said activity, is evil or "bad" intended. More than half of the time, we get scared because it's a natural fear of the unknown. Which is why I would like to encourage you to remain focused on your emotions, thoughts and surroundings of each situation.

I understand the fear of the unknown and how it can make you feel helpless when encountering something you cannot neither see nor control. But I would like to gently remind you that you are *not alone* in this world, and *never were.* Even if you thought you were, you would be greatly surprised just how many Spirits are actually hanging around, and you would never know. Not trying to spook yah but you very well could have a Spirit next to you right now but you'd never know because they don't bother you. Just because the paranormal activity isn't happening, doesn't mean that Spirit isn't present. It just means they are respecting your boundaries and would like to exist in peace, while being in your company.

Below I have presented a list of the most common to even the rarest of activity from Spirit. The paranormal activity experience list, however, is only a small sum of the endless possibilities from Spirit...

- *Physical touches on your body*

- *Objects moving without an explanation*

- *Objects/ electronics turning on and off*

- *Music playing that one cannot explain*

- *Echoes of laughter that one cannot explain*

- *Chills/ goosebumps that cause one's hair to stand on end*

- *Hair/ body pulled from an unseen force*

- *Shoves/ pushes from an unseen force*

- *Animals reacting/ behaving suspiciously such as barking or hissing at thin air*

- *Animals trying to avoid something unseen without explanation*

- *Toys turning on and off by themselves*

- *Lights flickering or dying often inexplicably*

- *Batteries/ electronics dying inexplicably*

- *Feeling a cold breeze that cannot be explained*

- *Suspicious aroma/sent that cannot be explained*

- *Objects shaking, flying across the room violently*

- *Objects/ people/ animals levitating inexplicably (VERY RARE)*

THROUGH MUSIC OR MOVIES

Okay, this topic is quite skeptical for some at first, but the further I go with this, you may see the bigger picture. I will not say that every single thing is influenced by Spirit, but I will say that indeed most of it is. Just through my own experiences of signs from my own departed loved ones, I have received countless ways of being able to hear their love in many forms. And although they have many creative means of being able to show us their love, it is also our awareness and our open hearts that help us notice them.

THROUGH MOVIES

Spirit has a way for us to take witness of their messages even through a TV show, or a movie. Have you ever kept seeing a movie play in your head, all the way to the point to where you just have to watch it? You don't know why, or where this comes from, but you just know that you have to watch it? Or, you turn on the television, and you suddenly notice that a certain phrase, scene, or character role, actor, singer or person somehow resembles your life in some bizarre way? Most often when this happens, we automatically brush it off. We think, "Wow, what a coincidence." When in truth, this is Spirit using the influence of Telepathy, to help us see their messages through movies, and or television. It doesn't matter how off the wall or random it may seem. Spirit always seems to have an exceptional approach to giving us their love by surprise.

Even as a Medium, I still have a hard time wrapping my head around the fact that they are able to, not so much manipulate us or time, but use the course of our lives in favor for us, in order to give us the message of love that we so desperately need.

Personally, this happens to me way too many times to count. Almost on a regular basis, I come across television shows, specific scenes, or a movie clip that sparks my soul. Something always seems to bring my awareness higher whenever these moments occur. Never before was this a daily routine expectation. But throughout my journey with Spirit, I have come to find that this happens to us way more than we ever realize.

When these kinds of Spirit, "Aha" moments take place, my approach is to thoughtfully consider what your loved ones may be saying.

THROUGH MUSIC

Have you ever felt a sudden urge to turn on your radio to a specific station, and then find that there is a song playing that you feel you can relate to? Or that it relates to a departed loved one? Or have you gone to a location and when you arrive at your destination, a song is playing that brings you back to memories of a departed loved one? Spirit requests that you carefully consider these moments, as these are Divine messages of love from them.

It doesn't matter if I am in my car, or in the doctor's office. I will suddenly notice a song playing that brings me back to good memories of my loved ones. The song "Mirror" by Justin Timberlake is one of the more common signs for me. This song plays almost everywhere I go. Not just because it's a wonderful song, but because my friend Chad makes sure I hear it as much as I need to. I could hear it at my doctor's appointments, in the grocery store, or even the next time I turn on the radio at home or in my car.

As long as Spirit is always around, (which they forever will be), then be rest assured you will always have amazingly beautiful messages from your loved ones on the Other Side.

THROUGH OTHER PEOPLE

There's a saying I like to express when it comes to Spirit, "When they look like them, it more than likely is…" Spirit has a supernatural ability in being able to have people come into our lives that will sincerely look and even act like them. Even crazier, they can actually have themselves come back as the body they last were, in order to cause you to wonder the "impossible" being in fact possible!

This happens to me *way* too many times to count. I have had a delivery guy come to my home one time, and when I took sight of his face, my heart dropped to the floor just as fast as the package did from my hands. The guy laughed and asked, "Are you okay?" I giggled and replied, "…Yeah…just a bit taken back is all. You look like someone I once knew." All I could think about was how much he looked like Aaron who had died not a few months before this bizarre coincidence.

It will always happen when you least expect it. Which goes along with my next encounter of Spirit. I happened to be getting a lot of anxiety back in March 2015. When these anxieties occur, I have to take notice immediately of my surroundings, for I've learned it's a sign from Spirit that something is about to happen. Not knowing what exactly was going to take place, I allowed my day to go along as planned. Without any idea, I suddenly had this need to go outside to check if we had mail in our mailbox. Again, you could debunk this as a mere "coincidence", but what came next baffled me. As I am nearing the mailbox at the end of the driveway, while chewing on a few chips, my peripheral vision caught a moving figure in front of me. It was a jogger but not just any jogger, it was a man that was the spitting image of Chad! I was caught in such disbelief, that I literally froze. Catching eye contact with this person, I then realized he was also wearing the same exact shorts that Chad also used to wear! I can only imagine how dumb I must've looked to him, standing clueless with a bunch of chips in my mouth. *One can only wonder.*

Now I know for sure this man wasn't Chad himself but a man that looks incredibly like him, for once in a while I see him jog in my neighborhood. What's even more important to note on this "coincidence" is I had never seen this man before, that is, not until after Chad had departed.

Spirit again, manipulate the course of our lives in our favor in order for us to interpret their messages more clearly. In this case, Spirit influenced me to have the "need" to go outside exactly at the same moment this handsome mystery jogger came by my house. If I didn't respond to this Divine influence to go outside, I never would've seen this man. This man resembles my friend SO much that the sight of him *literally* took my breath away. This was a gift in remembrance of who he used to be physically. A gift of seeing his face one more time to convey a message that he is still alive in another form. And by accepting this message I am able to receive the gift of love and reassurance that all is well.

These moments will be when you least expect it, and it will almost always knock your socks off. Not to mention make you wonder if you just saw a ghost in the middle of the day. For Spirit even have the unsurpassed potential of appearing before us as they once were but this is to say fairly, not as often as most would like. But for what it's worth, Spirit doesn't have to be all mystified and creepy, to appear to us to make their point. They almost always make it happy and memorable, to give you that feeling of surprise, and a supreme amount of love that you will have no choice but to smile the rest of the week.

THROUGH THE GIFT OF SMELL

This here is perhaps one of the most profound experiences one may encounter when being contacted by their departed loved one. It is fairly simple but without a doubt, especially personable when indeed faced. When our loved ones attempt to contact us they will do something that one may not realize at first is a spiritual communication but it most definitely is! From time to time, our departed loved ones will arrive in the presentation of a pleasant smell that we can relate to or that will arise certain positive memories of that individual. For example, some will describe smelling cologne, perfume, flowers, or even to other smells that will remind you of them. It will be specific. It will be a sent that is intentionally brought forth for you to purposely think and be reminded of them and when this happens and you can't seem to explain it, thank them for they do so especially for us on a personal level through love.

A COMFORTING THOUGHT

This chapter is one of my favorites due to the incredible odds of how Spirit will be able to give us the love that we once had when they were alive in human form. It can arouse emotions that you either once had come back, or new feelings that will give you a deeper sense of relief, or closure that you needed for many years over. Their intention is to give you validation that you're not crazy, and they're never far away. Spirit will stop at nothing to give you what you ask, or need in order to feel their love and presence in almost all cases.

I say, "almost all cases" due to the fact they won't always do what you ask. It can be something as simple as this, but give you just as much of the validation to help you move forward in your life with affirmation that they've never left you. All of the ways Spirit can communicate their love to us is not limited to just what I have listed. These were only a small few of the MANY ways Spirit can come forward with their absolute love within the course of this unlimited Universe. If you were to find yourself in a situation where you may feel as if you aren't receiving messages "yet", Spirit asks you to remain patient as all happens in Divine timing when we are in alignment of what we are in need of. When you receive these soul-warming messages from your departed loved ones, be sure to thank them as they take great care and consideration in all messages sent.

Remain The Same

One of the more repeated questions I receive is if their departed loved ones are the same person they once knew and loved here. I can tell you from countless readings, they most certainly are the same, but just with a bit more love *pizazz.*

During the process of crossing over, our loved ones will grow into the soul they were meant to become, in order to bring light to all within the Universe and to humanity. And even though they will advance in wisdom, knowledge and unconditional love, they're still their own individual soul. Without their own individuality, not only would this make Heaven boring, but wouldn't aid their souls in learning with the help of another. Thanks to individuality, each soul is able to continue their path to oneness with Creator, without being limited.

Imagine a school, and there's twelve teachers for the same topic, let's say English. But if they all taught English the same way, with the same tone of voice, same attitude, same logic, same strategy, even the same personality, most likely none of them would entice the students individually or personally. Thus, the statement is, we need variety when learning. We have to have variety, otherwise there would be no reason to exist at all. If we were all the same, then there would be no point in being different from the other person, or in this case, other soul. So with the benefit of individuality on the Other Side, Spirit and our loved ones are given the advantage in continuing their advancements in Heaven. All the while, being supported by fellow souls on how to enhance, as well as keep their own spice to life on the Other Side.

GRANNY PAT

When my grandmother, Granny Pat crossed over, my whole family was crushed. We all missed and honored her with so much love. She could make you light up, just by her smile, accompanied with her warm greeting as her arms outreached to embrace you with the tightest hugs ever. She was a good woman with a strong Christian background, forever her heart set on Elvis Presley.

And as much as I knew she was in a good place, I couldn't help but wonder at times for many years if she was okay. I'll never forget the impact it had on my dad, losing the one woman in his life he could never steer from. His heart was torn more than I had ever seen before. This was a guy you would never see cry at funerals. But when it came to the loss of his beloved mother, I knew there was a bond stronger than the eye could see.

As the years went by, and our memory for Granny Pat grew fonder, there was a moment on my journey I had lost hope. When I lost my beloved daughter, Victoria from a miscarriage, I had lost all of the light inside of me. This was a very dark moment for me. I had felt as if all of my happiness was ripped from my clutches. Though I knew logically this was untrue, my heart and faith had fractured nonetheless. But during one night after days of hospitalizations, hours of doctor visits and what seemed like endless treatments, I was finally able to sleep easy. I must've slept what felt like days, but on one of those days my Granny Pat came to me. The funny part to this visit was she didn't come to me in a dream dressed all in white, or with feathers from her glorious wings. Nope, instead I hear a loud, hard to miss Southern accent saying, *"Oh, honey...you'll be fine!"* Realizing what I had heard, I woke up knowing that too recognizable voice was my grandmother. Even though I was so distraught from the loss of Victoria, I was more focused on the fact that my grandmother still had her Southern charm. She still possesses the same personality. And not only did I hear the same voice she had when physically alive, but I could feel as if she hugged me. It was a memorable moment I will forever treasure.

"Their love for us is forever growing, filled with everlasting laughter, even if that means at our not so classy moments."

OMG!

It's not too unusual for me to hear messages from other people's loved ones, but it can certainly be a table turner when I hear a message from mine. After I had realized that Chad had passed away, I was instantly *mortified.* All I kept thinking in my head, was how embarrassed I was for him to come into my messy home as a Spirit. And how silly I must've looked, trying to curl my hair with curlers, and not to mention how much I stuffed my face like a couch potato. I was in the middle of depression, so of course I didn't look my best. Gosh, I must've looked like a doormat. I couldn't even walk through my own house for weeks comfortably. All I kept seeing in my head, was this person who I had dreamt of meeting, to only realize, now he's in my house, and without me knowing what he's either saying, or thinking. I was mortified with all of my silly, dare I say…girly worries.

To be clear, Spirit will give us our privacy, whenever we are doing something that would be considered private. However, I knew that as a Medium, my experiences of feeling privacy, was never going to be my normal as before. Of course I was embarrassed. But to be forward here, I had to accept that we shouldn't be ashamed of our humanness, and in this case my basket case-ness.

We are all here to experience human behavior in all aspects, no matter how embarrassing it may seem. But more importantly, even when they cross over if they poked fun with you, *bet your bottom dollar* they're still keeping up the same characteristic. Their love for us is forever growing, filled with everlasting laughter, even if that means at our not so classy moments. Of course they would never make fun of us in a way that could cause us pain, or humiliation.

INDIVIDUAL SOUL PRINT

The path of becoming more of who we are, is something we will strive to understand more than any other lesson. More often we continually forget our true selves and why we were created to begin with. The purpose of our lives here is to hone who we are in all angles, good and the not so good. And with those lessons, we are able to bless others by sharing our knowledge, and experiences.

Within each of us, is what I like to call the **Soul Print**. Just like our fingerprints, *we each are gifted with this essence inside all of us that no other soul possesses.* That's what makes each and every soul unique. Each of us are gifted with our own individual identity that makes us stand out from the rest, while still blending together as one in the Universe. Main reason why I, and many other Mediums are able to identify the souls individually is from the *Soul Print*. From the soul Print, I am able to understand the different characteristics that make each soul special from the other in their own way. Most famously the definition of a *soul is an eternal essence of one's being that is forever immortal.* Some even believe based on certain religious and spiritual beliefs that only humans possess a soul. Throughout the book you will notice I say soul when I am referring to departed human beings in order to establish an understanding of what I am speaking of when in the formlessness state.

If you compare the soul with the idea of the consciousness you would quickly find a level of similarity. **Consciousness** *is already conscious, aware of itself. It is eternal. It's the unmanifested beingness of oneself.* The more used phrase of oneself, the soul, has been so loosely used yet not very many people are able to really comprehend let alone describe what it is. But when we look at the consciousness, we are able to discover the undoubtedly obvious link between the two. Consciousness itself is timeless which would then support the theory behind the concept of there being no time but the present moment when in Spirit form that is essentially formless. So when I am connecting with a specific soul, simply put, I am connecting by intercepting into a spiritual communication of the consciousness that is connected for all eternity within the Universe. As we are all connected with one Source, this relationship leaves no room for error in the connection of consciousness for all consciousness are connected to the same Source.

It's very important to Creator that we hone in understanding, that He would never want to take away our individuality. He appreciates us as what He created us to be, which is a parallel energy Source with our own uniqueness.

Spirit on the Other Side is not just one Source, but many, through a grand scheme of creation. They're not just one type of being, but of many. When born into the person you are, regardless of how different or imperfect you may feel towards the world's view, you're always important regardless of the differences. We are all an important part that the Universe needs in order to be whole. It doesn't matter how much you love and wear the color pink, or if you're a person that strives to be around animals in a way that would be considered taboo. The truth of the matter is, we are all created, to bring a different kind of lesson for others, to learn unconditional love.

Come on...what is taboo anymore? Truth is, from Spirit's perspective, you're the exact person you were created to be, and for a larger purpose than something the human eye can convey. We are created to be the creator of something new, and forever evolving. We're created to create a new way to love. There is no other better reason to be alive than for this, don't you think?

So if this is true (which it is), then why would Spirit, God or anything on the Other Side try to destroy that beauty within you? Didn't make sense to me either. Which is all the more reason why Spirit encourages that when crossing over, we don't change, but grow to a more wiser and loving soul.

THE GOOD, THE BAD & THE SECOND CHANCES

It's not God's, or Spirit's plan, nor is it your destiny to inflict harm on another person or a another Source of creation. Nor do I believe, that when we cross over we are going to remain that way on the Other Side just because that's who we were here. But what I have learned from Spirit, is because we are granted the blessing of free will, we're still granted that choice on the Other Side. Now, does this mean that a person who committed murder, will stay that way on the Other Side? No. But it does mean, that person has a chance in learning why it was wrong, and how they can trust in themselves in learning what love truly is.

Spirit teaches us love from love. There is no other better teacher. Even the worst kinds of characters in this world, are granted the opportunity to understand the differences between love and the not so loving. Depending on the soul's drive, and will to learn love for the better, it may take centuries, to eons to understand love. And even though Creator would prefer us to understand love now (sooner the better), He is still a patient being with mercy for all.

ONCE A SINGER, ALWAYS A SINGER

I will never forget a session I did for a woman named Tiffany, who later became a very good friend of mine. We hit it off instantly, especially when her mother's soul, Melanie came through. She is such a sweet soul, evolving so well in her lessons that she clearly was on her way in becoming an Angel. During the connection with Melanie's soul, I kept hearing singing, which sounded as if there were a choir in the background. Finally I shared this with Tiffany, and to our surprise she said that her mother used to sing all the time! But the even funnier part, was Tiffany shared further… "I used to tell her to stop singing because she sounded horrible. But she didn't sound bad at all. I just told her that to make fun of her." I was then told by her mother's soul to tell Tiffany, with a swag I absolutely don't have... *"Hey, I CAN sing! And I'm even better now than before, honey."* Tiffany was so relieved to hear these words for she always wondered how her mother was. Wondering for years whether or not her mother was still the same person that she didn't get along with as much as she had hoped before. And although in their life when her mother was physically alive they didn't see eye to eye on most days, she quickly learned that all the negatives in their past were no longer going to separate them. Thanks to her mother Melanie's validations, her daughter was able to receive her love without allowing the past transgressions to repel her memories any longer. Not only did Tiffany hear from her mother's soul, but she also got the reassurance that no matter how long it's been, she still sings her heart out on the Other Side. It was such a rejoicing moment in being able to be a part of it, and I'll never forget it.

So if your uncle loved to eat raw onions, be sure he's still doing it on the Other Side. The point will forever be, that no matter how long it has been since their passing, they will remain to be the image you remember, and even more on the Other Side.

"They acknowledge each and every soul in Paradise, simply because their point in learning to become whole, is by embracing others."

THE GRUMPY GRAMPS

As Spirit evolves, so do their relationships with other souls they may not have gotten along with here on the physical Realm. Their differences will be a way of complimenting each other, instead of creating a division. They will begin to understand how to appreciate one another, and love without judgment. With that, they will begin to show loved ones here on the physical Realm their reconciliation, by appearing together during a connection with Spirit. This exact example happened during one of my more memorable moments with Chad before he passed. He had asked me if I could connect with his grandfather if able.

Understand, this was when I was still learning of my abilities. It was Chad's idea in allowing me to practice, by connecting with his departed family members on the Other Side. Learning how to interpret the messages from Spirit, Chad would call or text message me regularly, asking if anything had yet surfaced. His method was to allow the information to come forth on its own. He was the one to teach me not to force the process and I strongly trusted his judgement. The ironic part, is he had no idea how to hear Spirit, but he always had this natural intuitive sense, in how it worked.

Days went by, no messages or images were coming through, until one day I woke up with countless insights. It was almost bugging me to tell you the truth.

The images were of two males arguing over something minimal, but I had no idea what. This wasn't making much sense to me until finally I had realized, the two souls were Chad's grandfathers. There were two souls coming through instead of one. When I understood this was a possibility, I sent Chad a text, telling him that both of his grandfathers were coming through. But instead of talking with me, they were too busy arguing, instead of communicating with me.

This was a significant point in the connection towards validation for Chad, for the next thing I know, Chad called me right after I sent the text message. Without hesitating, he shouted, "What do you mean *–both of my grandfathers?!"* Repeating again, I followed with, "Yeah, both of your grandfathers are arguing about one of them smoking a cigar, but the other one doesn't like it," I said confidently. He then remembered that he never told me that both of his grandfathers had passed away, but only informed me of *one.* Taken aback without much resistance, my friend started to tear for this was something he'd always imagined. Occasionally, his grandfathers would come to mind but without putting much thought to it, he never figured however they'd still be so much alive in the life after this.

As he was openly expressing these emotions and deep thoughts of this life changing experience, without warning the same grandfather enjoying his cigar started drinking from a small glass. So again I shared this new tip from Spirit to Chad to only astound him further. He was bewildered to learn his grandfathers were still doing the same things they were doing here physically.

From his memory, neither of his grandfathers ever got along. But even though they didn't get along on Earth, doesn't mean they didn't make amends when crossing over.

This brought Chad such relief along with more resolution to his heart. Both of his grandfathers were showing me a reenactment of how they responded to one another when physically alive. But as they grew more within themselves, the more they grew closer to each other on the Other Side. And it certainly hasn't changed the one enjoying a cigar every now and then while the other wafts the smoke away in annoyance.

ONCE A FLIRT ALWAYS A FLIRT

One memory that definitely comes to mind, is a soul named Jimmy whom I had connected with for a client named Rebecca. Her friend had come through, and out of the many souls that stepped forward for her, he made it the most interesting. As humble as I am, I admit it's not uncommon for me to be hit on once in a while, but oh JEEZ was this soul a *flirt*. He would be hip to hip on me, always looking at me up and down. I laughed with the reddest cheeks, telling Rebecca… "Awh…lol who's the flirt?? 'Cuz this guy is somethin' else." She busted out laughing, saying, "OMG THAT'S MY FRIEND JIMMY!" During her session when trying to send messages for dear Rebecca I couldn't help but notice a feel of something touching my side. That's when I realized it was Jimmy. Explaining this to Rebecca, she then told Jimmy to stop. Yet what's even more interesting was he did! What astounded us both, was the way I had next described his attitude… "I keep seeing him very nonchalant. Someone with this vibe of being calm, casual, but knows what he likes." She giggled more, confirming that was the type of person he was. Not only was Rebecca able to hear from her friend Jimmy, but learned that his attraction towards women hadn't subsided *one bit.* It was remarkable to me, being able to witness this beautiful reunion of Rebecca and Jimmy. Especially how much their bond together had never changed, nor depleted.

FOREVER GROW NEVER CHANGE

Our loved ones never change who they are, but instead are grown into a more loving soul. Our departed loved ones still enjoy the blessings that they once enjoyed here, that are essentially positive. Does this mean that Chad's grandfather actually smokes cigars? I don't know for sure. But what it does mean is they are granted the ability to reenact the way they used to behave, in order for their loved ones to understand and recognize the soul that is stepping forward.

Normally they don't do things such as smoking or drinking, at least not excessively. They do things in moderation as any other good thing should be. And even if they do smoke a cigar or even have a glass of wine, it doesn't affect them the way it would us in the physical Realm, for they're no longer bound by a dense physical body. Essentially, they are simply blessed to enjoy life to the fullest on the Other Side, while enjoying the company of other souls. Just like here as we grow up into the adult that we are, so will the souls in Spirit. They won't necessarily change who they are by their Soul Print, more of adapt in wisdom and knowledge with love as their guide in their ascension. To elaborate, the person that we remember, the characteristic, personality is only a very small part of their true Universal essence. Their wholeness that is interconnected to all on the Other Side like us as humans is merely a tiny expression of the soul's limitless potential. Like us, their likes and dislikes as humans were just a speck exposed of who they are which is ultimate energy connected to Source. While growing into who they are it is teaching them the beauty of teamwork, sharing, companionship and how to love without judgement.

It can be hard to truly picture this, but it's something in Spirit we're all destined to understand, and is forever encouraged. Every time this comes into my mind, it's always when I watch the world go about its business. But instead of a person walking past another person without acknowledgement, each soul is greeted with smiles, laughter, sharing positive energy. They acknowledge each and every soul in Paradise, simply because their point in learning to become whole is by embracing others.

The only exception to this, is if the soul chooses not to escalate higher, then they would not be growing for the better. Please understand, I don't say this negatively, for we all have the light and love inside all of us to continue growth. However, the way towards growth, is by our own free will here, as well as in Paradise. And thanks to other positive souls, they're driven to guide the less aware souls higher as they learn lessons.

Souls in Spirit will never change completely. Just like if you're a loud person, and you learned how to fix a car, doesn't mean you still won't possess that extended side of yourself. It only means you have gained a piece of knowledge that you didn't possess before, which allows you to take a step further in wisdom. As the soul grows, their own individual selves will remain intact. Countless souls that I have had the gift in connecting with, have come forth to express this universal authenticity.

They're still the same person you remember them being here on the Earth Realm. If the soul once loved cake, don't doubt they love it even more in Heaven. If they appreciated the peace and quiet of being alone, that soul will still appreciate the same gift in peace. Just like how Tiffany's mother, Melanie enjoyed the gift of singing here, she still does in Spirit. But she adds, she's better now than ever before! And as Chad's grandfathers are still enjoying their life in peace, they now enjoy it even better with the company of each other. Likewise, just as Rebecca's Jimmy was a major flirt here on Earth, it's only natural for him to possess that dashing side of himself in Spirit. All souls remain to be their individual selves on the Other Side, but just with a bit more *pizazz*.

$\mathcal{M}$an's Best Friend

Spirit relays daily that our loving pets are with us even on the Other Side. Their love for us is eternal and unconditional, which is why they were created in the first place. During my sessions, Spirit will bring my client's pets forward that have departed. Each time this occurs, the client will be hit with an overwhelming relief, knowing their loving pets are safe and at peace on the Other Side.

BUDDY

Growing up, my identical twin sister, Carolyn had a cat named Buddy. We loved his big fact cheeks, which we believed made him more special. He had this way of crawling up on your lap that just made you smile on the inside. It didn't matter what we did, he would always make the attempt to sit on our laps, curling up in the cutest ball ever. I loved that loving ball of fur, and even though other people made fun of his cheeks, our family found him to be unique in his own way.

As the years went by so did his health. Tragically, Carolyn was faced with the decision as a teenager to put her beloved kitty down. We were all broken hearted over this reality and knew that it was for the best, due to a horrendous cancer that had swarmed inside his jaw and mouth.

More than ten years we were blessed with the company of our beloved Boo Boo. We missed him dearly, and couldn't bear the thought of him not in Heaven, or safe on the Other Side. We often wondered as children where he went, and how he was. Weeks went by, but our hearts were still raw. Devastation ravaged my sister's heart, for she found a true friend, companion and best buddy in her beloved feline. She was truly attached to that cat. And as there were days that seemed slow after his passing, there were also nights that seemed too unbearable. During the middle of the nights she missed his meow. You know that one, the creepy meow cats make for some reason in the middle of the night? Personally, I don't know why cats do it, but the fact was, it was another memory that she favored.

But one unexpected morning, Carolyn wakes me from my sleep. Startled, I awoke sitting up instantly asking, "–What's the matter?" She then shared that she dreamt of Buddy, and how he was okay, and his cheeks were cured! We both had tears of joy, with a great sense of relief to know that he was in fact okay and was no longer in pain.

I had dreams of our cat on numerous occasions like my twin, only never before was I aware that this was the message he was sending. While receiving another hint to indicate his soulful existence were instances that my sister and I both experienced a feel of something small and round, laying on the edge of our beds at night. For weeks we figured this was just a mere "coincidence" or flatly a source of our imagination floating to the surface of the physical sense. But after this dream visitation from her beloved Boo Boo we were given the affirmation that he was in fact alive and well in Heaven.

ANIMAL NEGLECT & CRUELTY

As a pet owner, I cannot tell you how much it pains my heart when I witness, or hear of animal neglect and cruelty. The neglect of poor helpless animals is not something to be acceptable, by any means. Spirit states adamantly, the purpose of an animal on Earth is to be another source of unconditional love.

"Animals don't hate and we're supposed to be better than them."

-Elvis Presley

We are human beings with the blessing and Universal Law of Free Will, which can either influence us to be positive, or negative. It is not God's will or intention, for an animal to be neglected or beaten in any case. In truth, this is the animal's understanding before being born into this world. To teach the animal how to love, even the most despicable kind. It can be hard to embrace this understanding, to hold compassion for a person who chooses to harm one of God's creatures. However, before an animal is born into Earth, they're shown the possibilities of what could be their fate and why, depending on their pet owner.

Based on the Universal Law of Free Will, we are all held accountable for our actions, even the ones we bestow onto innocent animals. The person that does the harm, will thus be shown how much harm they bestowed onto the animal. The person that commits neglect on an animal, will be shown how their mistreatments and misunderstandings of the animal was not of a loving nature, and why.

Embrace Where We Go In Spirit On The Other Side And The Unbreakable Bond

The purpose is to expand our awareness, allowing us and the animals to forgive, love unconditionally, embracing all there is to understand and to accept. No matter whether you feel it was justified or not, mistreating anyone, humans or animals alike, we are all responsible and held accountable for our said mistreatments and mistakes.

Have you ever seen those incredibly sad commercials by the ASPCA, where they're trying to raise money for neglected animals? I can't look at those without getting emotional, for the truth speaks in the eyes of each creature. I mean, if you look at the animal's eyes, you can see the effect the neglect has on them. Me personally, I always want to reach into the television screen and just swoop all of their unhappiness away. It breaks my heart. How could a person truly believe in their core that this kind of treatment is acceptable? *How? Why?* It honestly angers me to tell you the truth. These types of people have a lot to learn about what real love is and what it is not.

Point is, no matter what you may think, all animals have emotions and even memory. If I can recall correctly, animals have the emotional level of a child. So even when we may think they don't feel emotional pains such as sadness, rejection, depression, loneliness *–think again.* They have all of the same emotions we humans too experience.

The overall lesson for each pet owner is to remember that animals are placed on Earth to teach us how to love something different from ourselves. To teach us how to respect the different nature, the different level of communication and how to love without judgement. No animal's experience from neglect happens in vain. Spirit emphasizes that no matter how horrible the experience was, even if the animal passes during the neglect that is taking place. The animal will still learn to embrace the lesson it came with. Not to say that neglecting an animal is good. *Never* is it good by any means. But that when there is a difficult experience, comes a complex, yet highly invaluable lesson learned and wisdom gained.

And as there is a lesson for the neglected, there too is a lesson for the neglector. So keep in mind, nothing happens in vain when it comes to Spirit. Each person that does such a negative deed on another creature, will also experience an invaluable lesson. Whether the lesson is honed on Earth, or on the Other Side, no experience comes without a lesson attached to it.

HEAVEN WELCOMES ALL

Just like humans, our pets will go through a similar process when crossing over. As humans will go through a *Soul Cleansing Period*, or a *Previous Life Review*, so will our beloved pets. Each will be shown how good they were during their times of difficulty, expressing their loyalty to their master.

However, like humans, some pets may have been a bit untrainable due to certain life experiences. As the animal is spoken over with God, Angels and other souls, the pet is granted multiple opportunities to learn how to enhance their wisdom and love.

No matter the level of negativity brought on the animal, or onto their master from the animal, they too are not judged on their previous life experiences.

Each soul, including animals, is treated with the highest levels of dignity, respect and unconditional love. Like humans, the animal could be harboring unhappy, or unloving emotions based on their levels of past life experiences. Thankfully, the soul will also be healed during their arrival back to Heaven, giving the animal a chance at renewal.

When the individual animal soul is ready for their arrival back in Heaven, the pet may be granted a visit to their master in appropriate time. This will allow the departed animal soul the chance at saying goodbye –of course temporarily until they meet their beloved master again on the Other Side. But similar to humans, animals may be greeted by their master if the human departed before their pet. Which in turn, can be a beautiful unification period, granting both the previous owner and pet, a chance in reconnecting their bond.

NEVER LEFT BEHIND

Just yesterday I had a session with a man named Paul who was originally in need of guidance from Spirit on his journey in life. However during this time I couldn't help but notice that an adorable dog was peeking through the veil of my spiritual connection. I can still remember how sweet this female dog would appear with her tongue hanging out with a look of absolute happiness and joy. Finally after debating on why this was happening, I went forward by relaying to Paul that a dog was stepping through and if this made sense to him. He confirmed that growing up he had a dog that was female that he adored most definitely, and was sincerely crushed when she had departed. He then became more intrigued and followed with, "Do you know what color she was or is?" I confirmed with, "I keep seeing tan or light brown tones." He then agreed in comfort that was indeed how she was.

I could tell he was becoming more relieved to hear that she was at peace on the Other Side, but then I could notice something hanging in the air of his consciousness, so I followed with, "She is stepping forward for you to know that she is happy and at peace in Heaven. She is not lost and never was. She was immediately taken to Heaven with the company of Angels." His Spirit rose when I shared this information for Paul then replied, "That is such a relief because I was always worried and wondered if she was somehow stuck or even lost on the Astral Realm." I continued with, "No. Not at all."

No animal, insect or any other creature that is essentially not a human is ever lost or stuck anywhere –especially on the Astral Realm. The reason is because they are pure. They are the purest of all creatures on this planet due to not becoming distracted by the continual chaos contaminating their soul frequency. They are never lost, never forgotten or left behind for each animal and insect, reptile etc. are all a major priority and never would be neglected in Spirit.

To add, human souls that choose to remain on the Earth Realm or the Astral Realm is due to not letting go of the physical material illusions. But because animals have always been spiritual in nature primarily, they are not and are never bound by this fate.

ANIMAL SPIRIT CONNECTION

Animals, insects and many others have a Divine connection to the Other Side. They have the awareness of the Spirit Realm due to not being distracted by the ways of the world that are continually influencing us humans. The purpose of animals is to allow us to respect their connection to the Other Side, as well as being part of Source's alarm for danger. Their Divine connection with the Other Side, grants us the opportunity to be aware that something is present whether it is physical, or spiritual.

Dogs, cats and basically all animals have this certain way of knowing when someone is not to be trusted. They can show signs of warning in various ways such as, hissing, clawing, growling, or intensified staring with alertness. All animals whether large or small, especially cats and dogs, are granted the ability to tend to and protect the human race if needed. It allows not only the human to understand the concept of loyalty and friendship, but so do the animals. They too are here for lessons to understand their relationships with mankind.

Some people ask if animals have the ability to detect Spirit in their midst, and the answer is a big, "YES" the animal connection to the Spirit Realm is similar to humans. The difference however, all animals have this Divine connection, whereas only a select few humans do. The common house pet such as dogs and cats are more linked to the Spirit Realm, due to them also possessing Psychic abilities. These specific pets, are known to pick up spiritual entities that are not usually detected by the human naked eye. Such as demonic or negative entities, dogs and cats are more easily able to pick up these types of spiritual energies, based on their natural connection to the Other Side. I like to suggest owning one of these animals, for those that don't possess the ability in uncovering the less positive of entities, or energies.

Below is a list of the more common reactions from dogs, or cats that may indicate a presence in your home or area. Pay close attention to these reactions and behaviors. If your pet has never done these types of behaviors before, especially without cause, then I would take special heed the probability that these may indeed be spiritual warnings...

❧ *If you witness your pet's hair stand on end with no reasonable cause*

❧ *If you witness your pet trembling for no reasonable cause*

❧ *If you witness your pet running away from a certain room, location or area*

❧ *If you witness your pet refusing to enter a room, location, or area*

❧ *If your pet refuses to refrain from barking, growling, or hissing at an unseen force*

❧ *If you wake up from sleep, suddenly finding your pet staring at you or someone in the middle of the night with angry/ suspicious intentions*

❧ *If you discover your pet's diet, or behavior change without reasonable cause*

❧ *If your pet suddenly becomes violent without cause, towards you, or others*

❧ *If you witness your pet refusing to move from a certain spot in your home, location or area, while staring consistently at something suspiciously*

Embrace Where We Go In Spirit On The Other Side And The Unbreakable Bond ❧

If you unfortunately discover your pet unable to walk, or find deceased without a logical, or medical health explanation

If your pet's health suddenly plummets without a reasonable, professional health explanation or cause

If your pet cannot control it's bladder without cause, especially if whimpering during this reaction

If your pet or animal doesn't like a certain object, and continues to reject it, based on the animal's natural behavioral reactions without reasonable cause

If your pet suddenly draws itself away from you, or other people in the family or in the room, without a sound explanation or cause

---

What I have listed above are just a few of the many examples of how your pet may react when a specific entity is near. No animal will react the same as the next, nor will their behaviors be the same as the other. All animals will react differently, based on their own individual soul personality. Each animal is here for a Divine reason. For us to love, honor and respect their loyalty to us. Take heed if you unfortunately are witnessing these abnormal animal behaviors. Of course, I urge each pet owner to move forward with seeking professional assistance from your local veterinarian first, before suspecting these to be spiritual in nature.

ANIMAL SPIRIT GUIDES

Later in time on the Other Side, our pets can become what is known as an *Animal Spirit Guide*. *Animal Spirit Guides are departed animal souls that agree to guide, love and aid lesser experienced and knowledgeable animal souls. Animal Spirit Guides can assist fellow animals on how to love and honor their pet owner, while also teaching humans the importance of an animal's unconditional love.*

Like humans, animals will have their own Animal Spirit Guide, to guide and comfort the animal that is here on Earth. All animals have their own Animal Spirit Guide, or even an Angel as their guide, while here and on the Other Side. The purpose of an Animal Spirit Guide for your pet and all animals, is for the good for both the animals and mankind to assist in knowing the true meaning of unconditional love. Once the animal, or your pet understands and masters their lessons, they're then granted the opportunity to become someone else's Animal Spirit Guide if chooses.

People are also granted the Divine blessing of an Animal Spirit Guide, while here on the Earth Realm. Their goal is to assist us to understand how to love our pet and other animals in our experiences, that we may have yet learned to master.

THE ENERGY DIFFERENCE

There are many people who wonder if a human soul can reincarnate as an animal, or an insect of their choice, in order to experience things like flight, or other sensations. But Spirit states that's not the case. In my work with Spirit, we are granted the gift in experiencing the same emotions and sensations of the animal, but cannot become the species. Spirit expresses, instead of reincarnating, we can experience the animal's lifestyle by living through or within the animal. But we cannot essentially become the animal or insect. We are all set in our purpose, which is to hone the energy levels that we essentially are.

So to become something that is lesser in vibration than what we originally are is simply not the case, for we only continually grow, not shrink. And because animal souls are a lesser vibrational level than the human soul, we human souls would not become that animal but only are given a taste what it's like. Whereas with animals, even though they are a lesser vibration and one would think they could grow to become human, again it's not so likely. For the animal souls were created to hone their purpose which is to be who they are. And like humans, we are created to be the energy source that we were shaped to uphold.

However if the animal wishes to understand more of the human behavior, they would be granted a similar insight by the gift of experience through this, to say through mirage or illusion. Like the Previous Life Review, animal souls are gifted a chance at understanding the life of a human by experiencing emotions and sensations or life trials by seeing and feeling it all through a human soul's life on Earth without having to become one. Equal to animals, human souls are given an opportunity to know the sensations of things like flight through a bird, or lifestyle underwater while seeing and feeling the life experiences through a dolphin or from within a starfish.

Spirit shares in depth that animal souls are lesser than the vibration of human souls. Not to say, they're not as good, or as worthy. But that they're limited in their abilities vs the human's unlimited energy. We are however, gifted the experience on the Other Side to look and feel through the eyes of the animal we wish, in order to give us a deeper sense of love, companionship and a Universal understanding of that animal.

OUR PET'S WISH FOR US

During many sessions, I will experience a client's pet coming forward, showing that their owner was thinking of getting another pet. And even though our departed animals encourage this, Spirit will show me that the client will be feeling guilt, or fear that they're replacing the pet that had passed. However Spirit shares, that is not only a false truth of your intentions of why you want another pet, but that in fact our pets on the Other Side, encourage it. They love the fact you want to take care and love another animal soul, even if in honor of the one that is departed.

What many people are shocked to hear is more often than not, it's their pet from the Other Side, that will bring that new pet into their life. Having Spirit on the Other Side assisting you to find your next perfect pet, is what it's all about. Animals in many cases, drive us to be the best version of us. And even if that means one pet, or four, you're receiving a Divine love and guidance from them in Heaven.

Animal souls don't become the jealous type, nor do they struggle with the feelings of rejection when you do in fact get a new pet. Once they move forward with God in Paradise, they continue to fulfill their purpose, which is to continually encourage you to experience unconditional love. Their wish for you is to continue to discover love in all forms, even if that means with a new animal that you'll treasure and adore. I like to think of this as your animal in Spirit being the cupid for that next meet-cute for you and that new pet.

SACRIFICE NOT

The purpose of animal life, is to enlighten the soul's vibration and lessons. To enhance all that life has to offer within yourself, and within your belief in others. One of the few, but largest misconceptions about the purpose of animals, is the false belief that in order to find salvation, or worthiness from God or Spirit, an animal sacrifice would have to take place. Not only is this extremely barbaric, but outdated. God *would never demand or command anyone into doing such a horrendous act,* in order to be accepted into Heaven, nor His love. Creator's message is to *enhance life, not to destroy it.*

Ancient black witchcraft is most commonly known to practice conjuring rituals, where the blood of a dog or cat is needed in certain processes. The blood will be drawn after a person of this group slays the animal and drains its blood, leaving only the carcass for later uses if required. Of course, this isn't something that is done by those that follow God, but instead those that follow His opposite. However, even God Himself repeats whole heartedly, this is not the way to gain His attention. By no means is this something God had intended for His beloved creatures on Earth.

The purpose of life is to grow, not to destroy. To do such a thing in the name of God, is not only against the Universal Law of Love, but of Spirit's true calling and message. It is not in God's will to allow such horrific doings against His creatures. And because of the Universal Law of Karma, it only comes back to those that bestow such mistreatments in order to give hope of insight to why this is not only unnecessary but unloving.

ANIMAL SOUL CONTRACT

Our pets also have a *Soul Contract*, similar to that of the human Spirit. Just like us, they agreed to their intentions, goals and aspirations in order to grow and move higher in lessons and love. Their responsibility is solely for the understanding of love in all angles, no matter the difficulty that may come their way. When reaching to the Other Side after their time here on Earth, they too with Spirit Guides, may be taught to understand how they did, and what they may have to continue to learn about the role they were granted.

Animal souls do have the option of being reincarnated, if they choose to do so with the approval of their Spirit Guides, and Creator. Some will choose to reincarnate back to Earth, to experience things that they may not have had the privilege of honing. Such as running free and wild, flying without the pain of a fractured wing, or being adopted by a new family. All animals have their own experiences along with their own unique desires.

They're given the chance at understanding, and experiencing life here in many areas to understand the impact of unconditional love.

HEALTHY LOVE VS UNHEALTHY LOVE

There is a wonderful feeling when being able to enjoy the simple pleasure of playing with your dog, or riding your favorite horse. But

Spirit exclaims there is a fine line between loving, and obsession.

Throughout my walk with Spirit, I couldn't help but notice the level of companionship with our pets. The more common relationship with a pet and owner, is one of a loving nature where the owner loves their pet with the utmost dignity and respect.

However, Spirit confesses, that there are some pet owners that're not in the majority. And as a result, these people tend to have a relationship that the majority would consider unhealthy, or even severely dysfunctional for the pet and the owner. In defense of both, I can understand if you feel a sense of relief when being with your pet, however some people take it as far as over indulgence, like owning too many. And in consequence, more often it ends with the owner becoming neglecting, to starvation, physical/ emotional abuse, or even death of the pets. When this becomes the owner's reality, that is when Spirit likes to encourage them to look deep into themselves as to why they crave the company of animals to the point of co-dependency. Spirit understands our emotions on all levels, but urges us to look deep inside of ourselves to discover the core of where it all began, and how to accept it, then release it. The reasons for this kind of relationship with pets, *(generally speaking as an observer. Not as a clinical psychologist or psychiatrist)* is a result of an unfortunate negative traumatic life experience in the person's past, causing the person to emotionally, even physically retreat in this manner.

Again, I am not a doctor and do not hold any of these statements as factual evidence. Only stating what I believe to be some series of the many cases where these types of co-dependencies occur with animals.

Hiding behind our pain, whether it's with animals, material items, or even drugs and alcohol, pauses our spiritual growth as it does the brain. The purpose of animals in our lives is to enhance and grow ourselves with love and acceptance. When the animal shows and expresses their unconditional love for us, it should be a reminder of how much we should also put love into ourselves. Not only are animals here to show us love, but to remind us of how to love and honor ourselves, despite the differences and negative rejections of the world. Spirit's wish for you is to hone who you are in every aspect, the positive and the negative. When you can accept yourself in all areas of your life and of your past, you're then fully accepting the true person, heart and soul of you from all angles.

I'm not saying you can't allow yourself to have as many as even five dogs or cats. But what I am saying, is the more we request to have in our lives, the larger the responsibility and accountability that will be placed before us. The more we acquire in our lives, including the blessing of pets, the more we're being shown how much devotion, love and loyalty is expected of us. Animals are a wonderful life lesson in understanding this truth.

I am not a doctor, and do not prescribe any case in which would describe you, or anyone as an unhealthy or dysfunctional person. I have no say in that area, and want to encourage you to seek professional aid, if in a situation that you feel could be considered unhealthy, and or dysfunctional.

THE FORBIDDEN LOVE

Bestiality is *nowhere acceptable* in this life, and so it goes on the Other

Side. If you, or some you know is doing something of this nature –let me tell you, it's **not okay in any means**. I remember a day when I was working as a cashier in a thrift store, and on the radio I heard a person was arrested for sexually abusing his sheep, and having inappropriate interactions with his animals. There is nothing good about this. Love is our goal here, and when there is an inappropriate sexual arousal of an animal, then that is a moment Spirit encourages you take a step back and reanalyze yourself very carefully. If you have inappropriate thoughts, feelings or sexual intentions with an animal, then I would urge you to seek out professional help, in order to discover the root of this behavior. There is nothing wrong with you, even if this is your case, but what Spirit relays is that, *"love for animals is that of a respecting one."* And going as far as having sexual relations with an animal, is nowhere respecting the animal. The animal itself is a soul of its own like you and I. This is something that would be no better than child molestation. Of course, as I have mentioned before, I am no clinical psychologist, but this does scream, "control" in my head. Anyone that does this, needs serious help in discovering the root of the reason. In any case, nowhere is this acceptable to Spirit, or to the animal that is being forced into this kind of activity with their master. This is a betrayal of trust, loyalty and respect of the animal, and the person committing this crime (because it is a crime) must be held accountable no matter the cause.

Spirit doesn't judge the person that commits this kind of act, but will remain solid in the seriousness of this kind of behavior. So even if either you, or someone you know has done something like this, please understand it can be undone, by asking for forgiveness. In no means is this behavior acceptable, but mercifully, Spirit will do all they can to teach these souls the difference.

THE SUBJECT OF NEGATIVE INFLUENCE

The probability for an animal to become either possessed or influenced by a negative Spirit is not in their nature, and is not of a spiritual factor. Many have asked me this, and to what I hear from Spirit, is *"..There is no pressure, or urge for an animal to become evil, or negatively influence by Spirit in any means."* Can an animal become influenced by an evil force to do bad things? I don't believe so. From Spirit, it has been my understanding that animals are of a Divine connection, and are immune to spiritual influences. They are of a pure heart to which evil Spirits do not have a hold on the animal's free will. To add, the true evils on the Other Side, are not concerned with the animals, or any other creatures that is not human. The goal of certain negative energies, is to enslave souls that are closer to God, which are the human soul. Animals are immune to their attention, and are granted a simpler, lesser aggressive pull towards, or against the negatives that coexist.

THEIR DIVINE PROTECTION

Animals here and in Spirit, have the potential to rescue people, similar to the role of a Spirit Guide and Angels. I've heard countless stories of men and women being saved by their pets, or stranger animals in many scenarios. Their experiences are of the animals bringing them to a safer distance out of danger, or rescuing them by dragging them to safety, *literally*. Some have even witnessed their pets going and getting help from an outside source, to aid the person that is in trouble. The animals are not necessarily sent here to do only that, but if the moment calls for it, the animal may come to your aid. One story I had seen on television was of a woman saved by her pig, which guided her out of her apartment building that was engulfed in flames.

She had woken up to her pig squealing in the middle of the night, warning her of the potential danger. Because of the flames, the smoke was impossible for her to seek a way out. But miraculously, her pig guided her out through her home, practically dragging her to safety. If it wasn't for her brave piggy, she more than likely never would've survived.

All animals are given the ability to detect the imminent dangers that lay ahead, and with Spirit's help, they can do things that many would almost disbelieve. The gift of animals is most often taken for granted. We can so easily forget how incredibly brave and loving these animals can be when urgency calls for it.

THE BLESSING

There is absolutely no mistaking that Spirit has an incredibly unique way within the Universe. To give an example, I asked my Spirit Guides to grant me a sign that I was on the right path in this section. Just a few minutes later, I hear tireless tapping in my hallway. After a few minutes of this relentless tapping, I finally went to investigate. And to my disbelief, there, sitting on the other side of the window sill, I discovered a bird was the cause of the hindrance. Bewildered by this bizarre timing, I began to laugh to myself over this. But in mid-laugh, a thought arose that perhaps this bird was hurt and couldn't fly. At the time, the weather was overly windy that night, so it only made sense in the moment. Being the humanitarian that I am, I decided to gently bring the small bird into my house, however soon I discovered this was another one of my *great ideas*.

I was on the phone with my girlfriend Tiffany during this moment, and as she was laughing at me, she shouted, "–Melinda, it could have lice!" Freaking out, I finally managed to get the bird out of my house after nearly two effortless hours of this tiny bird frantically avoiding me. For over a week, I couldn't stop itching from the fear of having adopted the bird's unfriendly guests. Luckily, it was a false alarm.

I can only imagine how odd I must've looked to my neighbors in my window, waving my hands in the air for over an hour by myself. I'm almost certain I must've appeared like some *crazy* person. And I thought talking to dead people would be the icing on the cake of "crazy". Only I would decide it a good idea, to bring the bird in the house. Even Spirit told me, *"Melinda, the bird was the sign, but you didn't have to bring it in the house."*

Even though it was my idea to bring the bird inside due to my free will, it was Spirit that brought the bird to give me the reassurance I needed. The blessing of animals is *huge.* They're here just like humans, to gain and give back love in all forms. And what a beautiful and an eventful sign that was! The ultimate gift of animals, is to allow our hearts to grow on a deeper, and a more spiritual level. To gently remind us that love comes in all shapes and sizes, even breed. With the loving support, unconditional love and appreciation from our pets, we are blessed each and every moment on this planet. Love and appreciate them, for their flaws and mistakes, for they're no different than that of a child. Forgive their misunderstandings. And remember when you get angry, impatient or frustrated with your pet that they were chosen either for you, or by you, for a very Divine reason. Love and honor them the best you can, and ask for their forgiveness, in return for your mistakes and misunderstandings. Love is not without companionship and loyalty, on both sides, no matter the difference in breed.

Lost Not

It saddens me when someone is fearful that their loved one could be trapped in their death sate, or lost and don't know where to go after they pass. But this is farther from the truth about crossing over.

When we cross over, there are other fellow Spirits that will greet us to meet God in Paradise. The process can be a bit rough for some souls, depending on whether the soul is ready to leave the Earth Realm. Once the soul receives the comfort that it's okay to move forward, the soul will have help by being guided through the process without any struggle, or fear. The process of crossing over is very graceful and quick, without any pain, or uncertainty.

Each soul has the free will of choice, whether they want to cross over, or not. This is something that is never forced, but is guided with absolute love and understanding from Angels, and fellow souls.

SUICIDE VICTIMS

One friend came to me, that I could feel was a bit distraught with the idea that their loved one committed suicide. He expressed to me of his fear of the Biblical response to suicide victims, and how they would be condemned to Hell for all eternity. But I relayed to him that Spirit says this isn't true.

I too feared the same for others, but Spirit has shown that this is not factual, and was something they wanted me to express to my friend. God knows our hearts and how we love so strongly. And when a soul chooses to end their life, convinced that others would be better off without them…is *never* something God wants for anyone. But even so, God does *not* damn us because of this choice. Not to say this is okay, but that God won't punish you for it. He has a compassion for those with this kind of weakness and loves them just as strongly as those that don't commit suicide.

When a soul decides their own fate like suicide, the process of crossing over will be different from those that died by destiny, or fate. Committing suicide, is never God's choice for someone, but done by the soul that does the action through free will. It is then spoken over with the soul and God, of why they made this choice. With Spirit Guides, and loving Angels, they may also be present during this healing process from the Earthly pains the soul has been harboring. After healing has taken place, this soul will then be given another opportunity by a few options, to learn how to love themselves better and others.

If the soul chooses to go back to Earth, then it would be reborn, (reincarnated) to try to learn lessons more. Or they have the choice to learn how to love, by learning on the Other Side with the help of their Spirit Guides, and Spirit family. A foundation is created for these souls, so as to guide them in their healing with unconditional love and peace. There is no humiliation and ridicule, for God is what many have forgotten, is merciful. His love is fearless and mighty, but He is merciful for all of His children, and will do all that He can to help us through our lessons to be closer to Him. That is His goal.

During the learning of my abilities, there was a man I came to know and we were dating at one time. His Spirit was fragile and his hope was almost lost when it came to God and faith in the afterlife. His faith depleted after learning of his cousin's suicide as a reaction due to his girlfriend braking up with him. This broke my heart and so I decided to reach out to his cousin's soul, asking him to bring anything validating to heal my boyfriend at the time. While I was still learning of my abilities, I tried something I had never done before. I put my hand on his, and we both sat in silence while waiting to see what would come forward. When I placed my hand on his, I could see everything clearer than I usually am able. His departed cousin's soul showed me how he ended his own life by using a leather belt, hanging himself in his bedroom, leaving only a letter to his family. Tears ran down my boyfriend's face, when I said things that no one could've known. Things that even I was surprised his cousin shared, because it was so personal. Spirit knew this was very evident for my boyfriend to know that his cousin was okay. His cousin's soul shared this was the only way he knew how he could end his pain, but that he regretted it *indefinitely.*

It was so emotional for both of us, that it was difficult for me to keep my composure in order to continue relaying the messages. The further I went into sending these messages, the more I felt my boyfriend's soul embracing healing from Spirit.

When I thought the messages were over, one last thing came forward from his cousin's Spirit that needed to be addressed. Then I asked my boyfriend, "Do you feel as if your cousin is in Hell because of doing this act?" He then said with tears running down his face, "Yes. And it scares the Hell out of me. He was such a good person. How could God do that to someone?" Taking his hands into mine, he wept further as I said, "He says to not hate God for this. This was his choice, not God's. He also says…that you need to regain your faith in Him, and he is going to help you do that. But also…he says *please don't only remember me in this moment. Please remember the times when I was happy and laughing. And, no, I am not stuck in Hell, for God has forgiven me and is only full of love and mercy."*

The image of losing a loved one is very hard, but even more so, is the idea of a person being branded or damned to a place based on how they died. It's not fair to you, or to anyone to fear this. If anything when we cross over, we are freed from that memory for all eternity, without the pressure of feeling guilty.

Angels, Spirit and God all state clearly that even if a soul departs from suicide, the soul is always welcomed in Heaven. So with that, even suicide victims are always welcomed in God's Paradise, *never* damned to a place such as Hell.

I just had a client today named Curt who was seeking guidance in his life regarding a few things he needed reassurance on. More importantly, Curt was looking for messages to come through from his friend who had unfortunately committed suicide. As I was nearing the end of the reading I was told to send affirmation to Curt that no matter what, his friend was not in a place that was "bad" in consequence for taking his own life. But in a Paradise with Angels while no longer in pain. This comforted Curt. He was able to receive pleasant validations with a reassuring hand from his dear friend from the Other Side. I surely wish the best for them both in this difficult transition but I have faith that with this, Curt will be able to move forward in his life with positive motions.

God understands that when there is tragedy, there is pain. He knows that many souls go through hardships, pains and traumas that can have a negative impact on their emotions. When souls depart, arriving before Him from such a tragedy, He only welcomes them with mercy, unconditional love and forgiveness. He even shares, *"There's nothing to forgive."* He doesn't look at this as a fault, but more of a learning experience for the soul after their departure. For when a person or in this case, a soul, embarks on ending of their gift of life physically, there are unresolved pains deep inside the individual.

Source understands that when there is such hardness to our inner being, there is needed a grander healing process for these delicate souls. In order to heal these precious beings, there is only absolute Divine love, understanding, and empathy present.

TRAUMATIC PASSING

Even if the death of someone was very traumatic, impacting either emotionally, or physically, it doesn't cause the process of crossing over to be less quick, or less peaceful. When the soul departs from something traumatic, the soul will have a chance at leaving the body usually before they experience things that are emotionally, or physically painful. But some are not so fortunate, and are faced with dealings of such a negative nature before their soul departs, which can leave the soul having to forgive the unfortunate events. Either forgiving themselves, the souls that did them wrong, or the situations that occurred. Souls that pass from something traumatic, leaves them with emotions that they may need assistance in healing from the grievances. In this moment, Angels, Spirit

Guides and other departed souls on the Other Side, will help them through this difficult time, in order to regain their self-worth and unconditional love.

At one point there was a man who came to me, expressing his guilt for not being there for his young niece, who departed from a tragic murder. The images that came through from Spirit were so vivid, that I too wept for compassion of the unspeakable pain inflicted –this little girl went through *Hell.* Not only was she murdered, but beaten and sexually abused before her passing occurred. It was an experience that no child should ever go through, and it was a *serious* passion of mine to see that this man got the healing that he needed from Spirit. Being a mother of a young daughter myself, it was *extremely* difficult, just seeing what the parents had to go through, to accept this tragedy, was nothing a parent should have to face.

His terror was his niece reliving this horrific scene for all eternity and he felt timid on how to handle this possible fate. Lovingly, his niece came through, giving him the peace of mind that she was going through this pain no more. And no longer would be a victim of such a horrific fate. She was free of pain, free of fear, free of tears, and could see only happiness and love in Heaven.

She also told him how she had forgiven the people that harmed her. And she would hope that in time, her uncle would be able to do the same. Not only did she give him the answers that he needed, but also gave him validations that she has never left him, and has never been trapped in her death state.

It is evident to voice, that no matter how terrifying, or painful someone's passing is, they won't be stuck in that state forever. I can understand if something were to happen to us here in our lives that we tend to keep that memory subconsciously. It becomes a broken record repeating the same sounds, images, feelings over and over that don't seem to cease, but this is not the same with our life on the Other Side. No matter how shocking, or painful the passing was, the soul will still be able to release those memories of the physical and emotional pains, once the healing begins on the Other Side.

"It is more of an experience for the family to learn how to embrace life, no matter how short lived."

-Spirit

INFANTS, ABORTIONS, MISCARRIAGES & STILLBIRTHS

The hardest tragedy is a parent having to say goodbye to their own child. I don't believe it matters what age when your child passes, the process of letting go is unbearable nonetheless. It doesn't matter if you raised your child since they were born all the way to adulthood, or were only given the blessing to have your child in your life for a few days. The pain is *real*, because the *love is real*, and no one can ever take that away from you.

I lost a child when I was pregnant for only a few months and I can tell you from personal experience, it was something that I would never wish on my worst enemy. We are here to love and when we lose our own kin, we are faced with a pain that can cause us to become filled with anger, or hatred.

But your child is not in pain, and is living ever so strongly on the Other Side in Spirit more than you or I could ever imagine.

Within a matter of months, a week before my 2nd trimester, I had lost my daughter Victoria and had to face the emptiness that so many parents unfortunately experience. I share this personal experience with you, for I knew that if I was going to write this book, or any of my other books, they'd have to be based off of my own personal experiences. So you and many others would know first-hand that I too know what it's like to lose different levels of loves in my life. And I can tell you that even after losing my own child, it brought me to a place that was very dark.

Many emotions roamed within my heart and my head, to the point where I told God to go f%!k Himself. I couldn't understand why He would allow this to happen to an innocent child. Forgetting that everything happens for a Divine reason, I became severely depressed, and almost suicidal. Losing Victoria in early October of 2014, I was then experiencing other severe health complications around Halloween that same year. When Halloween arrived, I was still bedridden and was unable to walk without crying most days. Even though I was in severe pain from the miscarriage, my first daughter Josslyn, had been waiting patiently for this holiday to come and couldn't wait for her mom to join her trick-or-treating. At first, I had told her I couldn't go and was in too much pain to walk, but the moment when her eyes began to swarm with water, I knew I couldn't say, "No". With that, I took an extra pain killer that my doctor had prescribed to me, and went on the venture together with my parents, as they were taking care of me during this time.

Letting my 5 year old daughter trick-or-treat at one of our local malls was doable, as I would take breaks by sitting down, watching her from afar while she went to each store. After the first hour, I will never forget it because I swear I thought this moment was my last. I had never fainted before and I wasn't aware of what the signs are when one is about to. But thanks to Spirit, I knew something wasn't right and I had told my mother I couldn't breathe. She then suggested I sit on a nearby bench, but it wasn't working, for in the same moment I was losing my sight and hearing. My mom being the good person that she is, tended to my consciousness by asking me questions.

Sitting on the bench with my mom by my side, I knew something was terribly wrong, for the further I remained conscious, the more dozed off I got. Without looking at her I said, "Don't hesitate to call 911, Mom. *I'm serious* – call the second I pass out because something is *seriously wrong.*" Like most parents that love their children, she said, "No, you'll be fine. Just stay focused on something and stay with me." However, the harder I tried to stay conscious, the more challenging it was to stay awake. Sure enough within the next five minutes, I collapsed in the middle of the mall. When I had fainted, all I can recall was losing sight along with my hearing. The next thing I remember, is waking up to my mother screaming my name, as she caught my head before it reached the hard floor.

Thankfully, the paramedics and security guards, helped me through this experience. Later I had been told by the doctors at the ER, that I had fainted due to dehydration from taking a laxative and my pain medication, at the same time. And due to the dehydration my brain had also lost oxygen which explains why I had fainted. Boy, that info would've been nice if my doctor that prescribed my meds at least could've warned me. Yeah... let's just say, I'm *never* goin' back to the same doctor again.

Some people ask if I saw Spirit when I fainted, but I can tell you honestly, "No." And the reason is because, they knew that if I saw them, I wouldn't want to stay on Earth. But,…I do remember that just before I passed out, I told God under my breath, *"You serious?? I'm gunna be so pissed if I die right here, and I haven't accomplished anything."*

I do personally believe that with this experience, I was not only able to understand the gravity of losing a child. But forced into a harsh wakeup call that I was most certainly *not ready* to go. I went through a moment that forced me to remember I have family here that I love, and people that love me. I always told God, "If this is my last life (which it is), then I want to go out with knowing I had accomplished all I was meant to – with a *bang* so to speak." So with that, I know God won't let me off the hook that easy.

Of course, not everyone will lose a child based on the same situation, but for me it was a Divine reason just like all of our experiences are. And with those experiences, comes a great deal of love, lessons and wisdom. Never in a million years did I imagine that this would happen to me. And even so, it brought me to a real wakeup call of just how much pain so many other parents go through when losing a child. I can't imagine losing my first born. Josslyn is 6 years old now, and just the thought of having to say "Goodbye" to her makes my soul cringe. I can't even fathom the idea, for the pain would be absolutely *unbearable.* My heart and soul goes out to all parents that are faced with this tragic reality every single day.

This taught me how to be stronger within myself, and how to love others no matter how short lived. Reminding me of the loyalty between a mother and a child. It was a humble reminder of how much I and many other people are willing to go through, in order to bring life to this planet.

The bond between a parent and a child is so strong and no one, nothing can *ever*, and will *never* be able to break this unshakeable bond that God intended.

When a child passes and comes to me in a reading, it breaks my heart ten times over. I cry during almost every session when I connect with a child, because they are the innocence that is meant to establish the true beauty in this world. We crave that kind of innocent influence of their laughter and for their smile to spread like a positive flow. The parents will normally express to me how they feel lost without their child, feeling as if they cannot live without them. Even though we all grieve differently, the fact is your heart is the key to healing. When a child passes and their parent is with me, they will get the messages and validation that not only do they want their parent to live on, but to remember how much they are with them, even now while in Spirit. The sense of peace comes over the parents when this healing takes place.

When I relay to the parent that their child was never lost, it will bring a large sense of relief to their soul. Like most parents, we want to make sure that our babies are able to go Home safely, and Spirit shares they *most certainly do*. Shocking enough, even infants will come through, showing me that they are older than their parents, that they are all grown up. Laughter comes from both the parent and the departed child, when they get to share these moments together.

A great example of this is a woman I had helped just a few weeks ago named Sandy. She had contacted me in hopes to connect with her departed loved ones, but who came through had nearly caught her breathless for it was her son Joseph's soul that had departed and was barely a little over a year old. From what I had seen from his soul, was him being a baby then grew up by showing me is baby clothes. I had then asked Sandy if she had lost a son that was very young. She confirmed by saying, "Yes, we had lost a son that was a little over a year old from a stroke of all things." I was shocked to hear but knew that she most definitely needed to be healed from this tragic loss of her beloved son.

Without delay her son then added how he had not blamed anyone for his passing and had wanted his mother to know that he doesn't put fault on anyone. Her emotions began to flow with tears as I told her, "He doesn't blame you or anyone for his passing and wants you to know that."

I then followed with, "Do you have a husband?" She said, "Yes." Then I continued with, "Joseph wants to emphasize by saying –*tell dad it wasn't his fault mom.*" Not only was Sandy able to receive amazingly healing affirmations and validations that her son's soul was well and at peace, but more importantly that he does not label anyone to blame for his early departure. Which was remarkable to us both that he brought this for her and her husband for Joseph's father had blamed himself for years believing that he had caused the stroke from giving his infant son a bath. But thanks to Spirit, Sandy, and the rest of her family were able to receive more than validation but sincere loving messages that left no gaps.

During the session Joseph explained to his mother that he had signed up to depart early due to a life lesson that he had to learn in order to continue his growth in Spirit. He understood the chances of departure, and how, and when before he signed up for his life with his mother and family. He stated to Sandy last but not least, *"I know it was short lived but I wouldn't change it for anything and I would do it again if I could."*

While writing this, believe it or not, Joseph is standing near me asking over and over, *"Hey tell them how stunningly attractive I am too."* He says with a side smirk that lays confidently across his face. *PPFF...men.*

So even when an infant departs, Spirit explains that the mind may be young, but their soul is wisely advanced at times. With the soul moving forward, the child will quickly grow up, enjoying life on the Other Side in Paradise.

The Spirit of a child is so incredibly pure in their connection with our Creator. They have this uncanny ability in bringing their parents undoubtedly obvious signs of their presence in their lives.

I can say honestly, I never thought I would ever hear from Victoria. Nor receive any kind of messages, because simply... I was under the false impression that her soul never existed. Instead, that the pregnancy was there, but not her soul. –Boy. was I *wrong.* Not a few months after my miscarriage, (to me it was a stillbirth experience) I had to go see my doctor again, for further tests to ensure my health was up to par. And during this appointment, I was seen by a nurse I had never met before, in order to assist me with my ultrasound. About ten minutes into the ultrasound, I couldn't help but notice that the screen above me that had my name, also had the name of the nurse that was assisting me. Sure enough, her name caught me off guard, for the left of the screen said, "Melinda" and then on the right was, "Victoria".

How in the world could that be a coincidence?! Seriously, what are the chances? I laughed even more when I brought this up to the nurse and she said, as most skeptics would, "Oh, what a weird coincidence..." Believe it or not I have never met another Victoria in person before in my life. So meeting this nurse, especially at the time that I did, was something remarkable to me that I will never forget.

That moment was so special, for I was finally able to get more validation from Spirit and especially from my daughter, that she is always present.

Signs from our children, no matter how short lived, will most often be those little coincidences, to give us the faith repair that we so desperately need. Reminding us that they're forever loving and guiding us from the Other Side.

God personally meets all and every child that passes, no matter the age. Children are the apple in God's eye and the smile in His cheeks. Regardless of how short lived, or how they passed, for they're always welcomed in Heaven. Never forgotten, never left behind.

Same goes for souls that are aborted during pregnancy. For the soul to be aborted, is never in God's plan, but is done by the free will of the parent. Each soul is greeted in Heaven, even ones from abortion. Spirit expresses over and over, that no soul during an abortion process will ever feel the termination of the pregnancy. Instead, the soul will be guided out of the womb before the procedure is taken place, to rescue the soul from the unfortunate process. It is discussed with the children's souls before they are born into this world of the possibility of being aborted. Each child soul that is born into this world are aware and have agreed like you and I to experience those said "happenings". Whether you either regret or wouldn't change the decision you made in having an abortion, Spirit encourages you to seek hope and faith in the bigger picture that is ever evolving to create a new and better you. I cannot say that what you do or did is "wrong" when it comes to abortion, but I do believe that with every difficult decision we make, comes an invaluable lesson of the true gift of life.

Stillbirths are usually for the blessing in experiencing the gift in creating life, and then letting the soul go. It sounds a bit harsh at first – trust me it was very difficult for me too. But after a long look into the bigger picture, I was able to embrace this beautiful and sad experience. It's a reminder to us that we are to grow from these experiences not with pain, but with more love and appreciation of life. After I had lost Victoria, I was found to feel a lot of guilt, thinking I had done something wrong, that caused this to occur. But Spirit relays, no person that endures stillbirth or miscarriages, are being punished for anything, nor is it their fault. It's more of an experience for the family to learn how to embrace life, no matter how short lived.

If you have had to experience this kind of loss, whether from a stillbirth, abortion, miscarriage, or when your child was previously born…my heart goes out to you. As many believe, *no* parent should have to bury their children. But in truth, life is filled with many unexpected experiences, which comes with lessons on how to love. If you are dealing with a loss of your child, Spirit encourages you to remember the moments that you shared with them, and embrace the happier times. We will all be able to reunite with them again…and when we do, it will be like they were never gone.

EARTH BOUND SOULS

Now, depending on the intentions of the soul, a soul may decide to remain on the Earth Realm, which causes them to become what is more commonly called, ghost or **Earth Bound Souls**.

Personally I *despise* the word "ghost" being as it doesn't give them enough credit to why they are here and more so, it's turned into such a negative label. For the sake of keeping their integrity intact, I will continue using the phrase, "Earth Bound Souls".

Earth Bound Souls are individual human souls that decided to remain on the Earth Realm, refusing to cross over. No soul is ever forced to remain on Earth, and is greatly encouraged to cross over to Paradise. But like humans, many souls on the Other Side can become quite resiliently stubborn. When dealing with Earth Bound Souls, the job of Angels, is to guide these souls in understanding that they are no longer physically alive, and to cross over to God. If the soul refuses to cross over, due to being either too focused on Earthly materials, being negative at best, or from fears; that is when the soul is left to harbor the negative emotions and or experiences from their previous life due to not proceeding to the Previous Life Review. In order to become an Earth Bound Soul, it's done by the soul's choice from the Universal Law of Free Will. Again, no soul is technically "lost", but is either refusing, is fearful to move on or does not know that they have crossed over due to a sudden passing.

Another reason why a human soul may choose to remain Earth Bound, is due to having "unfinished business." This may sound a bit cliché, but the truth I have learned is there are many souls that feel it is their responsibility to finish what they started. Whether it's taking care of a job, making sure a living person knows how they died, or something else, many will choose to stay. As I have mentioned before, the soul that is Earth Bound *chooses* this, but is greatly encouraged to move on into the Light with God. Many souls may even have trouble from fear of moving forward. This can also be caused by the human fears they're still harboring, that are no longer a reality.

Whether the soul chooses to stay for one reason, or many, the truth will remain, that God, and their Angels, will come and guide them to the Light to seek healing, love and peace.

LOST NO MORE

Do you ever wish you could have a compass for your life? Know exactly where to go and how to get there, telling exactly how long it will take? I sure do. Even though we may not have that luxury here on Earth, the great thing on the Other Side is we don't need a compass of where to go. Spirit gives supreme love and guidance to help us through the difficult transitions, so as to not lose ourselves. Crossing over is *that easy.*

"They all go to the same place in the end of their lives here on Earth, as we all do when our time comes."

I once was friends with a woman named Amanda, and later as we got older, we went our separate ways. But back when our friendship was solid, she asked me about her father figure, Rick, who had departed from an accidental overdose. She relayed to me, that she would have dreams of being back in her old house, where he passed away. When she was in this dream, she searched the entire house, but couldn't find him. She said her fear was that her moving away would cause Rick's soul to not know where to go without her. However, Spirit gave her the permission that it's not only okay to move on, but that it's a must. Spirit shared that she had to move away from that house, in order to not be haunted by the past of his death as a constant reminder. Rick brought this image to Amanda, for her to know that he was not bound by this location and had indeed moved on to Heaven. More so, he gave her the answers she needed and the confirmation, that he was at peace on the Other Side and didn't blame her but encouraged her to move on.

Even if someone had suffered from brain damage, or had memory issues, Spirit assures these souls too have no difficulty with crossing over. Earlier departed souls may help these newly transitioned souls know they're no longer hindered by certain physical setbacks and are more clear-minded with freedom than ever before.

People that suffer from mental illnesses such as Schizophrenia, PTSD (Post Traumatic Stress Disorder), Alzheimer's, to even fear of small spaces, are all gone once they cross over. I am no doctor as I have said, and I don't know anything about the severity, or the necessary treatments for someone with these kinds of illnesses or disorders. But what I do know, is our loved ones are no longer a slave to the body with any kind of physical, emotional or mental ailments once transitioning into their true form.

When someone's departed loved one expresses this kind of release of the human restraints, they will show me things that they're able to do there, that they weren't able to do when alive here. For example, a little girl will show me that she can dance again without getting dizzy. A parent to their adult child, will bring me images of them being able to know their own name, without having any trouble. Or a soul will appear with a wheelchair then pushing it away as a symbol of no longer needing the chair to get around. Or a soul that had undergone cancer will show they have all of their hair and even better than before. Some may even approach a session by opening their eyes to express how they are able to see again more clearly.

No matter the passing our loved ones are in the secure hands of Angels, fellow departed souls and Creator, to greet them on the Other Side. Each of our loved ones are awakened to a new life that is eternally unlimited. No soul will go unnoticed on the Other Side and they are always given the choice to cross over, living happily in Heaven.

NO MATTER THE DEPARTURE

It doesn't matter how our loved ones pass, how fast, nor how traumatic it was. What matters is that God, and the Universe allow them to flow to the Spirit Realm in a gradual, pain-free process. While meeting their other departed loved ones on the Other Side, in order to know there is nothing to fear. If it was from a horrific murder, a devastating illness, disease, cancer, or even from passing in their sleep. They all go to the same place in the end of their lives here on Earth, as we all do when our time comes.

Let's face it, the idea of crossing over can indeed be a bit scary. But the truth is, there is nothing to be afraid of. To me, it's scarier believing there's nothing after this. Now that's *scary.* And although we may have a hard time accepting it, our loved ones in Spirit are guiding and loving you here. No matter the age, the way they passed, or how difficult it was, Spirit continues to share that their love for you has never ceased. Whether the departure was from something unexpected, traumatic or expected, each soul is welcomed in Heaven with open arms from our Angels, Spirit Guides and most of all …Creator.

Divine Protection

It's extremely important to our departed loved ones that we are just as safe and comfortable here, as we hope they are there. Their wish for us, is to remain faithful in their Divine love as long as we live here on Earth. Spirit loves us so much, they may go as far as delivering messages in the most incomprehensible ways, in order to express their loyalty to us. Even so, they may go as far as even putting in a helping hand, *literally.*

Sometimes, Spirit may personally intervene in our lives, in order for their physically alive loved ones to fully understand the messages that are being brought to them. When I deliver messages from a person's departed loved one, most often their messages will be to not make the same mistakes they did. All messages come in the form that will speak the most personally to the individual that is receiving the Divine affirmations from Spirit. It can either be a departed loved one, a departed friend, their departed boss from a past job, all the way to Angels, and even God Himself. All messages from the Other Side have one major purpose –to guide, love, honor and protect all in the name of love.

SPIRIT KNOWS BEST

There was a person completely taken for a loop from this very experience during my earlier years of Mediumship. Personally I believe with all of my soul, that he will change for the better, because of the major impact his departed loved one had on him. It took place at a local restaurant in Alaska. I was enjoying my time at my table, but I couldn't help but feel an energy *pull* towards this particular group of young males. Not understanding where, nor why, yet I had this strong feeling something interesting was about to happen. Then sure enough, one of the males in the group approached me. And being as they're all friends, the rest of his company followed.

They were a very bright and polite set of young men. As the conversation moved along on its own course, all of a sudden I could see in my third eye, a soul of what appeared to be a grandmother stepping forward. Soon after that, I had realized the man that approached me originally, was her grandson. I didn't know what to do. I had never seen a soul come to me amongst strangers before, so instead of reacting, I merely listened.

She was sweet and obviously strong willed. I can still remember her wardrobe, wearing what looked like a nightgown that she had favored when alive. However it became a tad difficult to engage in conversation with the group, when not too far in the distance, this guy's deceased grandmother was waving for my attention. She smiled, laughed sincerely, and asked me to send him a message for her. I could feel she understood my lack of confidence, but she kept pursuing. She kept repeating that she wanted her grandson to stop drinking, or he would be joining her sooner than preferred. His grandmother's soul came to me to specifically, but I was still nervous to say anything for I wasn't confident yet in my abilities. With that, I pushed her aside, but her soul was persistent. I could visualize her in my head, as if she were standing before me alive. Verbalizing how much she wanted this gift for her grandson and how I was ready to send this message to him. She also added how she didn't want her grandson to make the same mistake she did, but I *again,* dismissed her at least three times shaking my head.

I'm almost positive I looked like a complete whack-job, as the words, "No, I'm going to look like a complete idiot. He's not going to listen to me," flew from my mouth in discouragement in the midst of the group. Thankfully, I was saved by the men's present conversation which suddenly went into an uproar, so they didn't take notice of my crazy banter. But again, still smiling, she said, *"No, Melinda. It's okay, he will know it's me. Trust me...you're ready..."*

After a few more minutes arguing with her and myself, I gave in by saying, "Fine, but he's gonna think I'm nuts!" I stuffed down my anxiousness and turned to her grandson and blurted out... "I'm a Psychic Medium, which means I can see, hear and feel people that have died." He and the rest of the men halted in their chairs. You could practically hear each of them take in a breath as they listened to what came next. I continued. "Did you lose a grandmother around the age of 60 to 65 years old?" His eyes widened in utter disbelief.

His expression was as if I were speaking with three heads, as he answered, "Yeaahhh?..." I then replied, "Okay, well she's here standing across the room waving her arms, asking me to send this important message with love from Heaven. She knows you want to make friends and she is very proud of your progress in your life. But she says, if you don't quit your drinking every night, you'll end up like her."

This poor guy was so shocked and caught off guard that he deliberately put his drink down, and went to the bathroom *crying! I felt horrible!* Not to mention the amount of eyes staring back at me, astounded by what they've just witnessed. Even they were lost for words.

Yeah… talk about *aawwwkward…*

After a few minutes in the men's bathroom, he came back and explained that he had been drinking more since his grandmother passed away. He didn't know how to quit, so he prayed to his grandmother to give him a sign. He exclaimed how his grandmother had died from liver problems, due to her own similar drinking behaviors. With this, he not only was able to hear from his loving grandmother, but more importantly, to receive the wakeup call that he desperately needed. But he admitted openly by saying, "…I knew I would get a sign from her buuuttt… didn't expect this."

When our loved ones answer our prayers for protection or guidance, it won't always be about something we don't have any control over. At times, it can be about us changing our own lifestyle, in order to find a safer route to happiness in the long run. Love from Heaven isn't going to always be about stars and feathers falling from the sky. But just something as simple as a whisper, or in this case, "Hey –quit what you're doin'."

Now does Spirit have to answer our questions and prayers by using a Medium? No, absolutely not. However, for certain messages, it can be a bit more challenging to tell exactly what it is Spirit is trying to say without one. With the help from a person with the *gift* like myself, and many others, people are able to get more specific messages from their departed loved ones. This is one of the more classic experiences many people receive from Spirit. Because our departed loved ones are now more understanding with their higher levels of insight from the Other Side, they may take time to help us learn from their own similar mistakes. Using a Medium, just allows Spirit more of the freedom to express their messages personally, without confusing the living person that is in need of the message.

THEIR SPIRITUAL UPLIFT

Although Spirit can be expressive in their loving notes to us, sometimes words from Heaven won't always be what we may expect. Other instances will be where the living person that is in need of their prayers to be heard, require an extra nudge in reassurance of faith.

There was a moment where I was told by a friend of mine that she was praying, and *praying* for something good to happen for her. I heard in how she felt that she was passionate about it, however there was a leap of faith that she was missing. I pointed this out to her with love, and told her, "I know you're praying for what you need help on, and I think it's great that you're doing this. Although, I couldn't help but notice that you said, you keep praying and *praying*. But…do you really think that you need to pray more than once, if your prayer was already heard the first time? It almost seems that you're unconsciously fearful that God hasn't heard your prayer, if it hasn't been answered in the time that you would prefer. I am not trying to insinuate anything negative. Only trying to give you a piece of insight that maybe you could be missing. God only needs to hear your call once, and it shall be done. That is all that is required of you, along with your faith to patiently wait, and know it will happen." Her eyes grew when she heard Spirit's words to this. She then relayed that she actually was thinking that for a while, but wasn't sure. Ever since then, she has been moving forward with her prayers in a simplistic way, with a more strengthened faith as her foundation to her belief. Even better, a few weeks later, she joyfully shared that her prayers had been answered.

Faith is a big deal when it comes to Spirit, which I personally believe is the key ingredient to all that is spiritual. I'm sure you're probably wondering, *"What does faith have to do with this topic, about Spirit's love and their protection?"* Well to answer that, it has *everything* to do with it. When we're looking to be guided or protected, looking for an answer to our uncertainties, this is where faith is number one. When we carry more faith, that is when we're able to open the door to further insight to endless possibilities.

See…when one doesn't have faith, they lose hope in almost anything and anyone. Faith isn't about just God or Spirit and I'm not referring to a specific religion either. Faith can be used when you're relying on the mail person to bring your daily mail. You also carry faith, that your employer will provide you with a proper paycheck by the end of the week, don't you? You may not know for sure how it will come about, or where it is coming from, but you carry a belief that it will be provided for you without fail. Some may argue and say, "But I know my check is coming in, because it's something I can physically touch and see." Then I always follow with… "Hmm…not necessarily. Just because you know you are due a check, doesn't mean that your employer will give it to you. Many employers take advantage of their employees, steal the money and run away with it, while leaving those hard working people without a paycheck." But even then, with the risk of having both the possibilities, you remain to have faith that your check will arrive in due course. And because you worked hard for that paycheck, you also *believe* you *deserve* that payment in return, as you were promised. Having faith in the Universe, in Spirit and in Creator is similar. The only difference is, the amount of faith that is being asked of us.

Faith is where we carry hope and a strong sense of belief, that everything will be the way it should be. Of course, this is just my own interpretation of faith, and everyone's is going to be different and that's okay. The message here is that Spirit wanted my friend to understand what it was she was missing. Spirit brought forth what would stand out to her the most personally, and in this case it was her faith. Giving her the insight to where she needed to be more faithful allowed her the gift in letting go and letting the Universe do its thing without fail.

DIVINE MESSAGE RECEIVER

Everyone's take on Spirit's protection is different, and everyone will experience it at least once in their life. This is where we have to consider that there are many different ways Spirit can protect us. The previous experiences I had just described above were based on how Spirit can protect us by speaking through a Medium, or another live person. But there are many other people that will speak of being protected by a force, that they couldn't see, nor physically explain.

Some have spoken of seeing a bright light that kept them safe during a car accident. Others will talk of seeing nothing, yet still feeling the physical force of something pulling them from harm's way.

"With this unshakeable bond, we are Divinely connected to all that is Spirit, to all that is the Universe."

-Spirit

This isn't to say that our loved ones are the only ones keeping us safe, they have plenty of help. We are not without Angels, Spirit Guides and our loved ones. We have plenty of protection from the Universe. By the influence of Spirit, we are protected even to the level of physical protection that can also come into play if necessary. Through help of Spiritual Protection, humans are continually guided to a safer circumstance every day. Not everyone may understand this is indeed happening during the moment the protection is taking place. Most often it's unseen, and so easily dismissed. Below will be a short list of ways Spirit can protect us, physically, spiritually, emotionally and even mentally...

Giving you gut instinctual feelings to NOT pursue something, or someone

Giving you gut instinctual feelings to NOT go somewhere, or TO go somewhere

Giving you time to get to safety by delaying situation or person

❧ Giving you time to get to safety, by distracting the attacker, animal or group

❧ Giving you a sudden urge to run, jump, duck, or whatever deems urgent for such survival activity

❧ Giving you, or someone else insight to think creatively during a crisis in order to survive

❧ Giving you creative thought to prepare before a natural disaster, personal crisis, or accident

❧ Giving you a sudden deep insight on how to speak, or respond to someone, or something with bravery beyond your norm

❧ Giving you intense physical strength that is beyond your body expectation to avoid, prevent expected bodily injury from something or someone

---

When it comes to being Divinely protected, Spirit may come to our aid without us either knowing, or realizing it. You do not have to be a spiritual person, or be a part of a religion, or ritualistic practice in order for Spirit to influence your situation. It's all a matter of whether they see that we are in need of their safety for the best of all concerned, will they take heed on this venture.

No, this is *not* when Spirit takes possession of you. This is completely different and I must relay this firmly. This is only done from your departed loved ones, Spirit Guides, Angels and other Higher Deities. They do not do anything against your will and are always in your best interest at all times.

Have you ever planned on going somewhere, but then suddenly you get a strong, unknown feeling that you shouldn't? Then you finally decide not to go and later discover that a horrible car accident happened on the same route you would've taken? Or you discover the accident was at the same time you would've been on the road? This is a prime example of you being Divinely influenced by Spirit's Divine protection. Their way of helping us to make special decisions, in order to keep us safe, is through the power of intuition. This is also based on the way Spirit speaks on the Other Side. Words are not used in the Spirit's true form, as we discussed in the **Crossing Over** chapter. Each person has a very Divine connection with the Higher Realms, with God our Creator. With this unshakeable bond, we are Divinely connected, to all that is Spirit, to all that is the Universe.

Most would consider this just luck. Or they'd so flatly say, "You just followed your intuition is all." But then you have to wonder…*where does intuition come from?* You can't say it's "common sense", because this is based upon a feeling. Intuition is based upon your "gut feelings", whereas it's your energy seeing with its mind's eye, of what is good for you and what is not. It is your energy receiving negative and positive vibes. When this happens, this is your intuition (energy) responding to Spirit, giving you those feelings in order to follow that "gut feeling", for you to be safe.

The feeling may be amplified, if you're in serious danger and at times, they may even be physically forceful. This requires extra amounts of energy, in order to influence the means of the physical Realm. If Spirit were to intervene for a living person in this way for example, the Spirit would have to be a very high energy frequency. Or, receive help from another soul, or entity that is capable, like an Angel or a High Deity. When this takes place, it's for a very brief period, giving the living person a few seconds of an open window to move to safety.

There are absolutely NO guarantees that Spirit, Angels or departed loved ones will intervene for our safety, even if prayer is involved. I am informed by Spirit and Angels very delicately, they may or may not intervene, depending on whether it is necessary for all concerned. It's a highly complex topic indeed. Spirit gently also reminds us, depending on our *Soul Contract*, we may or may not be destined to deal with certain unfortunate events. It's all a matter of what the soul had previously signed up for, and whether they are allowed the help from the Divine or not.

There is so much involved when it comes to Spirit's Divine Protection, but the one thing they do guarantee, they're *always by your side*, no matter the situation. They will do all they are either allowed, or are capable, in order to ensure your security with their enormous, bountiful love.

Fortunately for me, Spirit intervened in a time of need for myself. There was an evening where I agreed to meet up with a person that I had known for a few years, at his house. But as the night progressed, I was beginning to feel negative vibes, which told me to leave. When I decided to depart and was walking down the road to my home, this person unexpectedly grabbed me from behind, wrapped his arms around me and was keeping me in a lock. I asked him to let go, but due to his heavily drunken state, he ignored my plea. After this moment, I heard from Spirit that something would happen to make him lose his grip. And without fail, a vehicle drove past us, honking their horn. Thankfully those few seconds of distraction was enough for me to swing one of my legs underneath his, pulled my leg hard forward, causing us both to land on the ground on our backs. Normally that wouldn't work, but because he's around my height, it was doable. And with his chest against my backside, it was easier for me to have a slightly upper hand. Because of his heavily intoxicated state, he was unaware that the fall was by my own doing. Without delay, I scurried away, just as he was attempting to grab me for a second time.

"The intuitive mind is a sacred gift and the rational mind is a faithful servant. We have created a society that honors the servant and has forgotten the gift."

-Albert Einstein

This not only gave me the chance to get away, but the fact was...Spirit was giving me the chance to leave in time for that vehicle to be there, that would release me from a possible worse fate. If I didn't leave at the exact moment that I did, that vehicle wouldn't have been there to help me get away safely. This influential protection of Spirit wasn't by a possession, but by a deep negative feeling for me to recognize when to depart in time, in order to be safe in the long run. That is how Spirit's influence keeps us safe. Spirit's love for us is so incredibly deep and they urge all of us to understand those gut feelings, our intuition is our *Divine Message Receiver*.

I can't tell you how many times my "gut feelings" have most often been right and have saved me and others, more times than I can count. Never, ever forget this message and I can promise you nine times out of ten, they will never steer you wrong either. Take your "gut feelings", instincts seriously, for they are Divine messages from the Higher Realms.

The further I go into the way Spirit can protect us, the more energy talk is involved. We are all made up of energy, thus allowing us to be able to feel, see and know Spirit is amongst us. This is the communication we have with Spirit and with our loved ones. Our emotions go a long way when it comes to the Spirit world, which is why we were given the gift to feel, in order for us to know what message to hear and to acknowledge.

COURAGE WITH THE DIVINE

I will never forget a particular session I had done for a woman who had lost her mother. And during this session, I began getting images from her departed mother's soul that nearly brought me to tears. I was being shown of a moment where my client had to confront a man who had threatened her with a knife against her throat. With slight apprehension, I asked her if what I had been seeing was indeed factual. She then confirmed this previous encounter. I then shared, "Your mother shows me that you put your hand on the knife without fear. And you gently talked this man out of a horrific possible act. …You even took the knife from his grip?" She began sobbing. I too felt these emotions from her mother and continued to send her further validations, but what came next, shocked us both. "Did you feel as if... someone was holding your hand, while you took the man's knife...?" Gasping for air in disbelief, she shouted, "OMG YES!" I then followed her mother's message with tears of my own as I said more... "I am told by your mother to always know that that was her you felt. Guiding you to make this brave, courageous attempt. Your mother put her hand on yours, granting you the strength to overcome this man's intentions. She is so proud of you, and you're so strong." My client was soulfully moved and forever will keep this loving memory on her journey, with her mother by her side in Spirit. Not only is she emotionally, spiritually guided, but knows even physically by the power of love with her mother's soul as her Spirit Guide. She always felt deep inside that the strength she had felt wasn't just hers and now she knows this without question thanks to Spirit.

LOVE'S LIFESAVER

Even now, this memory still shakes my soul, for this was something you would only see or hear in movies. How could this be? The power of our departed loved ones is something of a grand power, that we humans will never truly understand, at least not as long as we're human.

Spirit protects us with the force of God's help and the Universe. They don't only rely on themselves to keep us safe, but from the ultimate force which is God. Frequently, reminding us on a daily basis that no matter the level of need, we are always encouraged to ask them for their loving guidance and Divine Protection. We can overcome any obstacle as long as we continue to carry the power of love within our hearts. Spirit's loudest echo within the Universe, is to *use love as your shield and sword in this chaotic world we call Earth.*

Always hold it in your heart, the truth that you are never alone, even through the physical trials of this Realm. And even though you may feel physically alone, remember that this world is the illusion and our true form, is on the Other Side in Spirit. We all have loved ones from the Other Side, helping us to be the best version of us, and will be there for even our worst versions and situations.

The gloom in the rain isn't to defeat you, but to give you tremendous courage, to override anything and everything. So remember...when it gets cloudy, dark and thick with a wave of fog amongst your surroundings, you're *not alone...no matter how dark it may seem.*

Through the power of Divine love from Heaven and the Higher Realms, we are continually guided back into the beautiful positives of this world and the next. You are never left without their undivided attention in your direction, and they are forever loving and guiding you. And with that, I will end with this…

"Where there is love, there is life."

-Mahatma Gandhi

Universal Law Of Free Will

Free will is no different on the Other Side, than it is here. Reason being, is simply because you have a choice to respond or to react. You have a choice to heal, or to break everything, everyone around you. It is your choice to build, or to destroy the good of man, in the heart of all there is. Not only does free will have the power to build or to diminish one's character, it's the power within oneself to establish awareness through the act of doing and experiencing. Whether you are here physically alive or departed, free will remains to be a Universal truth based on one's consciousness.

YOU DECIDE YOUR DESTINY

Many people forgot as a collective that God doesn't choose anyone to do anything. He doesn't control you, and certainly doesn't control me. He does however, have the power to influence the good inside of us, with the choices that we make.

Let's not confuse the two. We are not in control of what happens to us, but we are in control of the decisions we make and how we choose to respond to those "happenings". The need to control, is not in God's nature, but He does influence the essence of your decisions with how, and why you make them. You can either allow them to be negative (unloving), or God (loving). It all depends on you. He doesn't choose that for you…only you do. He is the Source, the answer to all that is good and loving. The misconception that is so commonly believed is that God controls you, and your surroundings. But that is a misunderstanding. It's not that God controls your life, your destiny, or the time at which you live or die. It's all based on how you choose to live your life, and what you choose to do with it for others.

In the past, I used to spend time with two friends whom I knew had a lot of potential for greatness. They possess a fair amount of pocket knowledge, and wisdom that makes them really inviting. We had a lot of genuine likeminded conversations that were deep in nature, laughing over memories we shared.

But one memory that stands out the most, was a moment I will never forget. It was the moment that I realized how much people really had no idea, how much they're so important to God. We were sitting in their living room, and one of them said something that struck my heart. It was about their choice in where they stood in their spiritual beliefs. Changing themselves from Agnostic to Atheist.

Before I continue here, I want you to understand, *I don't label anyone. It is the person that chooses to label themselves.* Here, I am only quoting from my experience with them, and many others. I don't label, and don't care for labels. I care for who they are, and how they see themselves.

My friends and I were sitting on their couch, and one of them announced to me their spiritual belief. I listened adamantly, but knew in my heart that this was unfortunate, for they believed that they were here by accident. Both were certain they had never seen, heard, nor ever had an experience of God, or anything about the Other Side. One of my friends said, "I don't believe there is anything, but this here and now. I have never seen, heard, felt or experienced anything to give me reason to believe otherwise. God is just a figment of the imagination. It is only natural for people to want to believe in something greater than themselves. God wouldn't allow bad people to do bad things if He were real."

It only brings sadness to my eyes, and brokenness to my heart, when I hear such words. But I also agreed with them. Hear me out. They had a valid reason to doubt the Other Side, so I understood where they were coming from, for I used to question and was once convinced of the same thing. However, I listened, hearing the urgency in their words. I then carefully said, "God isn't responsible for your life, and He isn't responsible for other's wrongdoings. Just because someone killed another, doesn't make it God's fault, and certainly doesn't prove that He doesn't exist."

Their biggest issue that I recall clearly, was one of them said, "I don't let anyone tell me when, and how I will die." But He doesn't. God isn't sitting anywhere in the Universe, deciding how you will live your life, and where you will die. He doesn't have a desire for that. He is an all knowing being, with great power to love, create and to grow, but what He is not, is a destroyer of life. *Source is a creator of life,* not a destroyer.

Going back to the *Soul Contract*...we agreed to the lessons that we wanted to learn, but that doesn't mean that how we learn them, will be all His doing. It's hard to swallow at first, but the point is...maybe you signed up to learn how to love in the most difficult situations, but the way you learn them...doesn't mean it was because He made it that way.

He put you exactly where you, and Him agreed you would most likely learn those lessons, while the free will of *you*, and *others* would determine *how* you would learn which will too determine your fate or destiny. All those that carry a life as a human are given the choice of free will which allows them favor on how to live presently, which may or may not constitute a factor of one's passing. Our choices that we make *now*, in this very moment, is setting the bar of where and how we all will pass. No one is in more control than we are in this *now*. Literally at this very moment, is the moment that we all are given ever so graciously along with previously agreeing to our Soul Contract that sets the *how* and *when.*

Let's say however, you lived your life exactly like something out of a storybook. You brushed your teeth three times a day, slept early, saw your doctors regularly, was loyal to all of your friends, spouse and family and even went as far as being five minutes early for work every day. But then out of the blue, BAM you suddenly die from something you didn't expect. Then you ask Spirit that greets you, "I don't get it, I did everything right, why did I die sooner than I hoped? What did I do wrong? Did I not do enough of something?" But gently the Spirit that is listening puts a comforting hand on your shoulder while saying, "It was your time." No matter how young or old we may feel, we will always at times feel like "our time" is just too soon. But the fact of the matter is as we discussed, our Soul Contract is a binding agreement of the experiences and lessons you agreed to hone. And once that is said and done, and perhaps your purpose has been fulfilled, you will transition to the Other Side for further growth. So even though it may feel that it's something out of our control, to sorta say in a way is –it is. But, in hindsight we were given and consciously made the choice years before we came into this world, by already deciding when our time will be. It was never initially God's, but ours.

FREE SPIRITED

Once we reach our end of this physical life, that is where real life begins. Being here is only a taste of what is true, and what is real. Like many realities in life, we are faced to make choices and in the end of those choices, come the results, whether we wanted them or not. Like life here, there is free will on the Other Side.

If you haven't noticed, there are many Paranormal Investigators out in the world, and they are proving and providing useful information that the Other Side does exist. However, as wonderful and as helpful as the teams are, they have yet to prove *why* some Spirits still remain on the physical Realm.

Like the many P.I. I too have experienced much of the said paranormal activity, however for years I yet understood why Spirits are here, when they could be in Paradise. I wanted to make sure I had this information. I was on a mission to understand this questionable mystery. However, when I had finally discovered the answer I admit, I wasn't prepared for it. To tell you the truth, the answer shocked me, as Spirit said, *"...Because they can."*

Now the next question I'm sure you're probably thinking is, *Why?*

Seriously. If I knew that I had the option to go to Heaven, then my Spirit ass would be there in a flash, and that'd be a smaller ass mind you.

But the truth is, my Spirit Guides say, is because free will remains, so do their choices. Let's not confuse the fact that when we die, you all of a sudden can do whatever you want, without the consequences. Consequences exist even on the Other Side. If you are naughty here, you will reap your karmic consequences here. Same with if you are naughty there, you will too reap based upon your choices.

The loop that was startling to me to understand, is when you pass to the Other Side, you have the choice to go to Heaven or stay here. True. I know, right…sounded crazy to me too, trust me. But the fact is, you still have a choice to accept God's love, or to reject it.

FREE WILL'S VIBRATIONAL OUTCOME

When a soul chooses to stay on Earth, there's going to be a negative outcome upon the energy of the soul. It's a tragic fact that many souls don't want to cross over, and with this, they will remain Earth Bound, never exceeding in their lessons. Souls that choose to remain on Earth are more commonly known as *Low Vibrational Souls.* However, when a soul is ready to cross over to God, and accept God's love, they will then grow higher, lighter in their frequency, which allows them to be what is most known as a *High Vibrational Soul.*

Below are the distinct differences with the souls, and why they are, the way they are. Here you can learn to understand why it's so important for souls to continue their growth, with love on the Other Side…

LOW VIBRATIONAL SOULS: *Souls that choose actions/ feelings that are the opposite of love. Examples are hate, anger, jealousy, deceit, thievery, materialism, greed, harm, selfishness, judgement etc. Souls that choose to reside on the physical Realm, remain a lower vibration of energy, and or, have yet to master life lessons depending on the intentions of the soul. Soul unaware of thyself. Unaware of the consciousness that is limitless, entranced upon the physical illusions and delusions of the physical.*

HIGH VIBRATIONAL SOULS: *Souls that choose to go to Source, allowing love to heal, and transfer them to a higher energy frequency, a higher level of consciousness of thyself that is no longer bound by the Ego. A Soul no longer possessed by the illusions and delusions of the physical. Through learning lessons, and mastering love in all angles, they become closer to a Godlike energy. Examples are love, forgiveness, accountability, compassion, sacrifice, gratitude, loyalty, nonjudgmental views, selflessness, empathy etc. Further the progression through lessons with love, the more the soul is closer to God and ultimate oneness within the Universe.*

Now that you know the difference between *Low* and *High Vibrational Souls,* you can now see why it's so important to cross the barrier of here, to the Other Side. Staying here isn't ideal for anyone at all.

YOU CAN'T GLOW IF YOU DON'T GROW

I will never forget a reading I did for a woman named Betsy. She's your favorite kind of Southern girl, from North Carolina, that loves three things. God, her family, and good home cooked meals. She was lovely. She was nervous, but I knew deeply she needed to know that her loved ones were not only happy on the Other Side, but that they freely visit her. Connecting with both her departed fiancé, and father, she was able to get the closure and validation that she needed. But what startled us both, was how Spirit did this for her. During a point in the session, I was told to bring up about her pets barking at nothing. And to our utter disbelief, when she confirmed her dogs have done that on numerous occasions, one of her dogs then began barking at thin air during her explaining. We were floored! Betsy then stated that there was no one around, so why did the dog bark? Coincidence my rear! Spirit made sure, that during her session, she not only would get the comforting reassurance that her loved ones were safe, and at peace with God, but that what she was experiencing was in fact Spirit.

What's even more remarkable, is the way Betsy described her fiancé in her dreams. She shared how her fiancé would appear to her in visits as this bright, *glowing* Spirit. Her experience is a classic case of a *High Vibrational Soul*, due to the *glow* that she expressed. The glow is the essence of *Godliness* that enables them to continue loving, living and embracing life to the fullest on the Other Side. And the more they grow, the more they are able to have the speechless moments with us here on the Earth Realm. Spirits with high vibrational energy, is a sure sign they're growing with love while gaining the highest levels of wisdom and intelligence with Source.

Many people also express how their departed loved ones will *glisten*, to the point that it's almost hard to imagine. Almost as if the soul is *bedazzled* with endless jewels of every size imaginable. Spirit wants you to know, that if and when you see them *shimmering*, that is the essence of the Godlike energy frequency that they have gained from their lessons learned.

Choices that are loving, will bring a greater reward vs. choices fueled of a lower vibration, such as greed, jealousy, materialism, etc. In order for the soul to be of a glowing, or glistening energy vibration, the soul has to cross over to the Other Side, leaving the Earth Realm for a time being. Unless the soul does so, the soul will remain limited to only the Earthly limitations, which is not encouraged.

Free will is to enhance your soul, so as to become what we were meant to be, which is an unlimited being of consciousness. Many have come to believe, that once you reach the Other Side, you are automatically this all knowing being with ultimate wisdom, power and purity. Sure, the purity is in all of us, however if all of that were true, it would defeat the purpose of lessons. In order to understand between what's considered unconditional love, we have to have free will in order to learn the difference.

A NEW VIEW

I remember a conversation I had with my dad. We were discussing parenting, and the differences when I grew up vs. how kids are being raised today. And what he said was something that stuck with me. He said, "It doesn't matter how many years go by, the mind will always wonder why they couldn't do something when they're told not to." My parents' way of raising five of us kids, was to allow us to make our mistakes, in order to understand why not to make them. They understood that forcing someone to learn, is not the way to teach, but allowing someone to learn is better and more adaptable. Of course, they told us not to smoke cigarettes, drink alcohol or do something that would be irresponsible, unwise or unsafe. However, if they enforced us to not experience those said mistakes as adults, we never would've understood why not to. I'm not saying that doing something that's dangerous to our body, mind and soul is a good way to learn. But the harsh reality is, there are people in this world that learn the hard way, allowing life to essentially become their best teacher.

That being said, all religions and spiritual beliefs hold some levels of truth behind them in different cases. They all serve a beautiful message, aiding in faith for humanity. I am sure you may be wondering, what this has to do with free will. It has so much to do with it. When I first learned about God, I challenged the Bible constantly, out of the fact that deeply inside, it didn't make sense to me. I said at one point with a pastor, "I don't get it...why would God make us imperfect intentionally, but then damn us because we don't know any better?" The pastor replied, "That is why He made the Commandments, so you can understand how to be perfect." I then thought, knowing it still didn't make sense, and I again followed with, "Okay...but that doesn't make sense. What's the point of making us imperfect, if we aren't allowed to learn anything? How could He expect us to learn anything in the first place? Isn't that just setting us up to fail? Why would he damn us for being who He made us to be?" I was sixteen, and was always searching for more answers to all of my whys. My mission at that moment was to truly understand the concept of not the words of the Bible, but of why we are here. I know this is pushing the envelope a bit, but truth be told, it just sounded like a milestone that deemed impossible. And essentially, it is.

Realistically, it's just not factual to control every part of your life, and even our thoughts in order to learn lessons. If that were the case, then what would be the point of being here? Why would we be born to live in a world where perfection is required to go to Heaven if we were already made to be imperfect to begin with? With that being said let's take a moment to look over a few different interpretations of numerous religious and spiritual beliefs.

The word *"sin"* has been highly misinterpreted while severely misunderstood. Sin translated from ancient Greek in which the New Testament was written, to sin means *to miss the target*. To sin means *to miss the point of human existence.* Literally meaning *to live blindly thus leading to causing suffering.* Christian teachings from the expected collective, is of one of the "original sin". In other words, to be born imperfect and in order to become "worthy" or "perfect" is to not commit sin. And to not commit such "sinful" acts, one must follow the Commandments. Frequently the term *sin* is also suggested as, an *immoral act considered to be a transgression against Divine Law. A sin in the eyes of God. Wrongdoing, act of wickedness, evil or a misdeed.* Those that I have encountered both religious and non, agree that the word "sin" makes you feel as if you are unworthy, unloved, undervalued, and just downright disapproving due to the majority teaching this misinterpretation as such. This idealistic view, for so long has created a negative vibe. Thus, ultimately not aiding the rest of humanity to know that you aren't "dirty", no matter what you have endured. To say, it is not the word "sin" that has caused such a negative impression on the feel of self, but that the so loosely used misconception of the word is what is damaging at best.

According to the Buddhists' belief, the human mind in its normal state creates what is known as *dukkha*. Dukkha translated properly is known as *suffering, dissatisfaction* or *misery.* Buddha foresaw it as a characteristic of human nature. And that whatever one does, wherever one goes one shall encounter *dukkha* and it will manifest in every situation eventually.

Whereas in the Hindus' belief, it is a form of a collective mental illness, calling it *maya*, the *veil of delusion.*

Collaborating these select few beliefs, what may we determine? That the word *sin, dukkha* and *maya* are what are modernly known as the **Ego.** So what is the Ego? Ego in translation is of *one to walk in the world identified by form through thoughts. To be veiled of the truth of the essence of beingness, unaware of consciousness, of thyself and others as a whole in the Universe. Ego* in thyself is what creates separateness, limitations created by formed thoughts. The Ego can be considered the "original sin", the unskilled, the sufferer of the suffering within the delusion and illusion.

With such odds of the human condition, what does one do when in the presence of free will while continually faced with the Ego? Free will is the freedom to make a conscious decision. Again, there's the word *conscious.* The definition of the Ego establishes a basic understanding between being *aware* and unaware of the presence of our consciousness. And when we can become *aware* through our *consciousness* that is when one is able to distinguish between the "right" and "wrong" of *being* towards life itself.

EGO & FREE WILL

With our free will, we are granted the beautiful and amazing grace to understand the course of what love is, and what it is not. Wouldn't you rather know the truth of yourself, than believing that you aren't deemed worthy?

Don't you want to accept that you are worthy? Deep in the heart of millions throughout the planet they desperately want to experience the feel of true worthiness of unconditional love but without the understanding of the Ego, more and more are living within the ignorance, this unawareness.

From my deep dive into the Spiritual Realm, with my Spirit Guides, Angels and God, I have been given the opportunity to learn that our Divine reason for being here is to learn the *"sin" from our* **Lessons of the Ego.** Being unable to truly escape the *sin, dukkha, maya* or if even *Ego* we must remain aware of our essence in ourselves and without this experience as the experiencer, we would never fully understand the concept of being in the presence of now. With the gift of free will we are not only granted the precious token of moments but of a deeper understanding of ourselves and others as a higher level of consciousness. Free will gives the experiencer (you) the chance to hone all of life through your moments and to embrace the emotions for what they are.

In the King James Bible, Jesus states, *"Father, forgive them; for they know not what they do."* (Luke 23:34). Here Jesus is insisting that we put forgiveness on others based on the lack of awareness. When interpreted correctly, Jesus is referring to those that are unaware of the human collectiveness of the Ego. Unaware of the consciousness at which they are reacting upon out of lack of self-awareness. Most have misunderstood this to be based on the sinful acts which can still be understood correctly if fully embraced by the awareness of thyself. So if one were to commit sin, the sin at which that is being committed, *are the behaviors, choices through one's free will that are driven by the Ego that is essentially unaware of the bigger picture.*

So the question again is, *with such odds of the human condition, what does one do when in the presence of free will while continually faced with the Ego?* As we discussed, Ego is one that is unaware. As long as one is in awareness of oneself and of the bigger picture at all times with alertness, then the Ego can no longer become a factor. So even though as Buddha described that no matter where you go or what you do, you will always be faced with the Ego eventually, the good news is, as long as one *remains in constant awareness of thyself and of others through the consciousness of being,* then the Ego will only be a distant ray in the background.

This doesn't mean that hurting others or doing irresponsible things is an excuse for learning. Although the consciousness is able to be aware at all times, the consciousness that is us, can so easily be taken over by the Ego. While you or I are alive physically in this Realm we are to embrace what experiences come with it which would include the Ego. That is our test, to master the Ego that is a part of all of us while here on the Earth Realm. Once however the soul departs and is no longer a slave to this Egoic unawareness, what happens to their consciousness? Does it expand or shrink?

Spirit has expressed that each soul still possess their consciousness which in turn still grants the soul the freedom from the Universal Law of Free Will. And with that free will, they can still choose to deny or accept those lessons for what they are. To say, the Ego may remain present in the soul that has departed if they choose by free will, to be unaware. So as long as we are consciousness (which we are for eternity) we will remain to possess the gift of free will to either deny or accept those lessons of the Ego.

"I think that true religion is the kind heart."

-Dalai Lama

THE PURPOSE OF BOTH

The new message for us, is to be able to take the love by embracing the lessons from our Ego that is essentially unawareness of the bigger picture. The further aware one is of their essence when in Spirit, the freer the soul becomes. The less resistant of the "happenings" one is, the less reactive one shall be. And the less reactive one is, the more one responds to the now without the Ego overshadowing the judgment.

So does this mean that the Ego is a "bad" way to live? Yes & No. The Ego that I have learned from Spirit, is a reminder of who we are on the inside and who we are not. It is a reminder of why we make the choices that we make that are labeled "good" or "bad". The purpose of life is about understanding thyself through learning the Ego which is simply being unaware. Without the Ego we wouldn't have lessons to learn, for all of us would be already "perfect". It would defeat the whole point of honing your true *being* regardless of obstacles. And with the Ego, it gives us a chance to make a choice through our free will of who we want to be in this life based on the "good" and "bad" in the "happenings" of life. To carefully point out, one's Ego is the unawareness of thyself, the unawareness of the bigger picture. And it is the Ego that is essentially the harsh yet invaluable teacher of the true meaning of life here and the next. It is through the acts and effects of the Ego that will guide us to understanding who we are and who we are not. I am not saying that the Ego is what we need to learn by, but that those that learn the hard way by making the same mistake over and over again, at times is the only teacher left to learn from. As the Ego will always be there as Buddha described, one must remain aware of their *being*, of their *soulfulness* that is forever connected to Source that which is limitless. Remaining in the presence of now while being consciously aware of the potentialities of the bigger picture at all times, only then can the Ego be overcome. Awareness and Ego cannot coexist. Simply put, one cannot be unaware while one is already aware. And as long as one remains aware through free will that the Ego is always there, but is a distant ray in the background, then one will be able to overcome any obstacles through their free will.

In short, it is our Ego that can negatively affect our free will choices. As long as one is aware of themselves in all moments that is essentially not a part of the Ego but of a higher being of consciousness, then our free will choices will be that of a loving nature. This also would explain why there are many departed souls that are not of a loving vibration due to the soul following the Ego that is essentially unaware of the bigger picture.

It's free will that allows us to make mistakes and to understand the ripple effects of life. Without free will, we wouldn't know (being aware) that sticking a fork in an outlet is dangerous. We wouldn't know (being aware) that cheating wasn't the wisest way in getting out of a relationship. It wouldn't teach us how to make a left turn, instead of a right. Life is about teaching, it's about lessons.

Where free will and Ego is concerned, Creator doesn't force us to go to Him. With that, Source is understanding of the challenge it may be for some, to see through the Ego, which is why He is forever merciful in teaching us this bigger picture even on the Other Side. However, if one is to choose not to accept themselves and Creator with love, then they will not be able to ascend higher to a point of the highest frequency, consciousness possible. Love is the message to all that He is, and with that, comes the course of allowing you to learn with love,…even if that means loving you enough to let you figure it out by experiencing the Ego.

Heaven & Hell

As so perfectly put by my younger sister, Heather, "There is a silver lining in life here, as there is there." The concept of Heaven is vast in different cultures and beliefs, along with the idea of Hell. With my walk with Spirit, I have come to understand that the modern approach to these Realms is different than what has been portrayed. I know, again this is a large leap, but with your permission, I will continue here with a deeper, basic idea of what Spirit says about them. I will discuss each Realm to their core of who goes to each, why and how. These are just my own interpretations from what I have learned from God, Spirit and Angels, so you can take this or leave it. I will never say for sure that I am 100% accurate, for this is all based upon my interpretation from Spirit.

DESCRIBED THROUGH THE AGES

The Christian/ Catholic faith have a strong belief in being saved by the savior, while determining where you belong in Judgment. Judaism has come to believe in various versions of Heaven, some of which occur after the Messiah comes, and allowing the righteous dead coming back to life on the Earth Realm. The spiritual belief of Hinduism's oldest sacred text, are the notions of oneself and the afterlife, being developed over numerous lifetimes.

According to the Upanishads, our actions connect us to this world of illusion. The Universal Law of Karma can only bring you a sense of relief from death and rebirth. Reincarnation is done based off of your actions and reactions, thus only then can you be set free. Therefore, once you learn from your Earthly ignorance and realize that ultimately, you are not you, but Brahman itself, you can achieve release from the endless cycle of reincarnation.

Buddhism believes in the concept of reincarnation while the Ego or (desire) continues to burn inside of you as a flame, which prevents you from the truth of your ultimate self. Releasing the Ego (desire) will be the only source to truth that will allow you to ascend to Nirvana.

Each belief above that are only briefly described, may carry a bit of the version of what may be true on the Other Side. Can I say with 100% certainty that each one is absolutely right and one is wrong? No. A belief, or spiritual preference is what speaks to the person that follows it based on personal aspects, so I cannot say that one is right while the other is wrong necessarily. Being as I don't personally follow a set religion or belief system, I do feel however, that each carry some versions of what may have in fact been factual or is truthful to a sense today. Let's be real, yes, I can speak and hear from souls that have departed but even I myself don't always have all of the answers to say which one to follow. But what I have learned is that our Source is not a religious Deity, yes I talk about Deities such as Jesus Christ and Buddha but if you haven't noticed I don't set myself to either of their views…but look at each one openly with acceptance without judgment. I know Jesus did in fact exist and still does in Spirit, why? Because of my NDE.

However even so, I am not a Christian or a Catholic due to remaining open to all levels of spirituality so as to not close off the mind that then closes off the heart.

With that being said, I have indeed received information from Source and from the Higher Deities about the Other Side, including the Realms, *Heaven* and *Hell.* What I share is what I have heard and have seen in Divine visions from departed loved ones, Angels, Jesus and even God Himself.

Heaven

WHAT IS HEAVEN?

Heaven is a place that all souls have the privilege to reside. It's a Paradise that grants each of us the feel of pure freedom, love and true serenity. We are all able to experience Heaven, and are given that right from the time we were created by Creator. As I have described in previous chapters, Heaven is a blissful serenity without any means of war, disputes or pain. All souls that reside on this Realm are fueled by love, harmony and peace. Each soul is given the beautiful opportunity to experience this Realm in order to determine whether it's truly for them in Spirit. With this gift, more than most, will easily choose this Realm over Hell, due to the wonders this Realm possesses.

Heaven is such a beautiful place, that it will bring tears to your soul filled with so much joy. I have seen this glorious place, and the beauty is so *enchanting*, that it will *literally leave you absolutely speechless.* There is no justifiable way to describe how gorgeous this Realm is, but it's most *definitely a place where I want to be!*

In Heaven, I have been taught that it's a world of its own. The seasons we experience on Earth, also circulate throughout Heaven like I have never seen before. You can take one step and be in the season of summer, feeling God's grace fall upon your energy with such love. Then you can take several steps, soon finding yourself embracing the season of winter. All of the seasons exist on this Realm, and are amplified to the highest levels of magnificence.

I remember a time during my visit in Heaven where it began to rain. Like most women, I was trying to hide the rain from my hair, but Spirit communicated the joy in embracing your inner child, by dancing in the rain. Because the weather doesn't affect our souls as it does to our bodies on Earth, they pressed on for me to remember the simple joys in life without worry.

Same goes for winter, as in another part of my visit, we had the fun of a snowball fight without ever feeling cold. Each soul was able to enjoy each season, minus the negative effects to the body one may experience here on Earth when in doing so.

One of the more spectacular experiences in Heaven is being able to connect with all that surrounds through energy wavelengths. Each tree, flower, and blade of grass has its own life to it. They too breathe everlasting life on the Other Side. And Spirit has shown that each human soul has the ability to help make plant life grow in Heaven. They will sing to the trees, water the flowers and give them a nudge to exceeding their growth by using the most powerful push of all, *love.* The plants in

Heaven have their own energy frequency, not as high levels as human souls, but still require the help of us to evolve. Many human souls have a green thumb in aiding the plant life on the Other Side. With their own special abilities, they are able to give the flowers, trees, bushes and even the grass a green light to continue their shine.

Have you ever dreamt of what it would be like to fly? I have, and Spirit shares that you can do that on this Realm. You can fly, swim, jump over mountains and experience things like a superhero. You can do practically anything on this Realm. But if the simplicity to life has your fancy, you can enjoy a good book, accompanied with a nice cold cup of iced tea. Or, if you like the outdoors, you can enjoy the fun of fishing in the most beautiful rivers imaginable. Flawless rivers that will leave you speechless, captivated by the powerful greens, purples, yellows, oranges, reds, pinks, blues, grays and millions of others. Each color brings out the most beautiful of emotions for the human and animal soul, which is why God made this so purposeful. His mission, God's dream is for us to truly explore and hone that spectacular side of Him...that side of us by embracing eternal peace.

Because food is not a necessity, they're not required to eat. But the joy of food is a great way for the souls to join together in union, thanking God for the Eden, for the experiences of eternal life beyond our wildest fantasies. To add, they will eat foods like fish on the Other Side, but when they do, they say thanks to God, and thank the fish for the gift of taste and experience. So again, food is just another gift in experience. *No animal life is ever harmed* on the Other Side because essentially they cannot technically die a second time. Instead, the gift and the tastes of food is only another *illusion* that is simply for the souls to experience life as a human soul once again.

An obvious gap of difference in opinion lies on the topic of whether human souls eat food or not on the Other Side and I am only sharing what I know first handedly. No animal soul is ever actually harmed in Heaven but is only the illusion, the formlessness manifestation that is eaten for the human soul to recapture a memory of life on Earth.

There was a sincere debate on this topic that I once had encountered with two women. They claimed that eating animals in Heaven (and in general) didn't make sense and it must be Hell, that I was confusing the dimensions. Stating that anyone who chooses to eat animals are merely living in their Ego. One of the women even claimed that I was speaking of "evil" behavior that no God would allow such cruelty upon its creatures nor condone it. I listened to their exclamations graciously but simply responded with, "As there is an evolution in life here there is on the Other Side." Like I had said, we are all made up of energy and that energy continues its cycle as a never ending foundation for all life that coexists throughout the Universe. If God didn't want us to eat animals, then why do and did some of the most holy of men and women on this Earth eat fish such as Jesus Christ? And if I can recall correctly, there is a scripture in the King James Version of the Holy Bible where Jesus speaks, *"And He said unto them, Follow Me, and I will make you fishers of men."* (Matthew 4:19). Jesus in this scripture notes to teaching the people how to fish. But if He was so against animals as another source of food, then why do so, if this were against the Divine Laws? There was another instance in the New Testament (Luke 24:42) where speaks of Jesus eating broiled fish and honeycomb in the presence of His disciples after His resurrection. If eating animals or anything that is considered "life" that which inhabits a consciousness is Egoful or "evil", then why did Jesus? Does this mean He too was a participant in this "evil atrocity" as they put it? Naturally one would suspect that if such a deed were either "sinful" or "evil" then why would He have helped the men and women eat meat in the first place? Surely His holiness would not have condoned such a thing if this were against Source, Creator.

To remember, our Holy sister Mother Teresa who too was a non-vegetarian. Not only was she a devout Christian for her love of humanity through Jesus Christ, she too ate meat.

When we take a look at the Buddhist monk the Dalai Lama, from recent efforts one would discover since the 1960s His holiness is a meat-eater. Unlike most Buddhist monks, he tried being a vegetarian for a bit but had to give it up after he became ill with hepatitis. Buddhist monks that don't eat meat are founded on the belief it is wrong to slaughter any sentient being yet the most currently highly respected is not amongst this group. Now why is this? Regardless of their choices in life, their life calling to be who they were and are, doesn't change one's personal perception or perspective of what they can or cannot eat. I would imagine they're not one to disregard this difference amongst the others in their circle of belief, but it is indeed intriguing to lean towards this open mindedness of why vs why-not.

While the idea of harming an animal in order for one to survive may not be the best picture in mind of how the carcass is being "processed" or "prepared", I would encourage one to consider the natural worldly reality of the wild that too, are carnivorous. Many animals in the course of the world, including plants, eat other forms of life that indeed possess a consciousness. Now, forgive my push, but if this is indeed the case, (which it is) then why are we not also pointing to this atrocity? The carnivorous coyote eat other animals in order to feed their cubs, while the hippopotamus is an omnivore, eating both animal life along with plant life. If being a meat eater was such an unspeakable killer of life itself, while all animals in the world are pure based on their inner connectedness to Source for not being affected by the Ego –then why would Source give them the instinctual behavior to do the same to survive? One could say in fairness, "Animals eat for survival." Wait, but that includes the hippopotamus, while having the choice to eat both animal and plant life. But you don't see the hippo suddenly deciding to become a vegetarian. While probably less than a mile away from the hippo there is a zebra being chased and savagely overcome by the king of the jungle. If the lion wasn't supposed to eat animal life like the fellow zebra, then why make him that way? Is too the lion being entranced by the Ego?

The animals are not the only legitimate source of thought, but so is the plant life throughout the globe. Most forget to take into account that plants indeed eat insects that rest upon their territory even including rats and frogs if given the opportunity. These charming plants, categorized as carnivorous, trap insects and arthropods by producing digestive juices that dissolve their unlucky prey. After this they derive some, or most, of their nutrients from this process, from the prey itself. There are reported to be well over 670 different species of these fascinating plants. And some of these plants have over 200 species of just one kind but are different in their own ways. Despite their unique alluring appearance, each are deadly to the insect or other lively creatures that come face to face with one. While there are over 670 species, there are five basic trapping mechanisms found in all these plants: Snap traps, Fly Paper traps, Bladder traps, Pitfall traps and Lobster pot traps. To name a few of these plants, there is the most famous Venus Flytrap, the Utricularia, the Drosera and the Pinguicula.

As we are all a part of the Earth, the course of creation goes in its place at which it was created. Life is a gift. The established planet Earth, yet not so easily recognized is the master supplier for all that coexists. All life on Earth is a gift. All life has a purpose whether it is to live long or short physically, for each life is meant as a Divine purpose that is guided with utter precision to form the bigger picture that one must take time to witness that is present. There is life in all forms, besides animals but in the plants, the soil and all that you may not be aware of that once was life. Everything we own or may have used once, used to be a living organism. Such as the roses someone gave you for your anniversary. The leather from your couch, or the chair you are sitting in right now while reading this book accompanied with a pair of rather expensive leather shoes or heels was once was a living cow. Or the desk, table, floors, or other things that were made from the trees man had chopped down in order for human civilization to flourish, were all once a living organism.

To only pinpoint one life over another would be not only ignoring the point of life, but of the bigger picture that is ever evolving. Life is meant to flourish naturally, to the extent of even the animals evolving over centuries to be the animals coexisting today. Not all of the creatures on Earth were the same form of species centuries ago. Did you know that? Many in fact changed, dramatically, morphing their bodies to adapt to the changes of life itself.

Creatively, similar to plants and animals in the world, we eat what best responds to our own different characteristics like the rest of wildlife. When we look more closely on animals, plants and us, we are not that far from them. We are from a separate though similar species, yet we possess our own personal diet. Such as when we look at the famous polar bear, its diet is rarely vegetarian, mostly craving beluga whale, walrus and seals. Then compare the polar bear to the black bear and you will discover the black bear is an omnivore, enjoying roots, berries, and grasses along with the occasional insect and other forms of meat. Both mammals are in the bear family, yet both instinctually prefer their own distinctive diet completely opposite from the other. Like these bears, humans look different, come from different parts of the world, while too surviving on dissimilar diets respectively.

So by speaking genetically based on the instinctual bodily necessity that is in every living creature, not just humans here on this planet now, it would be safe to say that neither being a meat eater or a vegetarian is bad but is the reflection of the course of nature. Only through one's perception of what is "right" or "wrong" is it then labeled as such. Animals in the wild and even domesticated don't do what they think is "right" or "wrong", instead each pet and wild animal merely respond to their bodies and habitual nature that which defines said desires and needs without question. The animal and plant life are not set on inner dialog nor doubts their instinctual desires like humans for their consciousness is not affected by the Ego but are only responding to what they *were designed* to do.

Does this mean those that are meat eaters are bad, "evil", or unaware due to living in the Ego? Well, if that were the case, then that would mean that every plant and animal that is either carnivorous or omnivorous would also be living in the "Egoic evil". However, as we went over, no animal lives nor is ever affected by the Egoic behavior like mankind so with that said, it is highly unlikely to be so. Animals and plants cannot simply live through the Ego for they are untouchable due to their purity that is Divinely connected to Source. So with that being said, I will let you be the judge of what you believe.

We are all connected to the limitless potential grounded upon the infinite Source, not requiring a meal to survive on the Other Side. However, from going into the depth of my experiences with Jesus from my NDE and Angels during countless visits in Heaven, the likelihood that it is considered "evil" to enjoy the goodness of meat has not yet been confirmed by their Holiness.

Until Jesus Himself or Angels confirm this to me personally, I don't underestimate this particular possibility based on the boundless potentiality that the enjoyment of food is too in Paradise, but just in a different way.

Each soul, big, or small will always be treated with the highest levels of respect. And even so, the fish aren't alive, to say, like they are here. Food is more of a gift from God Himself, an expression of His love for us.

Truth be told, nothing is impossible in the Realm of Heaven, and is greatly encouraged by Spirit to never doubt the endless possibilities of His glory. This is God's true Eden. The Garden of Eden that many have been led to believe, does in fact exist, but only on the Other Side.

Another really neat note I learned about Heaven, are the colors. The colors are so intensified beyond measure, including the amount of colors that I had seen. The colors are so vast in Heaven that it goes beyond the color pallet. Each color has its own energy frequency as all things do on the Other Side. And with each color, they bring about their own waves that enhance other energy waves. So for example, imagine you are sitting in a green field. But instead of you sitting on that green grass, you're feeling the green vibration of that grass. Along with feeling the color of the grass in its entirety. The energy of the color makes the greens of that grass more vibrant to the point of bringing it more to life on the Other Side.

To elaborate a bit more, Angels are with us in Heaven. Angels that reside in Heaven have a Divine job in keeping Heaven balanced, along with teaching other souls that reside in Heaven.

Receiving the blessed sight of Angels is truly beyond this world. When I have certain dreams, I will *know* when it's a dream from my subconscious, or a vision from Spirit and Angels. I can tell you this dream was *definitely* a vision without an ounce of doubt. During this vision, I felt my soul gently flowing out of my physical body. Ascending higher toward what felt like multiple dimensions, I came to a gentle delay of movement and soon discovered I was in a place surrounded by an unspeakable golden blissful ray of illumination. Associated by an insertion of warmth and security erasing all disbelief as for what I saw could not be ignored. As all of my senses were adjusting to this higher Realm, I hear this mystic resonance bringing waves into the core of my being that brought utter tranquility that was unfamiliar. *"What is this magnificence?"* I ask myself in thought while searching for the assuming instrument that made such a sound. But I was wrong. For as soon as my thought arose, the majestic owner of this unworldly vibration came into view. It was an Angel. The Angels were singing harmoniously. This original tune brought tears to my eyes. An Angel's hymn in Heaven is *nothing* like one's ever heard as the hymn from an Angel doesn't echo out in the atmosphere, but within your core. The Angels were singing for my soul. As if, their melody was literally hugging my soul. The grace from Angels in the authentic form is *unlike anything* I had ever seen. What's more, I can still recall the rhythm of their movement within this dimension. Each sway they made was as if they were underwater. So swift, gentle and guided by the highest levels of energy possible. When they greeted me with their unsurpassed radiance, I knew this was a once in a lifetime encounter. The uncharted glow from their sacred contour was close to incomprehensible. I remember looking at this one specific Angel that shined so brightly with a glitter about her, that I swear I could see my own reflection upon her Godlike originality. Each sparkle danced within their smile, eyes and even hair. I remember still to this day how speechless I was when they approached me.

Unconditional love birthed from the depths of their indescribable pupils that were *unlike anything* remotely imaginable. As they came closer, I could make out the remarkable detail of each accent of their form. The golden remedy of their bodies was almost unforgiving for it stole your heart the second one witnessed this holy rarity. An Angel's essence is truly *beyond extraordinary.*

I can still recall the white, glittered garment lengths of perfection draping in harmony to their rhythm. Each wrinkle seemed as if it were on purpose to only encourage their holy remedy to retaliate your heart. *"How could such beings exist?"* I quietly asked myself as their eyes laughed with an inescapable bliss. It seemed as if no being, no skill through words could justifiably recap what I had seen. The longer I gazed upon what could never be truly described, another gasp of air escaped me as I took sight of their wings. Each feather was precise. This magnitude of precision through feathers couldn't be witnessed without a sense of humility. No marks or imperfections could possibly be identified for like the rest of their presence was *nothing short of spectacular.*

I *truly wish* I could show you what I had seen, but the good thing is, we all will be able to experience this when our time comes. Even as I describe this, doesn't even come close to how sensational an Angel's encounter is. To add, this encounter happened because I begged God to allow me to see the true beauty of Angels, for I am a firm believer that I have no right to talk about something if I have never experienced it myself first hand. And with this, the experience was something *so special,* I can guarantee *they absolutely exist!*

What's more, Spirit shares that even though beauty is not the most important part on the outside when here, however the true beauty from within our soul manifests the inner beauty on the outside. So, if you feel as if at times your physical body doesn't quite give your soul justice, you're right! The physical-ness of us, is to learn that looks aren't everything. To remind us that the truest points of love is from the inside of the person. And when we are evolving into our purest forms of ourselves in Heaven, that authenticity of your love manifests finally on the outside… giving you both glories of yourself. Which is why souls glow to begin with, for the glow is their essence of their love manifesting on the outside, as so does the inside. So as long as you love deeply here and there, you will forever be just as radiantly, eternally whole.

Souls that reside in Heaven have their own jobs, and a place they can call Home. Each soul is granted gifts like Angels, and they too are to bestow those gifts to others in order to help build a brighter, lighter energy frequency throughout the Realm. Some souls will greet souls in Heaven, while some will be the teachers for the lesser experienced. Then some will be the guide to the animal souls, while others will take on the responsibility and experience of helping new souls through past life trauma. They all possess beautiful attributes that grant them the ability to enhance each other within this Realm. We are all granted the gift in experiencing true absolute Divine love on the Other Side, and in this Realm you will get this and *more.*

Quite frankly, Heaven is a lot like Earth. We all have our own Home and Spirit family we can live happily with for all eternity along with sharing memories at the many festivals in Paradise. Each soul is given the Divine opportunity to experience what Earth was meant to be originally, which is a blissful place where everyone is loved equally. The more fun and exciting part is I have also been taught that each person is their own kind of celebrity. Unlike Earth where you have to either acquire money, or a special kind of status in the eyes of the world to become famous, people in Heaven are all famous in their own way! How great is that?! We all have our own celebrity lifestyle where we all can enjoy, and experience the kind of life that we have ever dreamed of for *all* are in complete support of each other *equally.* All are appreciated and are equally important on this Realm.

The bliss of Heaven is something I wish all people could experience. Even I am in shock, that what I had the privilege of experiencing was real. It's something that no one can truly, or really want to deny. *It's that amazing.* The food, the laughter, the ambiance, the beauty is so brilliant, that it would blow your mind. Even I have a very hard time truly believing in what I saw. But I can tell you *without* a doubt, it's *not* a place you want to skip.

Spirit expresses time and time again, that no matter who you are, you are always welcomed in God's kingdom. This shouldn't be a shocker, because God's message has, and will forever remain, that regardless of what the world says, you were always meant for Heaven.

JUDGED NOT

Love doesn't have a title, and neither should you. When you look at yourself in the mirror, you don't automatically think of your spiritual practice do you? No, and neither do I. No, we see ourselves and think, *"OMG I have new grey hair!"* Or, *"Where did that mole come from??"*

It pains my heart when people harshly judge others about their loyalty to God. Judging whether or not they love God enough based on their level of works. But God has shared that His love for us is not earned by our works, but on how we treat our fellow brothers and sisters. And when Heaven is involved, He and Angels will help guide us to this deeper understanding about the power of love on the Other Side. Even in Heaven, we are taught the value and importance of love. With that being said, when we die we are not judged based on our works, but are to ask ourselves how we treated others and why. He will ask us what we feel deep inside, and then give us a chance to look at how we measured fellow humanity in spite of our Ego. Believe it or not, it is not God that judges us, but *it is us that judge ourselves.*

I love meeting people from all kinds of walks of life, for each teaches me so much on unconditional love and how we are different for a very special reason. One of the most heartwarming messages I receive from Spirit, is that we are not our bodies. Love is not your face, hair, skin, height, religion, culture, background, history, race, sexuality, gender or lifestyle. If God wouldn't judge you on your physical form, why should you? There are no accidents when it comes to life. Whether you are African-American, straight, Caucasian, short, Gay, Asian, handicapped, blind, deaf, a Little Person, Transgender or even purple with green polka-dots, doesn't matter. For Creator made you *exactly* the way you were meant to be.

I remember a conversation I had with a friend about the Gay community. She didn't understand why people would "allow" themselves to be Gay, especially when it's against God's rules or laws. I listened and then simply replied, "I know that in some beliefs it speaks of a man being with a man is wrong, and a woman with a woman is considered wrong. But I have learned that since God is an all knowing being, with the highest wisdom and creation possible, then it's up to Him on whether He approves or not. And if He chooses to change those rules or Commandments, then He can, because He's God. And even though I'm straight and can't relate to the feelings a Gay person has, doesn't mean they're wrong on how they feel."

My friend heard but she quickly retorted, "God obviously made a mistake." I then responded with, "No. God doesn't make mistakes and He certainly hasn't made mistakes with a person being different from you or I." After a long pause, all I could say that made her think was this: "Maybe, just maybe, God decided to bring Gays and other people into the world, to give us another way to love, accepting others without judgment." Our Creator wants us to live and to accept love in all areas, even if that means something that is against His "rules".

We put so much pressure on ourselves when trying to be accepted, but the truth is you are already amazing, because you were made out of love. Creator doesn't base you off of your body, history, or the countless mistakes that you make.

Take the time to think about this concept for a minute. Seriously try to think openly about this with me as I say, *He made you exactly the way He wanted you to be.* And if so, *why would He damn you for being in His image?* Sounds silly now when you think about it doesn't it? And if it doesn't yet… hold on I have more.

"Whether one believes in Religion or not and whether one believes in rebirth or not, there isn't anyone who doesn't appreciate kindness and compassion."

-Dalai Lama

We're all in union with one another on the Other Side, and so is our Creator. When we cross over to the Other Side, we are all accepted accordingly with the highest levels of love, and compassion. Being accepted into Paradise is not by the number of works, or how you earn it, but *how you love.*

KEY TO HEAVEN'S DOOR – WHO GOES UP

When Chad was alive, I remember him asking me, "Do you believe you have to be saved or accept Jesus in order to go to Heaven?" I heard him, then Spirit's message was, *"As long as you have even the tiniest bit of love in your heart, you will go to Heaven."* He was confused, and to tell you the truth, so was I. For so many years raised as a Christian as a child, I personally didn't understand why Spirit would say that. Being an avid Jesus believer to be honest, it downright dumbfounded me. Later I had remembered a glimpse of a moment I had with Christ during my NDE and He told me, *"Tell the people that I was here. Share with them your experience sitting with Me. Tell them that I am still here and share with them of the love that is Me, that is in all, and for all."* He never told me to tell people to "go to Him" but to remember that His love was the only message, that love is the message.

Spirit's message is, *"Being accepted into Heaven is not by your works, but by your love."* Even if you don't know how, but still want to learn how to love, then our Creator will stop at nothing to help you understand love. We were created with love, and His mission is to *teach us love out of love.*

"Love is a better teacher than duty."

-Albert Einstein

How powerful that is, and so true beyond all measure. Your heart is not leveled by the amount of time you spend on your works, instead by your soul devotion to others for the best of all mankind. Sure, I get that people do nice things for others, and that's the point of it. However, I share carefully, there is a fine line between devotion of love for others, and devotion of love for yourself. We don't do things for others because we want something in return. We're encouraged to love for the sake of loving others. The more we share our love, the more we will have the gift in experiencing love.

Spirit does not measure love for humanity based off of how much money you make, or how much product you sold, or how many followers you have on social media. In fact, Spirit doesn't look at that at all, and could care less. But what they do pay close attention to, is how you use the gifts you are blessed with, and how you bless others with those gifts. The more you are loved by others, the more we are to share that love. And the more you are given from the Universe and God, the more we are expected to give back. It's a give and take, as a healthy balance in life and love should be. That is the true purpose of Heaven, to benefit others around you together as a team. And the key ingredient in entering Heaven, is by being the essence and vessel of love through the act and nature of love. As Spirit says, *"True success is not by how you are measured by the world, but how you choose to measure others in the world."*

Remember, God does not turn away any soul, no matter how "bad" they may have been here. However, God will teach the soul on how to love in all areas before they are allowed to go to Heaven. Each soul will be leveled based upon their own energy of love (God based). During their lessons, Creator will grant them access to Heaven when they have finally understood the truth about unconditional love. The way to enter into Heaven is by allowing God, Angels and Spirit to help the soul move forward with healing & unconditional love.

FORGIVENESS OF THE EGO

Even to say you went as far as harming someone physically or emotionally. Whether it is something so horrible like murder, sexual violence, physical violence, or emotional abuse, doesn't mean you are sent to Hell. It doesn't make you an evil person, but the actions you did perhaps are unloving, and that's where these next few things come in.

If you did something so heinous, it doesn't mean you are set to go to Hell. I have learned there is such a place. However, it's not a predetermined conclusion for your soul for all eternity, just because of bad, sinful or Egoful deeds.

The point of Hell is to enslave the *true* necessary evils that are pure in hatred, anger, and so on. But as a human soul, we are not bound to that fate. It's all based on our truth of what we dwell upon more. For example, if you are to commit murder and you're begging for a second chance, because you truly feel in your heart that what you did was wrong. The truth will speak in your soul, and God will hear, and know that truth inside of your soul. As long as you are *truly* remorseful, then you still have a chance in redeeming yourself.

I had a client named Mary, that I was reading and her sister's soul came through. I was seeing the word, "Salvation" and with that, I knew that Spirit's message for Mary was to not worry about her sister being damned to an endless fate, all because of a few mistakes. In reality, God is a forgiving God, so why would He put you in a place of evil?

Wouldn't that defeat the whole point of forgiveness and love in the first place? Of course it would!

Mary was able to get the reassurance that with love, her sister's soul was accepted in Paradise in an instant. Spirit said, *"There was no question. She was meant for Heaven."*

Throughout my journey with Spirit while undergoing massive amounts of meditative hours, came with understanding the balance. There is a balance of love (positive based) and Ego (unawareness based). Not to say that Ego is inside of you when you do bad things, but that you can become influenced by the Egoful nature that is unseen, to allow the capabilities. There is an Ego at work, unseen, behind the scenes that'll try to get you to believe that it is you that is right when doing bad or unloving things. However, part of that silver lining is it may also be a part of the malevolent influencers that caused you to be convinced in this false belief. We'll talk more about the malevolent influencers in a bit.

As we have discussed earlier, the Ego is based on your level of unawareness. Unaware of what one is actually doing, saying or thinking from lack of perception in areas of the whole truth. Lack of understanding, that we are all interconnected as a whole while still obtaining our own soul essence that is energy within the Universe.

With this, Spirit emphasizes that when one is acting upon another in anger, violence or an emotion that is negatively charged, it is happening due to the individual being unaware. Completely blindsided of the fact that it is the Ego that is angry, not them as a spiritual being connected to Source. Unaware of the Ego that has ahold of their lack of knowledge of their consciousness essence that is connected to all including the one that they harmed.

Because there is a balance of both energy levels within the Universe, is also why human souls are so easily manipulated even by the Ego. The positives to this however, is we have the power to control what we allow to manipulate us, or not. We have the power to control what we choose to believe. If you choose to believe you are special, loving, and worthy, then you will act out of love. If you choose to believe you are not special, unworthy, dwell on jealousy and hatred, then you shall act out through the unnecessary "evil".

I say they are unnecessary because they are. It's again back to the fact it's a choice whether we want to follow the Egoful nature or not. And with that choice, again come the consequences of those unnecessary evils that we bestowed upon others. Now I'm not saying that because you had a fight with your parent, and are no long speaking to him/ her makes you an evil person. That is only based on learning lessons and love. There is a vast difference between something so minimal vs doing something intentionally to hurt another with little to no remorse at all. To say, there are no "levels" of badness. That is, Spirit doesn't have a scale saying one thing is more bad than the other, so you're in more trouble for doing "this" vs "that". Instead, Spirit carefully examines all areas of the soulfulness of each person to understand their unawareness and awareness in all angles before making a determination of what this soul needs. So with that, if you do absolutely horrible deeds, then you shall be forced to answer to Creator, in what drove you to believe that it was okay. He will listen to your heart. If you don't feel remorse, and felt you had every right to it even after Spirit teaches everything possible with extensive patience and love, then yes…there would be a possibility that the placement of your eternal residence would be somewhere other than Heaven. To distinguish the difference: A soul that knows through full awareness of the negative impact they bestowed on another after Spirit expresses the whole truth, and still doesn't feel any kind of remorse, then this would be something highly probable. What I do know, is God won't allow anyone in His Heaven that doesn't care if they hurt someone else for Heaven is a place of eternal peace.

It all depends upon your soul's level of light, love and the desire to love. The silver lining is Source is a patient, loving God. He will take the time to listen to why you thought this act was justified. Then with love, He will take the time to teach you why it may not be. It all depends on the levels of the situation at hand and what is necessary. There is no room for faults on the level of Heaven for each soul is given room for explaining their reasons. No soul is judged nor denied the grace and mercy of Heaven for all are deserving of this precious gift of eternal life in Paradise.

Hell

WHO GOES DOWN?

How one is sent to Hell is determined by a few things that Spirit emphasizes strongly. The way Spirit describes it is based on how we are here, and on the Other Side. The way a person is viewed on the Other Side is by their level of negative energy, and positive energy. If the soul lacks love, then God will ask them a set of questions to help them see the side that they are. He has hope in all of us and does not ever send us there. I repeat –God does NOT send us or anyone to Hell, for it is one's choice to descend to such a place.

The way Spirit explains the process is with the Universal Law of Free Will, grants us the gift of choice. We have a choice of whether we want to learn love, or to dwell in the hate. We are granted the gift of love to change our perception, and to see the truth of who we are –but will not be forced to do so. Each soul has a choice of whether they want to be with God in Paradise, or not. He will *never* force a soul to do anything they don't want to. And with this, this is our "Judgment". The Judgment is based on who we feel we are.

The Judgment is the one we give ourselves. Again, I emphasize, God will give all the time the soul needs in order to fully understand both sides. To understand the truth of who we are in God. He doesn't give up on any soul, no matter how much of a lost cause one may seem or feel.

The Realm of Hell is not down, or below like we have believed for centuries. Instead, Spirit shares that like other Realms, Hell is another world between worlds, as Heaven. So it's not down anywhere, but within the Universe, existing harmoniously within the rest.

WHAT IS HELL?

Hell is a Realm of itself, and there are going to be things in this Realm that would be unimaginable to the human comprehension. I can tell you honestly, I had a taste of what Hell is (*'cause I had to ask*) and honestly it's *way more* than what I had initially thought. Hell is a place for the ones that damned *themselves*. I want to state that clearly. These souls chose this Realm. They chose this outcome. They chose this lifestyle for all eternity.

What Hell is, in my own interpretation and experience, is a place where you will experience your worst fears, but even more amplified. Trying to even imagine that in my mind, is literally incomprehensible, but this is what Spirit relays. They describe that Hell is so hard for us to picture in our minds, so instead of telling me, they gave me a glimpse in a dream.

–To be clear when I say I dreamt of this or that from Spirit, these are in fact visions. These are not dreams that you would conduct in your mind from your subconscious but from spiritual visitations from Spirit on the Astral Realm or higher Realms. Even though these visions are during my sleep state, I can tell you without a stutter that each vision is utterly profound! And I can state that it's a place that I wanted out of *immediately!* It's a Realm that brings about your worst fears the second you think of them in your energy.

It's a Realm that enables you, with other souls, who too have their own worst fears in the open, causing you to have to deal with their fears as well. When you do the math, that's a whole lot of chaos! It's a Realm where what you imagine, or think of from emotions, immediately manifests. This is a place that *no soul deserves* to experience.

I argued with myself on what kind of book this was going to be. I had to ask Spirit what exactly was the best route in helping you in understanding the Other Side, but Spirit reminded me that as there is a positive to life, there is a negative. And as many people would come to know me well enough, I've never been the type to sugarcoat anything. So when this topic came about, instantly I knew whether we want to admit it or not, it's something we should understand. I'm a firm believer that knowledge is power. And with this kind of knowledge, you will have the upper hand in understanding our relationship within the course of this vast Universe that is a part of all of us. Sure, I could just tell you only about the good things of Spirit and the afterlife, however I don't feel that would be the most beneficial in preparing you for what's possible. It's not like I walk around in life all emo, but I most certainly don't wear flower colored glasses either. To me, as we are to accept the ups and downs of life here, it is my Divine responsibility to educate, teach and guide others to the same Universal potentialities and realities of the Other Side. Trust me, you'd rather know these things, and be prepared than have no awareness at all.

Because we don't possess a physical body once we transition to our Spirit form, the fears are thus manifested in other ways. Instead of the outer parts being manipulated, or harmed such as being dismembered, the soul would feel this feeling even more brutally due to the soul feeling everything times a million. At least, this is a theory based upon the idea of Hell. And more so, based upon what I have come to understand from Spirit, and as a Psychic Medium.

My Spirit Guides along with Angels, have shared over and over again, that no set fate of Hell is the same for everyone. For example, the Christian religion believes Hell is a place of fire and brutal beatings. However, Spirit says that each soul's experience of Hell is based upon their worst fears. Then those fears are manifested, causing the fears to become their worst reality. So if you fear of being eaten by a bear, it will be you being eaten by a bear, but amplified. Or if you fear of being burned alive over and over, then that's what's ahead. What the soul's worst fear is, will be amplified immensely. Do I know how much? No.

But the fact is, it's not a place anyone wants to be.

This is not a place that God created. God did not create this place, the Primary Evil did. Spirit relays this piece with large intensity.

To tell you the truth, I have only gotten a taste of Hell, the idea of what Hell is. Spirit will never allow me there. Instead, they only gave me visions, and ideas of what one may endure. Again, no soul is "damned" to this fate by God, instead the soul chooses this based upon their own belief of their soul value. The other major factor of why Spirit won't allow me to see the authenticity of Hell, is due to not wanting us to focus on the negative of the Other Side. Sure, I'm describing it to you. But even with these minor descriptions, I have no doubt in my core that they don't even come close to the evidential realities of Hell. With that, our departed loved ones don't want us to focus on the negative side of the Other Side, but at least give us the knowledge of its purpose. Again, knowledge is power.

Hell can also be other fears. If the soul is terrified of being alone, then that soul will find themselves in a lonely abys of nothingness, but again this is their choice. As Spirit stated before, *"No soul will go unnoticed to God."* Each soul will have the opportunity to skip this eternal Hell that they chose. Such as, if the soul decides later that this is not what they want, they're then are able to go back to Creator with Angels as their guide. So even though this is something that *can* be eternal, doesn't mean that it *has* to be. It's all a matter of the soul's choice.

PRIMARY EVIL VS EGOFUL EVIL

There are evils that are meant for the place that is opposite of Heaven, but it would have to be a sort of evil that is beyond change. Such as Demonic energies/ entities, or other sorts that are not and do not hold any light in their energy. To understand it a bit more, we will talk about the *Primary Evil* and *Egoful Evil*. Each level of evil determines the soul's vibration, where they belong indefinitely, and why.

PRIMARY EVIL is of a negative force that forever was a part of the Other Side, such a Demons, etc. And or, a human soul that only exists for the negative side that is opposite of love and light by choice.

EGOFUL EVIL are the evils of nature made, human based that are done by people, to people, to animals due to lack of awareness through one's Ego. This lesser evil is able to be changed and have hope in God's eyes.

Primary Evil is an abomination that is originally beyond the Earth Realm. The level of this madness is beyond the human soul's control, which is where God must intervene. No human soul can banish this type of evil without the help of God, and must receive God first before able to do so. An entity that is of the *Primary Evil*, has its own agenda, which is to destroy humanity. It is the immorality of all negativity. Human souls that decide to walk with this kind of entity will do so at their own discretion. Human souls are *never* forced to follow the *Primary Evil,* but are so easily duped into believing in trusting these soulless entities. They are deceivers, manipulators, exploiters, thieves, inhuman beings (most often reported), and will do anything to destroy all hope and faith in humans. Their main priority is to take control of the human soul, by destroying the human's free will. By bashing down the free will, they have a greater chance at success. *Primary Evil* is an evil of itself that is far beyond measure of human existence. The energy level of the inhuman entities can be low at best, but more often are reported to be stronger than a group of five grown men. Their psychic powers are cunning, with a twist of a distorted nature that will leave the human soul in disbelief.

They know the person's worst fears, past regrets and will use these to destroy the will of their human target. The form of each is based on their own accord. Many of these distorted creatures will manifest to humans most often as a child, woman, or a lost innocent soul looking for help or a friend. But again, they are *deceivers.*

Primary Evil will never be positive in God's eyes, for they chose the opposite of love. Never having light or positive energy since creation, or destroyed that positive energy by choice. Some say they are fallen Angels of God. These inhuman beings, and human souls are the rebellion of love, light and Creator. They are not allowed in the Realm of Heaven, for there is no room for any kind of negativity, having no use for hope.

It essentially doesn't matter what you name them as, they exist and are a force not to underestimate.

Egoful Evil are the evils done to humans by humans, and by humans to animals. They're the lesser evils that are deemed hopeful in God's eyes. There is a chance in redemption by the mercy of forgiveness, love, and faith. The energy levels of humans are based on their level of understanding through wisdom, and love. Each human soul is never damned. Instead, they are taught based on their lessons throughout their lifetimes, to learn the truth about unconditional love, and knowledge while gaining ultimate wisdom. With the help of Creator, Angels and our loved ones, *Egoful Evil* will forever have a chance at redemption for understanding there is Ego at play causing one to act upon another through unawareness of the bigger picture. All human souls are gifted forgiveness and experiencing true love on the Other Side with mercy.

In order for a human soul to be sent to the Hell Realm, they would have to be an energy that is not driven by love or God. Even though people are made by God from love, the unfortunate fact is, we are here to be tested through life lessons to see which side we are to choose. A human soul has the choice whether to either become the primary evil in Spirit, or may essentially follow the nature of such entities when alive physically on the Earth Realm. But again, these dark forces are master deceivers. They possess great power in influencing the Egofulness of an individual to believe that what they are doing is in fact either justifiable, good or their right. When in truth, these beings are merely lying, fooling the unaware human soul that is already unaware of their Egofulness to begin with. Thanks to Source's mercy and unconditional love however, even if a human soul was either influenced while aware of what was happening or not, Creator and Angels will gently guide that human soul to understanding this Universal manipulation that is quietly and unmistakably forgiven nonetheless. And even though I speak of this in generality, one must be open to the objective individual care of each that is never the same scenario as the next.

The choice is the one a soul makes for themselves, and is not, never was God's. Creator doesn't, and won't force you to be a malicious intended or good person. It is done by those that choose to do the unloving, or loving acts towards life itself that is all a part of creation.

That was the toughest concept I had to fight to understand for many years. I would ask Source on a regular basis, "Why would people do bad things, if we were made in your image?" Then later after much study, and hours of mediation with Spirit, I have come to learn that we are still given the gift of free will.

LOVE CONQUERS ALL

Overall in the end it is up to us on how we want to be as an individual, as a person to others. Love outweighs any number of destructiveness, no matter how impossible it may seem. And the bright side to this, we are surrounded by Angels, our loved ones and Creator. I have experienced both levels of evil, and I can tell you *neither one is good*. But as long as we do our best in being a good person, no matter how negative we may have been, Creator will see in our heart of hearts, how much we want to grow for the better.

The bigger picture to keep in mind, is we are always given a choice in how we want to live. We are given the freedom to learn the value and importance of love here, as well on the Other Side. What's even more relieving, is knowing there's no such thing as, "too late." Anything is possible when it comes to love, and despite whether you have yet to learn love here, or there, we're always given the chance at redemption. Embellishing with large delicacy, no person shall go to Hell to say, only due to their Ego. The Ego is not something one will ever go to Hell for unless the individual's soul was, let's say, "swallowed by it" indefinitely. And even then, Spirit shares the goodness of love always prevails even that darkest of men and women.

Being the best you can be to yourself and to others is all that Creator, and Spirit ask of us. They don't focus so much on the mistakes that we have made in our lives, or the poor choices. More on *why* we made those choices. There's always a silver lining as I have said before, and within that lining come the reason of those choices. God knows when we are hurting. He knows when we fall off our wagon of life, feeling as if we fail at certain things. But Spirit wants you to know, that there is no such thing as fault on the Other Side. And without fault, there is no such thing as failure, but growth, and with growth comes the gift of experience, which comes with the birth of wisdom.

Becoming closer to Source, Angels and loved ones in Spirit, we are able to understand the importance of our free will. They have taught me and many people gently, that with our free will, we are given the most precious gift anyone could ask for, the gift of life. It is our choice of where we want to be here and on the Other Side. We have the gift in honing who we want to be, whether we know how to or not. And thanks to this beautiful gift, we are never denied by God in Heaven, as long as we simply go to Him with love in our hearts.

The Higher Aides

The complexity of Angels is vast. Not to mention the amount of Angels there are, that it would be impossible for us to keep track. The truth is, it's not our job to know how many Angels there are and certainly isn't our job to worry of what they're capable of. All they want us to know is that they're here. Their job is not meant to be our focus or concern. In fact, they are such humble beings, they are not concerned with taking the spotlight, but are grateful for the recognition nonetheless.

During my studies of Angels, I couldn't help but notice how many sources focus solely on the order of the Angel Hierarchy, instead of their loving messages that Angels have for humanity. With Spirit, I will be giving you a less intimidating view of Angels, and how they work for our Creator. I don't know about you, but if I read too much into something, I tend to get overwhelmed, especially if it's something so detailed. Heck, I can't even fathom the idea of doing math without a calculator. I've learned over the years there's only so much that is truly necessary to know. So what I've decided to do, is give you a simpler list of Angels, and at least give you an idea of what's about them.

Let's discuss the basic, need to know about Angels, and other Spirits that work alongside Angels. After that, I will talk more about their purpose, and how they influence us with their Divine connection with us in the Universe…

꙳ *ARCHANGELS*

꙳ *GUARDIAN ANGELS*

꙳ *ANGELS*

꙳ *EARTH ANGELS*

꙳ *SPIRIT GUIDES*

꙳ *ASCENDED MASTERS*

The list I have provided is not in an orderly fashion, for Spirit doesn't want you to focus so much on the order, but on their purpose for us. In this you will begin to discover a few of the similarities to each, and of their nature in how they can communicate with us.

꙳ *ARCHANGELS*

Archangels are a large part of the Divine connection to our Creator. They take on both the Spirit Realm, and Earth Realm. Their purpose is to keep the Earth Realm in balance, as well as the Spirit Realm. They can take on human form, or their own form when connecting with humanity. Archangels are large in size, vast in the highest levels of wisdom and knowledge. Archangels possess great powers and abilities to keep humanity safe during any time of need. These higher level beings work closely with humanity, as well as casting out Primary Evils from the Earth Realm. You can call on Archangels whenever you feel the need, and they will respond without delay.

Some have wondered if you can become an Archangel and I am told by Spirit, that it's possible. However, it takes eons in order to obtain this amount of wisdom, discipline, and love for God and humanity. It's not impossible, but does take much work and dedication from the human soul. They focus solely for the purpose to provide the highest levels of love, wisdom, guidance, protection and comfort. You can call on Archangels when you need these, and other types of reassurances. You can call on Archangels to help other loved ones whether they are aware of it or not.

GUARDIAN ANGELS

The role of a Guardian Angel is to protect, honor and love the person they are assigned to, since the human's birth. Every person in the world has at least one Guardian Angel. The purpose of each Angel, is to protect and guide you to a higher level of awareness, and to allow you to learn love in all areas possible in your lifetime. No Guardian Angel is better than the other, and neither Angel is in competition with the next.

Guardian Angels work in various ways with humanity, when the moment requires. Guardian Angels may be permitted the assistance from a fellow Angel, of either rank, in order to protect you. Some have this misconception that Guardian Angels only protect those of a certain faith, but Spirit says this is false. Angels including Guardian Angels, are all here to honor, love, protect and assist any and all persons no matter the faith.

ANGELS

There are different ranks of Angels that are vast in numbers and vary in qualities. There is no Angel that is not of a high level of vibration connected to our Creator. All Angels are of light beings, here to assist Creator, the Other Side, and humanity. All Angels are special with unique qualities that allow them the ability to help us and the Other Side, with supreme love and light.

There are so many different kinds of Angels, with different specialties. Each Angel is imbued with a specific specialty, in order to keep the Earth Realm in balance, while assisting the Spirit Realm with their unique qualities. Art, music, literature, hard labor, child bearing are just some of the few expertise, within each Angel. All allow assistance to the human race, granting inspiration when trying to achieve similar dreams, aspirations, life purpose and or careers. Angels will also be specific towards the lessons that we are in need of mastering, for our soul growth. Helping us learn unconditional love, forgiveness, courage, humility, grief, grace, endurance and tolerance, are just a few of the many emotions we are to experience. With their mastery skills towards the specific areas, they provide us the pillow of comfort, with the light of knowledge in order to pass through these areas, and many others successfully.

EARTH ANGELS

Earth Angels are of a nature similar to Angels in the Spirit Realm. The difference is they are walking amongst us humans, with the intent to give us inspiration filled with love, and lessons. They will be bright spirited, loving, patient, understanding, and greatly encouraging. Their purpose is to guide humanity to a higher light by being the walking example of how we should treat and value ourselves, and each other.

Earth Angels are no different than that of humans, but with a different aura about them. Earth Angels are Divine, just like Angels of the Spirit Realm. They are hardworking, loving, sacrificial, bright, forgiving, compassionate, patient, understanding, empathetic, and filled with laughter. Earth Angels can take on human form, or their spiritual form, when influencing the human race. Primarily, their purpose is to assist humanity without judgment. When coming into contact with an Earth Angel, you will feel a drawing, or a strong pull towards this person. It could by anyone, including a bum on the street.

They will possess immense amounts of love and compassion, speaking words of utter wisdom. They will speak to your soul the moment they look into your eyes. The connection with Earth Angels will be so undeniable, that you will have this indescribable feeling of companionship with them. They are something like that of a speechless wonder.

SPIRIT GUIDES

Spirit Guides are both purposeful for humanity, and the Other Side. Soul growth is exponential when trying to achieve spiritual oneness and success. With Spirit Guides, we are able to achieve that with their undivided attention. Spirit Guides are known to be both human souls that once roamed the Earth Realm, and animal souls. Spirit Guides can be loved ones that have crossed over, all the way to people that have lived hundreds of years prior to us.

Same goes with Animal Spirit Guides. All Spirit Guides have a goal for you, and for them, which is to allow love to grow in them and in you. They will work with you in all areas of your life, whether you are aware of them or not. Most Spirit Guides are assigned to Lightworkers, Psychic Mediums, Shamans, Nuns, Priests, Healers, Saints, The Pope and many other people that are here to bring enlightenment of the consciousness to the human race. Along with those that are here to assist humanity in their own creative and purposeful ways.

Many Spirit Guides are a part of our daily lives, but people don't usually think about them being a possibility. The Divine purpose of Spirit Guides, is to grant us the connection to the Other Side, as well to our own life purpose. They will work with you night and day, in order to understand love and lessons. Their abilities may be limited, which is why there may be moments where they may require the assistance from other Divine beings, such as Archangels, Angels or even Ascended Masters.

As the person grows in their lessons, so will the Spirit Guide. A person can have as many as two, or more Spirit Guides, depending on the calling which is needed by the living person's purpose on Earth. Some Guides are more knowledgeable than others, due to their level of lessons mastered. No Spirit Guide is more important than the other. Each Spirit Guide is assigned to a person in order for them to learn the same lessons and values with the person on Earth. Being a Spirit Guide to living people, is another way to redeem themselves after living a previous life in order to learn more internally and externally. Doing so, allows both the living person and Spirit Guide, to move forward with a deeper understanding of unconditional love in all areas.

Souls that choose to become a Spirit Guide, are granted the chance of living, loving and making better decisions through the living person they are guiding on Earth. It's a way for the departed soul to learn what better choices they could've made, if they were living and responding out of love.

ASCENDED MASTERS

Ascended Masters are the highest Deities you could ever come into contact with, that are just below Source. They possess greatness beyond the human imagination, with unlimited abilities in order to heal, guide, and love humanity. The purpose of Ascended Masters is to bring supreme enlightenment, throughout centuries for the greater good of mankind. Some Ascended Masters were never born by the process of conceiving. –there is a loophole where a human can become an Ascended Master, but would take eons to achieve. Jesus Christ is a Divine example of possessing the gift of life, death and resurrection. Other examples of Ascended Masters are that of Buddha, The Virgin Mother Mary, and many others. Not bound by time or space, Ascended Masters hold the freedom of coming and going to the Earth Realm without the need of rebirth. Each Ascended Master surpassed all Karma, remaining balanced in their energy frequency with Source. Their higher levels of consciousness, wisdom, and Divine love, heals the Universe for the better of all that is energy.

Each Ascended Master is available for our time of need whenever we feel necessary. They will respond to your prayer no matter the time of day, to grant you the highest levels of enlightenment, love and certainty. Spirit wishes for you to hone their love, Divine connection within the Universe, and supreme greatness. All Ascended Masters love, honor and appreciate all of mankind, no matter the faith. Their vision is to guide each person, in order to be what they were meant to be, which is an unlimited being reserved for unconditional love.

ANGELIC MESSAGES & SIGNS

Angels send us loving message and many of them are of a similar nature as our loved ones from the Other Side. Not all Angels will send messages the same as the next, for they obtain their own individual characteristics like humans. One Angel may send a loving message to you through music, whereas another Angel may send you a message through coins. All have unique meaning to them, and all play a giant role in how we receive, and appreciate their love, and guidance. Angelic messages are always filled with loving validations, and reassurance. Learning how to recognize when they are sending you these messages, grants you a more fundamental understanding that they are with you. Below, are short indicators of their Divine messages, and how it can be a positive influence to your life, mentally, emotionally, physically and most of all spiritually…

COINS

FEATHERS

PICTURES/ VISUAL REPRESENTATIONS

- ⁓ *STATUES/ SCULPTURES*
- ⁓ *NUMBERS*
- ⁓ *DOVES*
- ⁓ *MUSIC/ SOUNDS*
- ⁓ *DREAMS*

⁓ COINS

Just like our departed loved ones, Angels are able to grant us the simplicity of reassurance with pennies, dimes or any coin that you seem to find on a regular basis. No coin is a better sign than the next, and all possess a great deal of validation that our Angels are loving and guiding us. The gift of coins can be found anywhere that deems odd, or "coincidental."

⁓ FEATHERS

One of the more common yet powerful signs of an Angel message is that of feathers. Doesn't matter how the feather necessarily is found, or what bird it comes from, but when and how you discover it. Most people describe the feathers as being white, while some of a bird that they favor. Reason of a feather, is to grant the person a higher level of faith, based on the common description of Angels being that of a human, with grand wings upon the back.

PICTURES/ VISUAL REPRESENTATIONS

With the blessing of pictures and art, we are able to receive messages from Angels, through endless amounts of possibilities. Whether through a post card of an Angel, advertisements, paintings, drawings, or anything that sparks your soul –understand this is Angels catching your attention. These signs will arrive in Divine timing when we least expect it, and like all messages, they're creative at best. Their way in helping us know they are continually loving, and guiding us is by pointing us in the right direction in being able to hear, see, and feel their loving messages.

STATUES/ SCULPTURES

Through statues or sculptures, we are allowed the chance to delete doubt. We as humans, driven by our Ego have a natural instinct to delete the impossible, left rationalizing something "inexplicable". But thanks to their creativity, we are forced at moments like these, to wonder the "what if". Their message can come in many forms, such as statues, figurines, knickknacks, and many other items that resemble the obvious. When we come across these types of beauties, embrace the love they are bestowing, and appreciate the inevitable.

NUMBERS

From the power of the Divine, we are able to receive messages in perfect timing, no matter how "coincidental" it may seem. Thanks to Spirit & Angels, we are able to take simple things such as numbers to a whole new level. From the time on our clocks, to license plate numbers, you can easily identify the difference between a, "normal number" to a

Divine message from the Heavens. Numbers such as 11:11 on your clock all the way to, 333, 1133, 777, or other numbers in this similar pattern, you are being shown messages from the Heavens. Angels are important to our daily lives, and their purpose is to allow us comfort during our struggles. It doesn't matter where the numbers are being shown, or how, but why and when. When you see numbers that speak personally to you, make note of when you see them, and what you were thinking or feeling at that exact moment. These inclinations are symbols and even confirmations when asking for a sign. Dates of a departed loved one, such as their birthdate, date of passing and even anniversaries are also messages from Angels and departed loved ones through the gift of numbers.

DOVES

Another way of receiving messages from the Angels, is by the gift of doves. The dove is a sign of purity. Doves are also known as one of God's messengers on the Earth Realm, based on numerous spiritual beliefs. The sign of the dove can come in various forms such as photographs, feathers, or the physical dove itself. It is also widely believed in some cultures that if a dove, or a bird were to lay its droppings upon your body, it's considered a sign from the Divine as a blessing in disguise.

MUSIC/ SOUNDS

Music and sound is a large part on the Other Side, and they love bringing you the blessings in this form. Many people have described

Embrace Where We Go In Spirit On The Other Side And The Unbreakable Bond

*their experiences of Angelic messages through the form of music &
sound, but likewise, many also may not realize that they are receiving
these messages. Musical messages can come in many forms, such as a
ringtone, or a loving song on the radio. Spirit as well as Angels, can
send us messages through music by influencing others to sing, play or
incorporate the specific message, in order for you to take notice of its
Divine timing. Through the gift of hearing, specific sounds may also play
a gigantic role in influencing our souls. Sounds of animals, insects,
objects, or anything at all that speaks to you personally, also brings you
the reassurance that Angels, or a departed loved one are present.*

DREAMS

*Angels can visit us in an unlimited amount of ways, including during
our sleep. Angels can appear as a golden glow with a soft whisper. Each
Angel will have a different approach in dreams, but all will feel the
same, which is an incredible sensation of love and security. Not so often
an Angel will appear to us in the form we would normally hope, or
expect. Most often, they will appear to us as a humble human. The
difference of a loved one's visitation vs an Angel's, is the amount of
energy, and the feeling they give off. The energy will be of one of the
highest levels, and one way to tell the difference, is how loving and
warm you will feel during the dream. Other instances when detecting an
Angel's presence during our sleep, is when dreaming of things that make
us feel loved. Being surrounded by stars, feathers, flowers, butterflies,
birds or other things that give off a loving sensation to you, is a sure
sign of an Angelic visitation.*

Signs from Angels are not just in the physical form, but also come to us in the form of the unseen. Our bodies are a large prop that can give us the hint when there is an Angel in our presence. While there are physical sensations, there will also be the emotional and mental sensations that will arise during the presence of an Angel. Not everyone will experience them in the same way, or in the same time, or order, but all carry an equal amount of validation and reassurance…

AN ANGEL'S HUG

BEING ON CLOUD NINE

SWEET AROMAS

TASTE THE SWEETNESS

SLIGHT LIGHTHEADEDNESS

STAR-LIKE FLICKERS

AN ANGEL'S KISS

AN ANGEL'S HUG

Love is intensified when present in its natural form, as are Angels. The feeling of an intensified warmth will wash over your body and soul when an Angel is near. The sensation will feel similar to a tingling feeling from head to toe, giving off the impression of safety. Angels have this impeccable ability in aiding us, by granting us healing and love with their energy. This feeling will automatically make you so comfortable, that you may have a hard time standing up or concentrating.

(I urge you to immediately seek medical attention by a clinical/ medical physician if these sensations continue longer than comfortable. No Angel will make you feel like this longer than needed. Rule out the physical possibilities and probabilities before solely leaning on this as such. I am not a doctor, and do not possess the knowledge of the physical embodiments of certain illnesses that would suggest this side effect or others. This is only based on spiritual & paranormal behaviors & beliefs).

BEING ON CLOUD NINE

Here you are embracing the love and happiness from Angels, when they are in your midst. This feeling of being on Cloud Nine, leaves you with only laughter, serenity, and a great sense of peace. We are always at a loss for words when it comes to the chaos of the world, and sometimes Angels are pleased in giving us a slight nudge away from the realities for a day. Some describe this sensation most often after a pleasant dream, vision, or a message from Angels and departed loved ones. Another more approachable saying, is feeling as if you can take on the world, or falling in love.

SWEET AROMAS

The power of scent from Angels is overwhelming, and can be a wonderful way when trying to detect the presence of an Angel. Aromas *are one of their favorite ways to manifest their presence to us, for we can relate this sensation to a happy place, and or memory. Their intent is to bring you to a place of love, in all the senses of the human body, in order for you to piece the puzzle together. Some describe Angelic aromas, by smelling flowers, such as a rose or lavender or any sent that is pleasant to the nose. When smelling the scent of an Angel, make sure to thank them for the pleasant entrance.*

TASTE THE SWEETNESS

Another more spoken detection of an Angelic presence, is through taste. The Other Side is vast in every sensation imaginable, and Angels never want to miss out on a good sample. Love is in all forms, including the goodness of taste. Sweet tasting sensations are numerous, such as a sugary morsel, or anything that you would find satisfyingly sweet. Angels reach to us on personal levels, so what you find sweet, they will bring to your taste buds. On numerous occasions, I and many others will receive the liking of cupcakes, or even ice cream to the tongue.

SLIGHT LIGHT HEADEDNESS

When resonating the physical indication of an Angelic presence, we tend to become dizzy, or may experience a feeling of lightheadedness. Not all people will receive this kind of feeling. Most that do however, are due to their natural connection to the Spirit Realm. Angels are of a strong energy vibration that is purely positive, in light and love. Angels are such a high energy vibration, that it can be impacting to the human body, causing dizziness, or lightheadedness.

(Again, I urge one to seek immediate medical attention if this were to last longer than a period of time that is comfortable to you. No Angel will make you feel this longer than necessary for you to be aware of their presence.)

STAR-LIKE FLICKERS

Angels are of a higher frequency that can give off to the human eye, flickers of light, similar to lightning bugs. The star-like flickers may appear to us any time, day or night, allowing us the blessed opportunity to visually know they are present. Some experience this when are in dire need of assistance from Angels, such as near death experiences, accidents, time of injury, or deep depression.

(Be aware, not all moments when seeing these flickers will be your Angels. Be sure to rule out the possibility of illnesses that could be causing this to occur, such as Anemia, or others. Please be sure to rule these factors out first, for your benefit).

AN ANGEL'S KISS

An Angel's kiss is very bountiful, filled with grace, love, embodied with a forgiving heart. The kiss of enlightenment, feels similar to a slight cold spark on the skin. When the kiss takes place, the feeling should bring you a great sense of ease. No Angel's kiss should harm the person in any way. Whether you feel it on your cheek, forehead, or hand, they are gracing you with their presence, filled with unconditional love. They lack the judgmental nature, able to give us the chance to see ourselves *for who we truly are –no matter our mistakes or misfortunes.*

UNDIVIDED ATTENTION

Similar to our departed loved ones, Ascended Masters and Angels are not limited to time. We are graced with the blessing of their undivided attention, and I mean, *undivided.* They are able to be with us at any point in time, no matter the situation. With that, one Angel can help you, at the same time while you prayed for the same Angel to give attention to someone else. They're able to be here, and there, anywhere in the Universe without the limitation of time.

HOW THEY MAY APPEAR

Most often when one catches the sight of an Angel, there will be a few that will share that what they saw was almost disbelieving. Some claim to see a misty apparition that is floating in mid-air while slowly dissipating after a few seconds of movement. It must be clearly stated that when one is to come into the presence of an Angel, the Angel's presence when in an apparitional formation will be *only* of a white light being. To include, this is most common for people that catch the glimpse of their departed loved ones souls when being visited physically on the Earth Realm.

Very rarely –but does happen, will a person come into direct contact with an Angel that is a full solid being. When a live person experiences this they will describe their interaction and the state of the Angel's presence in different ways. No person will explain their personal experience the exact same way as the next when in the presence of an Angel.

It is exceptionally rare for a live person to be visited by an Angelic presence that possess or arrives with a halo atop of the head. In all of my encounters with Angels, never have I ever seen nor heard anything remotely close that resembled or gave the impression of a halo atop of the head of an Angel. More likely to what I have been led to feel, is the reason why halos are so commonly believed throughout the centuries is due to confusing the halo with their high vibrational energy that is in Divine connection with Creator. The "halo" is more so, the form of energy that is specifically a link to God in a Divine bond of oneness and absolute love. So if one is to come into contact with an Angel and this is what you may see, this is the purpose primarily for this "halo" appearance. They want us to focus more on the purpose –not on the status of who they are.

CALLING THE HIGHER HELP

No matter the time or day, we are granted the blessing of limitless availability of Angels, Spirit Guides and Ascended Masters. Connecting with them is no different than how we connect with Creator, or our departed loved ones. Communication, connection to Angels, Spirit Guides and even Ascended Masters does not require a set of specifics, such as a ritual, a certain recited prayer, or anything of that matter. Your heart is all they require when connecting, or attempting communication with them. Love is their calling and their true purpose. They do not demand anything, but simply respond to how you feel, and what you need.

When a connection is established, which is simply by your need they will listen, and assist you without question. In their works, they do what is best of all concerned including others around you. They're intent is to give you the reassurance, guidance, protection, along with a sense of security. In doing so, the Higher help will do what is best needed, rather than wanted. Sometimes what we want, is not always what is best for us and with that, they may deny our desired requests, doing the opposite of what is requested, or simply not responding at all, respectfully.

Our loving Spirit Guides, Angels and holy Ascended Masters, including Source ask us to connect with them through love, insisting we be as open as much as possible. Opening your heart, laying before them your level of vulnerability, while showing them your true heart's desires. Their plea is for us to remain humble when asking for their loving protection and guidance. They are continually loving and guiding us regardless of our mistakes or misfortunes in our past or present circumstances. We are their number one priority, and will never be denied no matter the faith.

The Power Of Closure

In order for us to receive the relief from Spirit, there has to be a process which requires the heart to open up. In this, there will be messages sent from our loved ones that will not only give peace, but more so, the love that you never thought possible. The closure we seek is only something our departed loved ones can give us, and as a Medium, I can say this is absolutely the case. You can have people all over the world tell you, that your loved ones in Spirit are near. But the reality is, it only matters when the words are spoken from the horse's mouth.

As a Medium, I am granted the beautiful gift in being able to give you, and millions of others, the opportunity to heal. What a better way, than to have your departed loved ones do it for you?! I know that God, and Angels understand we are able to heal with faith, but even God knows that we need a little reassurance every now and then. They know that we try with all of our might to continue moving forward. But let's be honest, we only do so because we don't have a choice in the matter. With Spirit's loving guidance, they're giving us their love each and every day, to bless us with the amazing gift of closure making life a little easier.

OF ALL PEOPLE

When our loved ones come through for us, more than half of the time, it's a soul that the client never wanted to hear from. They will say, "I don't want to hear from her/ him again." But what the person is unaware of is that Spirit is forcing their way through, –for you. They're trying to show their love they may not have been able to express here on Earth.

I had a session with a woman, and her father's soul came through. She was absolutely confused why he would, and it took a while for me to explain to her that he was trying to give her closure. My client said, "But we fought so much and never got along. I don't understand why he would want to come forward now." Spirit's response to her question was, *"I know I wasn't the best father, and understand your confusion. But I'm trying to express to you out of unconditional love, that I know now what I didn't see. I finally understand how you felt."* As the words came from my mouth, I suddenly could feel weight lift. I then asked, "Did you just feel a large amount of weight lift from you?" With tears, she confirmed this sensation. Thanks to Spirit, my client was able to get the emotional release that she so desperately needed.

It is so evident to our loved ones, that we understand and comprehend the amount of love they have for us. Their ultimate mission on the Other Side, is to give you the love and healing that comes with closure. The energy is pure, and the intentions are true. No matter the differences, Spirit learns to know the importance of love, besides the disputes. They no longer focus on who is right or wrong, or who's at fault. Instead, their primary focus is the truth, that love is the only answer to all things, no matter the level of dissimilarity.

FORGIVENESS

Spirit is not able to reach their full potential, if they don't pursue love to the fullest, by reaching out to people they didn't get along with in some way. So likewise, even in Spirit, without closure, growth would not be possible.

"Some of us think holding on makes us strong; but sometimes it is letting go."

-Herman Hesse

When we reach to the Other Side, there is no reason to hold grudges, or to not learn to forgive. There is no room for something to be held back. As they learn to accept their role on the Other Side, Spirit will begin to see what life, or situations were like for others. They will not only feel everything, but see everything from the physical aspect, all the way to the emotional, mental and spiritual. The goal in Paradise, is to bring a sense of peace, and harmony within themselves and all that exists. And the best way to achieve this, is by fully embracing other's experiences. There are going to be past experiences, that we may wish we could take back, and certainly, Spirit understands the heartbreaks accompanied with guilt. So where they come into play, is by allowing your heart to open up to their love, that they may not have been able to do here when physically alive. Their love for you is far beyond measure, and what a better way to express so, than to say, "I'm sorry."

Forgiveness is one of the most prominent releases to the soul. We all must learn not just to ask for forgiveness, but also to give forgiveness. As the soul learns the lessons of their previous mistakes, they're then given another chance at being able to reach out to us again. Insight into our hearts, our loved ones are able to understand now, more than ever, exactly how we felt and feel. With their words fueled by unconditional love, we receive intensified relief, with a great sense of peace. The reason why so many of our departed loved ones come through, is for the healing to take place first and foremost. More than half of the reasons why people spread apart from each other, are due to either not willing to let go of a dispute, or person(s) are not willing to accept something.

We have a duty to love people unconditionally, not just when we feel like they've earned it. If we all were able to forgive freely, more than half of all of the quarrels with people would be diminished —or nonexistent. Trusting in our ability to love unconditionally, allows the forgiveness train to take way into our hearts and others.

One of the hardest moments during a reading, is when Spirit is coming through for their loved ones, but then the living person refuses to hear from this particular soul. This always brings sadness to my heart, because the soul is trying to connect with them out of love. Reasons the living respond this way, more often than not, is due to the living person harboring anger, fault, resentment, or judgment on the departed soul. Spirit knows your fears and your frustrations. They know when we're feeling those emotions. However, their purpose of coming through, is to give you the peace in knowing that no one is at fault. That no matter how much you may feel guilt, resentment, anger, judgment, or sadness, they are here to express their unconditional love for you. Spirit only wants the best for you. It can certainly become a challenge to understand the concept of how Spirit thinks on the Other Side. How they can forgive someone for something so horrible, or how they can easily move on, without resentment, or regrets in themselves, and others. But that's what makes Heaven so *wonderful.*

Try to imagine that every step you take, all of the muck from your life that you endured…slowly leaving a permanent stain on the place at which you previously stepped. Doing so, you feel lightweight…starting to see the truth in all that there is about unconditional love, happiness, tranquility, forgiveness, inner peace, and so much more. And the further you go, the more you leave behind all that was weighing you down. All that muck, all of those unhappy feelings become unstuck. Your feet become soothed, along with the rest of yourself…revealing the true beauty that was inside of you all along. This is the experience that our departed loved ones come face to face with, when reaching to Paradise. There is nothing but goodness on all angles of oneness with Source, and the Universe. No longer do they look for faults, guilt, or any of the negative emotions we endure here. When they bestow the gift of forgiveness, we must also learn to accept their blessing, in order to continue growth happily here.

But just as importantly, Spirit states forgiveness is not just for the sake of others, but for yourself. Forgiving another is not giving the person the right to dig you deeper into despair. Instead you are releasing their mistreatments and are allowing them to take ahold of your life and heart no more. It is a release for you, to give you back your life. Whether it's from someone stealing your parking spot, or your innocence, forgiving them allows you the chance at living life without guilt, anger, and serious heartbreaks. Just because we forgive someone for something they had done to us, doesn't mean we are giving them permission for what they did. It is a conscious decision to take back your power. Deciding that you're no longer going to allow them to take control of your life in anyway, ever again.

Loving yourself is something that is number one, for no one can love you more than you. No one will understand you more than yourself, and no one can release you from those negative emotions but you. Not even God can give that to you, instead He too asks you to give yourself this gift as well, because *you deserve it.*

When we refuse to choose forgiveness, it can affect our emotions, and even our relationships. Without giving yourself permission to let go of the negatives from others, you are allowing them to take control of your way of thinking, which affects your feelings, which then affects your behavior, which then affects everything and everyone around you. It's a giant pool of ties that will be affected so negatively, that it can even cause you to become bitter. Don't allow these emotions to become who you are. Spirit doesn't want that for you, and neither do I, to be truthful. Plus, if that ain't a good enough reason, then read up on how much it can also affect yourself to age faster. It's *true!* When one becomes negative by nature, their whole body becomes affected, thus earlier wrinkles. *Eeek*, yeah no –I'm good. I'll choose forgiveness any day.

But know, this doesn't happen overnight and Spirit knows this. It's a process. Sometimes it can take weeks, months to even years. It all depends on the level of forgiveness that is being asked of you. And when or if, you are having trouble in doing so, Spirit shares you can call on to them. They are experts in this area, and are more than happy to help you to heal this part of you, no matter the amount of forgiveness that is needed to be released.

FROM THE UNEXPECTED

Too often there are experiences during sessions, where the living person will receive messages from someone unfamiliar to them. Even if they never met here on the physical Realm, Spirit may come forward to give you reassurance, that they do love and honor you. Whether you and the soul never met, or stopped speaking, the soul will come forward to give you the blessing of healing and closure.

The moment a soul comes through, that the client didn't expect is always unpredictable. It can be either a really hilarious experience, or one with tears. The purpose for all reasons when a soul comes through, whether you have known them personally, or not, is to heal. Their mission is to give you that time to let go. To take away the pain, and the thoughts of wondering how it would have been different. They want to release you from the guilt that you may have by deleting the, "what if's". Each point made from Spirit, is to enhance your ability to let go, and to allow the healing to take place. And at times, it takes someone that never knew you personally in order for you to understand the amount of worth and love they have for you. Love from Spirit is limitless, no matter how far when alive.

FROM THE *REALLY* UNEXPECTED

After Chad's passing, it took almost two years for me to let go of the guilt I had endured from his death. For almost two years, I had blamed myself for his passing, not being able to let go of the premonitions I had. When he departed, I knew there was nothing that could be done, for it was decided by him and God. But even though I knew this was his choice, his destiny, I still felt it was my responsibility in keeping him safe. I thought for two years, that because of the premonitions, I was supposed to stop this tragedy from occurring. Not to forget, his family had lost a beloved son and brother, that would forever leave a void in their hearts.

What Chad's family never knew, is I secretly prayed to God and Chad, for over a year after his passing. I spoke to them, asking for a very specific request, … "I know your family is grieving over your passing. I wish only to give them a gift in healing. Could you please give them a reading from *Theresa Caputo, the Long Island Medium?* If anyone could give them the healing and closure, please let it be from her as the vessel."

As our lives were slowly adjusting to the "new normal", as Chad's mother, Karen calls it… something miraculous happened. On June, 9th 2014, Karen posts on Facebook that she had gotten a reading from Theresa Caputo! Out of *6,000 people,* Theresa came to Karen asking, "Who lost a son from drowning?" Theresa captured how Chad and his beloved friend departed, and so much more. Going off *without a hitch,* Theresa made the message known, that Karen's son was not afraid to let go, and is safe and at peace on the Other Side.

I was so thrilled, and was shaken up to the point of hysterically crying at my desk. I was so overwhelmed and so happy, that Karen and her family were not only able to get the confirmation that he's safe, but that he never left. It was such a thrill to many that knew him. I could envision in my head, just how much they sobbed from this experience, from the sensation of knowing that the words Theresa spoke were that of their beloved Chad. This was such a beautiful experience, and such an overwhelming blessing, that even I personally will *forever* be grateful for.

The even more miraculous part, is Karen never planned originally going to Theresa's seminar in Salt Lake City, Utah. Instead, Karen was surprised by a few of her friends to take her along with her daughter, Kelsi to be able to witness the healing from Theresa in person. Little did Karen and her daughter know, that this would be the moment their lives would change forever. Never did they ever imagine that it would be them, that Theresa would send messages to them on that day. What's more awakening, is Theresa could have gone to anyone, but out of *6,000 people,* she came to them. I mean *seriously,* what are the *odds??* Still think this is all coincidence? This is just another prime example that Spirit's messages can come from the most unlikely. Even more crazy was I had a feeling for two days that something remarkable was going to happen, but had no idea what it was going to be. But then as I was writing this portion of the chapter for you, I was bewildered to find that today of all days, that this is written is on *June, 9th 2015.* Of all days that I finally decided to write this experience in this book, was on the anniversary date of that very day. I was in such shock, I screamed, *"WTF?!" I swear to God that I didn't even realize that till later.*

Not only was Karen and her family able to heal, but so was I. Being a Medium and a humanitarian, I naturally felt it was my duty and responsibility, to stop the bad things from happening. But in truth, we cannot stop the fate of our lives, even with free will. I speak from my own personal growth, that this was something that I thought was my responsibility to give. But I never understood how much I also needed this done. I was so focused on them, that I began realizing just how much I was holding so much guilt over his passing. Thanks to Theresa and Spirit, we were all blessed in receiving the gift of healing that day.

The reason why I prayed for the healing to be sent by Theresa, is simple. She has this undoubtedly beautiful connection to Spirit, and I can say hands down, she will always have thumbs up in my book, (no pun intended). Her way in being able to connect with Spirit, and the people around her is very unique. No, I am not saying this to get props of any kind. I just know a good Medium when I see one.

To be clear, I do not hold any credit for this miracle at all. I believe this was done by the grace of God's love, and Spirit's will. Karen and her family were blessed with this gift, only by the means of what God believed would be suitable. I don't take credit, and am humble enough to state so. What this was, was a simple answered prayer. And I am sure that I'm *not* the only person that prayed for this healing to take place for the families of both Chad and his beloved friends.

BREAKING THE WALL

Without the gift of healing, the blessing of knowing that you're worth every inch of what love has to offer, we become hollow. We become a person that keeps everyone at bay, keeping yourself safe from the potential future pains. We become someone that shuts anyone out, no matter how much we feel we would want to trust. This is not a way to live. This is not how God wishes for you to embrace life, because essentially, it's not embracing life at all. What's life without love?

I know this wall, because I used to live this way for years. I used to believe that everyone was out to get me, out to take advantage of me, the instance they had the chance. Granted, there *are* people like this in the world, but that's not everyone.

Embracing life, is not without embracing all that life has to offer, including the healing that you deserve. And in order to be able to learn how to embrace all of life, we have to be brave enough to take down the wall of fear, accepting that it's okay to be vulnerable. It's okay to love. It's okay to want to feel your emotions. Being vulnerable doesn't mean you become a target, but it does allow you the blessing of learning how to remain in balance in all areas of life. When people hear the word, "vulnerable" they automatically assume that you're a sitting duck, just waiting to be shot down. But that's not true at all. Vulnerability means you are allowing yourself to hone all of your emotions, by accepting all of yourself without limitations. This is a good thing. Being *vulnerable is a good thing.*

Spirit encourages us to know that being vulnerable is not a sign of weakness, but an inner strength. It's a decision that you, yourself make. That you're no longer afraid of your inner feelings, and true heart's desires. And thanks to the messages from Spirit, we are bestowed the brilliancy that life has to offer to all of us. We are granted the chance at living again, through their loving words of validations and affirmations.

ACCEPTING THE INEVITABLE

In truth, on the Earth Realm we are going to come face to face with individuals that, no matter what you do, will deem you never good enough. It could be your parent, sibling, Mother-In-Law, nephew, cousin, neighbor, classmate, or your coworker, the battle of differences will remain to be a factor. In this case, Spirit likes to encourage that when you come across these types, that we seek guidance, love and ask them to help us through these difficult situations. Spirit knows the pressure we may feel when trying to talk with someone that never seems to hear you. Sometimes it will be as if you are speaking totally different languages, no matter how simple you try to be. Growing up, I was forced to accept very early on that no matter how much you try to please others they're always going to bring up something that you may have done in the past. Granted, we will all make mistakes, but no matter how many times you may accept your own levels of accountability, you still find that's not enough for them. There are going to be people in our path, that regardless how much you take yourself to the lowest of lows to please them…it will never be good enough. The sad truth, is there are people in this world that feel a false sense of entitlement, and you are to earn the self-worth, by kissing their feet. Harsh –but *undeniably true*. In these kinds of cases, this is considered abuse, and neglect. And in no means do you deserve this kind of treatment. Spirit would never force you to have to reap your mistakes your entire life. And nor should you have to! We are human, and no matter how much the person believes otherwise, they're going to discover the hard way, that love is measured by our heart, not our works.

Life is not measured by the amount of money you make, how successful your business is, or how popular you are, but how you treat other people. And vice-versa, if you have been hurt by someone else's mistreatments, and mistakes, but no matter how many times they say they will "change" –never seem to. These are also classic cases of neglect as well. And even though you take them back, forgive, they still do it to you again, and again, and yet...*again*. Or, what's worse, they may make you feel like you're asking the world, causing you to feel guilty for the slightest of love you ask in return.

But again, *this is not a way to live.*

Even though we are here to love, doesn't mean we are to be the subject of their mistreatments and delusions from their own Ego. These people are the types I call, *"The Work In Progress."* They are *Lower Vibrational Souls* that have yet to understand pure unconditional love. Based not on their material gains, and or respect, but on the way they measure others, instead of themselves. Not to say they are "lower" than you in Spirit, vibration or as a person but on a different energy level which can negatively affect communication.

"Sometimes the process of receiving closure, is the closure you give to yourself."

Spirit relays, these types of people are not essentially bad, but may not be seeing the bigger picture for what it is. They may not be aware of their mistakes, or refuse to own them. Maybe they don't know how to love, thus pushing you away for the sake of safety. Or perhaps, something happened to them in their past, and they essentially blame any and all persons in their life. This can be the wall we discussed. They will push you away, believing they are better than everyone else, and in turn, believing you owe them their attention. This is another false belief that Spirit wishes for you to understand. This is not a way for you, or anyone to heal, no matter how unfortunate your past was, doesn't give you, or this other person the right to deem you less worthy. Despite the situation, you are not meant to have to lower your self-worth in order to prove that you love someone. And anyone that says otherwise *clearly* doesn't know how to love themselves, and others, with pure unconditional love. The process of receiving closure from these types of people, will unfortunately never be a reality. That's unless, this person completely accepts their accountability, responsibilities and decisions that contributed to the situations that caused the rupture in the relationship.

Sometimes, the process in receiving closure, is the closure you give to yourself. Accepting who you are in God with love, fully aids you to continue living life, without this level of negativity in your heart.

Spirit never wishes for you, or anyone to remain in a toxic relationship, especially if this relationship is potentially life threatening. If you, or someone you know is in a situation such as this, then I would urge you, and or this person, to seek counsel from a professional.

"Love is not a place that should bring you down, but raise you up."

In turn, the only way these types of individuals see the truth, is to pray for them. Love is not abusive, and certainly not on the Other Side. And the sad truth is, sometimes it takes them arriving back to the Other Side, in order to finally see the truth with unconditional love. Seeking closure from those of this nature, is like trying to pull teeth without the pain involved. You can easily swipe it under the rug, never resolving the issues that arose from the past. But the fact of the matter is, healing sometimes comes with closure. And if you're not allowed to get the healing that you need from this person, then the only closure you can get, is by moving on. And moving on is not a bad thing either. Sometimes we must depart ways, in order to continue growing, learning and loving unconditionally. Spirit won't punish you for separating from people in your life, even if it's your family. Granted, they wish for you to at least make the effort, but only do so as much as you feel you are truly able. Otherwise, all you are doing is allowing this individual to continue hurting you, due to their toxic vibration and large Ego. With that being said, sometimes the reality is these specific souls may never truly give you the closure you desperately need or deserve till their passing. And if they did in fact pass, rest assured they're learning now more than ever before with love.

THE POWER OF HEALING

Healing is such a powerful gift. There is no other way to describe it, for healing is the main ingredient for growth. When the gift of healing takes place into our souls, we are then able to have the ability to continue growing in our lives. And with that growth come more blessings, filled and fueled by love for others and yourself.

There may be certain experiences, memories that you wish weren't in your past. You may wish that certain things about you, or your life, were just not real. But the gift of healing allows us to accept ourselves no matter the misfortunes, mistakes and badness done to us. Spirit knows inside of our hearts when we cry asking for the pain to go away. They know that when we think about those unhappy thoughts, while trying to push them down, not wanting to relive it. Spirit understands your pain, grief, and most of all, the amount of love you may be missing in your life.

Healing every part of us is crucial, because without cleaning out the negatives in our lives, we will never be able to accept or believe in the positives. Without the healing process, we would forever be trapped in our misery, unable to allow love to grow. Without hearing an, "I've always loved you." Or an, "I'm sorry." We would not be able to continue living life to the fullest at times, forever blocking the possibilities of more love to enter into our lives. This is why healing is so important. For without healing, our core belief in ourselves, and in our loved ones, would forever be limited. And that is not Creator's wish for you.

Their wish for us is to fully embrace that we are forever loved, no matter the case. No matter the situations, experiences, or the Hells in our lives, we are to know they love us without question. Angels, God and our departed loved ones, shake their heads when someone says this isn't true. *They love you! They honor you. They appreciate you. They care for you*, because that's how much they love you. They even cry for you –did you know that? Yup, they will even shed their own tears for us because that's how much they cherish all of us.

No, they're not in pain, but it's because of their Divine level of empathy. Their dream for you, their wish for you is to embrace truth inside of yourself, for you deserve to be healed. You deserve to have closure, to know that you're forever loved–and are *never alone.*

Embrace The Present

It should be no surprise that this topic was going to surface. I mean –*of course* Spirit wants us to live in the moment, otherwise we'd be missing all of the wonderful things that surround us. I know it may be a big step to take, depending on your current lifestyle, or situation that you may wish were different. But Spirit cannot express this piece harder, for the benefit to this is greater than we can possibly imagine. Living in the moment is such a wonderful gift that we have!

WHY SO SERIOUS?

Something so funny happened while writing, that made me not only bust out laughing, but *literally bust open my blouse!* I decided to wear a button shirt with a tank top underneath, and as I was writing, I stretched too far forward, causing my buttoned shirt to rip open along my back! No joke people, that *actually* happened. Now instead of getting angry about it, I heard Spirit relay that when there are bumps in the road –or in this case a busted blouse, they encourage us to look at the positives to the potential negatives.

With patience and a dose of your inner child, you can begin to start to see things in a brighter, lighter view. Life isn't about being so darn serious. Sure you have to take your courtroom experience seriously, and other things that call for your undivided attention, but that doesn't mean that everything you experience has to be.

I used to take life way too seriously. In fact, people would look at me, and without me having to say a word, they would ask why I looked so serious. It took me years to realize that the more I took life too serious, the more it reflected on my aura and on my approach towards others. Life isn't about taking control of every little thing, focusing on what you can control. But more of how you accept what happens in life with faith, while learning how to respond to those *happenings* receptively.

I know it's easier said than done. Trust me, I *know*. Sure, you can't control what time your bills come in, or how your teen behaves at dinner in front of your boss. But you can control how you handle the situations that evolve before you.

APPRECIATION LEADS TO CONTENTMENT

Life is all about appreciation. When we appreciate more of what we have, the more the Universe will bless us, because of the goodness we spread to others from that feeling of contentment. However, if we were to forget what we are currently blessed with, we can so easily lose sight of the blessings we already have. Whether it's people, a pet, a roof over our head, or the food we eat, we can so easily write off those blessings without realizing it.

"Focusing on the future will rob you from the present."

-Spirit

The reason why I don't do future readings, or "Fortune Telling" –is for that exact reason. Spirit wants us to focus on the now, and to be appreciative of what we are blessed with here today. We can get so caught up in our ideals, that we forget what we have now. For instance, if you have a Ford Pinto and you're okay with it…but you keep focused on having something like a Cadillac Escalade, you will forget to appreciate your Ford Pinto. Eventually you will begin to neglect the Ford, because it's not personally ideal for what you had your heart set on with the Cadillac. Sure, the Ford isn't exactly running in style in your eyes… but before you can be blessed with the luxuries of the Cadillac in the future, you have to learn to appreciate the vehicle you have now. (example of appreciation.)

It's the same with relationships. So many times I get a client that comes to me for relationship insight, wanting to know what their next love is going to look like. I tell each person the same thing, "Spirit wants you to focus on how the person will make you feel, not so much on what they will look like." In fact, one specific client asked me what the future held for her love life. Spirit told her, *"Focusing on the future will rob you from the present."* She was confused, but once I explained to her that life is about appreciating what you have now, she began to understand that Spirit was blessing her with a very beneficial reminder. And even though she will be blessed with a love in the future, doesn't mean she still shouldn't be content and appreciative of the people she already has in her life today.

Going back to my busted blouse, I want to enlighten you a little bit further for Spirit emphasizes here that is so gratifyingly true. *"If we focus too far forward in our life, we can rip, or become unappreciative of our current blessings."* Think of that, how awesome of an example is that? I don't know about you, but I just got goosebumps like crazy. I just hope they make up for my busted blouse.

POPCORN ANYONE?

I will never forget a session I did for a woman named Yvette. During her session, I was beginning to get a little bit hazy, which is normal for me when a soul is stepping forward. And as I was feeling the sensations of this departed soul, I asked Yvette if she had lost her mother. With tears of relief she said, "Yes." While giving her validations of her mother's soul being present in her life, her mother showed me something repeatedly. Not understanding what this meant, I shared with Yvette, "This is so random, but maybe you'll find some reason to this, but your mother keeps showing me popcorn?" Yvette laughed in agreement following with, "My family and I are huge popcorn fiends. We love popcorn." Soon enough after Yvette confirmed this, I then was being shown images of Yvette and her family having movie nights and how she does this in memory of her mother. When I shared this information with Yvette, she agreed by saying that she does indeed do this in memory of her mom. Then quickly Spirit had me say, "Your mother wants to thank you for taking the time to appreciate your past, by living in the moment with your family. She shares that she is thankful that you honor her memory in this way. By doing things that you and her did together when she was alive." With this reassurance from Spirit, Yvette was being congratulated for living in the present, while still honoring the past memories of her mother.

This was a beautiful message of Spirit's undivided attention to our lives here, and how we should live in memory of them in our present time.

SABOTAGING YOUR *NOW*

Point is, life is meant to be lived now, or else we could end up sabotaging the present. As an example, let's imagine a father too focused on his previous life when he was a bachelor, before he married and had a son. Truth be told, some folks tend to miss the life they had when it was a lot less complicated. A life before bills, accountability, mortgage, kids, etc. As an example, the father then starts neglecting his kid and his wife, because he is home-less, and isn't emotionally invested, due to the focus on the previous life he had. And due to his past life tunnel vision, he misses out on his son's soccer games, birthdays, anniversaries with his wife and other special moments with the family. Sure enough, the family has had enough with not being appreciated or acknowledged, and the wife moves out with their son. Leaving the father to his empty wishes, that are no longer a factor, while left wondering what he did wrong.

This is a classic case of many people, when remaining in the past. Please understand, I get it when there are instances in our lives that leave us with a few scars. Maybe you feel cheated in a way from what someone else did to you in the past. But Spirit's message is to help us realize that the only moment we have any control over, is our *now*.

"All power is from within and therefore under our control."

-Robert Collier

THE DESTRUCTION FROM DIS-EASE

Some of us are left focusing so much on the negatives, or the positives, of the past that we may do things that cause dis-ease in our lives. Whether it's through drugs, alcohol, sex, porn, hoarding, or through gambling, etc. we can find ourselves lost, quickly sucked into this unhappy normal. I'm a firm believer that when a person suffers from the past, they're more than likely going to lean on something to numb the pain. But I can tell you from personal experience, *it's not the way to live.*

Being around the block with alcohol, I have come to understand that numbing the pain won't resolve your feelings, and most certainly won't stop the pain from returning. It becomes a vicious cycle that's never ending. You drink to numb the pain of the past, or present situations, but then quickly regret it, and drink more to numb that regret. Sure enough you wake up feeling like absolute Hell, focusing on last night's mistakes. Then, yet again, you put yourself worth and self-esteem down, and drink again because of that recent choice. It's a constant triangle of never ending pain, and no matter how much you try to drown it out, the memories continue to resurface –which then, only drives you to want to drown it out all over again.

I speak from personal experience. Going to substances that cause you to become disoriented will only leave you with a bad headache, and a stomach full of guilt. I know how life can suck when it really does at times. I know the feelings of never wanting to see the sun again, not wanting to eat, or even breathe. Sometimes I wondered when being emphatically hungover from yet another poor choice, asking God if this train of destruction would ever end. And I remember so many times, hearing His loving kindness, and each time He said, *"Yes... when you let me help you."* I understand from personal experience of my own struggle with alcohol that it is a disease in the body, as well as in the mind. It's not only a cause of destruction of the body, but of your surroundings that are manifested from the mind. You essentially become the walking, breathing disease that brings about the great *dis-ease* in your energy towards the Universe. The disease of the body does bring about *dis-ease* into your life when it takes over who you are.

The good out of this is Spirit understands those that struggle in their lives from diseases. Whether it's alcohol, prescription pills, street drugs, sex, porn, or whatever the addiction you may be struggling with, all carry hope. Spirit notices when we're struggling with these kinds of diseases, determined to bring us back into our present time. Helping us remember the beauty that holds us up each and every day with love without judgement.

Granted, I have never been in a rehab, and nor did I have to. I have been gifted an ambition to think of a goal and stick to that goal, and with my determination to remain sober not for me –but for all of the people in the world that'll need me. I was cured with the gift of awareness of myself. Spirit was my cure. Love was my cure. I have never gotten to the point to where I had to be detoxed to an extreme, or anything like that. But my pain was still very real, and the drinking problem was still a large reality. I knew I had a problem, but I kept rationalizing it saying, "I don't drink every day." Or, "I am in my 20's, this is just me enjoying the partying stage." Or my favorite was… "I know my limit, I just choose to ignore it." As if that even made sense. I was not very aware at all. Maybe that's partially true, but I also knew my drinking was getting me into dangerous situations, leading my health to nearly collapse. I'd drink so hard to the point of blacking out on a regular basis (simply because I thought if I didn't black out, then my high was weak). I would lose track of time, even ending up in the hospital more than once from my kidneys close to failing, *twice.* So yeah, I didn't have to go to rehab…but I still had a *serious problem.* Granted, I didn't drink every day, more like every few weeks but when I would, it would be to the extent of blacking out each and every time. This was a huge setback not only in my relationships but in my healing process from the many "bads" of my past.

People that are willing to associate the pains with their disease or poor choices are given the opportunity to heal thanks to the rehabilitation centers and countless facilities with wonderful people to help those in this crisis. In order to accompany the way to healing we must discover the reasons behind the said *dis-ease.* Most often people usually already know what it is they are grieving over and are still unable to either control or stop their addiction. Which is why it is greatly encouraged to seek professional help in order to heal physically, spiritually, emotionally and mentally.

RECOGNIZING THE CAUSE OF DIS-EASE

The unfortunate statistic that people lean towards substance abuse is due to harboring pains of the past such as sexual/ physical abuse or neglect or due to a traumatic experience and I happened to be one of those statistics. In my growing up in my still youthful of years I was raped numerous times and molested.

After undergoing such moments I was forced to grow up rather quickly for an eight-year old. However, because of my drinking to escape that pain, I then found myself in an unsafe and unwise situation where I was raped another time.

Do I say this situation, this "experience" was my fault? No. Spirit had brought insight to see that regardless of what was done to me, I was dealing with pains that were not done by my hand but of another's.

On the Other Side there is no room for who is at fault for situations but a matter of perception and personal interpretation of the situations. Each situation is based on how the individual views things and sees things either with, or without full awareness. And the lack of awareness or pains of the past situations, can cause one to behave unlike their true self. By acceptance of the truth that we are not our experiences "good" or "bad", but are the *experiencer* of those experiences, the healing process begins.

REALIZING YOU ARE THE EXPERIENCER

When I finally accepted I had to heal, was when I realized how much of my life I was missing out on. I was twenty-seven, still not knowing how to drive. I knew that if I wanted to learn to drive, then I would have to be sober. I knew that my level of awareness had to rise, but in order to do that, I had to stop drinking. When I finally let down my guard, asking God to help me quit cold turkey, (not a technique for everyone) so I could be the person He and humanity needed me to be...my whole life changed. Of course, not everyone will have their addictions solved, or more of, under control through self-awareness as mine, but with God's help, I was able to get my life back on track. What's even more, was I knew that if I didn't change myself, there was no way that I could.

Of course, there are moments where I think about going back to drinking the same way... *"Just for fun"* my old thinking tries to say. But logically, I know deep down inside of myself, I will immediately regret it the moment I go against my already known limitations. It doesn't do anything for me anymore, my heart longs for a longer, deeper high and that's God. Now does this mean I cannot control myself? No. It means that I am now fully aware of my limitations, to say, I am fully aware that I am no longer going to a drink to erase old memories. Now with full awareness I am able to attend a gathering with a glass of wine without the urge or false belief that overindulgence is necessary. My overindulgence of alcohol was due to me trying to escape old memories that had not yet been healed. But once I became fully aware of this I was able to move forward in my healing process in order to no longer have my past experiences take a hold on my present life. Not all people are going to have the same stamina and I completely respect this, and only urge you to remain strong if you are dealing with something similar. You are exactly where you're supposed to be, and God only wants the best for you. If He didn't, He wouldn't have urged you in some way to read this book. After all, I'm that amazing *(wink, wink)*.

When dealing with addictions, or situations that cause us a level of *dis-ease* in our lives, we have to come to a place of accountability. We have to be ready to take action, taking a level of responsibility, willing to change our lives for the better. I knew that the only way I was going to change, was if I finally acknowledged that I had a problem with how I was running away from old memories. I had to dive into *why* I was drinking. After much soul diving, I was able to discover that the reason I was drinking was due to running from my past. Granted, I knew that the pain of my past was always going to be in memory. But the blessing was I was finally able to no longer allow my past to become the negative impact of my present. No longer was I going to allow my past experiences to identify me as who I am. Coming to the conclusion that we are the *experiencer* of our experiences and those experiences do not make us who we are but are only a subject of a situation. When you can fully accept yourself no matter the misfortunes, you are brought the gift of unconditional love for yourself. I was finally able to accept that I deserved better. With this revelation in myself, I was finally able to be a mother to my daughter that she would be proud of. Finally being the woman that I forever dreamt of becoming, no longer bound by the fears and pains of my past. With this powerful revelation you are able to take back what is rightfully yours...which is *life.*

TAKING BACK YOU & YOUR *NOW*

Learning about yourself and the reasons behind levels of dysfunction, you are able to discover a way out by digging deeper into the *why* of yourself. Not asking the "why me?" but the "why not me?" As uncomfortable as this may sound, but when you no longer look at yourself as the person that was hurt, but as the person that learned a potentially invaluable lesson from your past experiences as the *experiencer* of your life, you no longer will feel so bad about yourself. You will begin to gain a higher level of awareness of how you grew up to be the person that you are and eventually may fully accept it so much that you may even tell the person or the situation "thank you" or an "I forgive you". After a while you may even discover that you don't ever think about it anymore and whenever if you do, it won't bother you as much, or at all because you will no longer feel you're identified by it.

Of course this is not going to be the case with all situations we may face but the underlying cause is things "happen" for a greater purpose than we may fully understand. Like I have said...*nothing* is a coincidence.

For me, I know that what "happened" to me was not "right" in any length but I have gained a higher level of awareness of myself sooner and of those around me before the majority of my class. With those experiences while being fully aware that I am not those situations, I have gained knowledge in how to help the healing process of myself. And without knowing this myself first handedly, I would not have been able to help countless clients that too have gone through similar trials in their life. *What some may see as a curse is also a gift in disguise for others.*

Asking yourself penetrative questions grants you a more in depth idea of the reasons behind these behaviors in order to solve what it is you need and don't need. I highly suggest that you don't leave anything out when you do this. Be brutally honest with yourself, of your essence of how you truly feel of a situation, timeline, encounter, behavior, people or whatever it may be, to help you truly dive into the pool of healing.

Below is a list of some helpful tools for being able to start your healing process; that is, if you feel this is what you may need, to be more actively present in your *now*. These techniques I have found personally to be highly effective as I have used them and still do whenever I feel I need to heal…

TALK TO YOURSELF HONESTLY each day about the feelings you have about something that is bothering you. Express don't repress. The more you hold in your emotions the less likely you will ever be able to let it go successfully depending on the topic or situation that is affecting you.

LET IT OUT. As corny as this may sound to some, allowing your emotions to flow naturally without resisting gives way for the healing process to occur. In truth, when you are full of emotion like sadness or grief, you are in the process of healing in that moment. Every tear you shed, whether it's three or one hundred, you will start to feel the release of negative energy leaving your shoulders, arms, legs, neck and back…and most importantly in your heart and soul. Doesn't mean that not feeling the need to cry means you aren't healing or moving forward positively, for each person goes through emotions differently. But don't resist this healing method if the feelings should arise. Accept them as they are without shame or guilt for all will need to do this at least a handful of times in our life.

SEEK A LIKEMINDED GROUP. Most may agree that when one is undergoing certain trials in one's life, going to others that are in the same faith, belief or likeminded-ness aids exceptionally. Whether it's a local church, a public or private support group, a sponsor, a meditation circle or whatever you feel may assist in your healing, gaining clarity or awareness of thyself, this brings much personal success. Having those to cheer you on without judgement, and understanding where you are coming from, really does put the kick in one's step towards positive vibes.

VENT IT OUT! Sometimes we just need to vent. Some may agree when I say, it's good to just let out the stress and the hardship once in a while. We're human, it's normal and by accepting that it's okay to be confused or frustrated by expressing so to another person in releasing unnecessary energy that may not be positive. If you don't have someone to vent to, then by all means vent alone in your home! However, for the best results –only express what is truly upsetting to your inner self. When you are no longer in need of doing so, feel as if you have fully expressed yourself –STOP. Continuing on becomes complaining or gossip (depending on what it is) and that would not be in the best interest of one being in positive vibration.

TALK WITH CLOSE FRIENDS or relatives who can relate but still look at the situation while not being emotionally invested.

Make sure this person(s) are nonjudgmental of your situation and emotions that you are sharing so as to be of service when in healing yourself fully.

KEEP A JOURNAL where you can store all of your emotions, frustrations and gratitude without fear or judgement. This is where you must be brutally honest with yourself no matter the situation. Then reread it from time to time while asking yourself if this situation, problem or pain is still bothering you. Your answer will help you to determine how much healing you have left to pursue and how long it may take for you. Make a mental note that when you write down your personal situations, issues, truths that you are doing so to "let go" of the situations/issues with a fair amount of forgiveness so as to release you from its clutches. Doing this will aid in allowing to forgive and move forward in your life without so much of it hanging over your head and heart.

CONFRONT THE PEOPLE that you feel have done you wrong. This will contribute to your inner strength in honing your own personal truths as a person and what you will and will not tolerate. I urge with sincerity to do so when you are "ready". A person that knows when they are ready to face the people that had hurt them is something that can take an individual a certain amount of time in order to fully process the emotions of the situation at hand. With great care, express yourself to this person(s) without the need to stoop to their level by stating your emotions soundly, responsibly and respectively of all parties including yourself. If you choose to do so, do it without any expectations of the outcome so as to allow yourself to be released of the hardships for good. Make sure this is a safe and wise decision before going into such an encounter. Not all people are safe to "stand up" to, so I encourage with caution to be fully aware of the levels of possibilities depending on the specific situations, reasons, locations and person(s) involved. This is not to take "revenge" or to promote a combative encounter. Make love your truth speaker and forgiveness as your shield.

STAND IN FRONT OF A MIRROR and look at yourself without saying anything. Look at who you are. After about one minute, ask yourself out loud what you see when you look at yourself. Answer honestly. Don't try to sugarcoat yourself. When you do this, don't answer things about your past. Focus on yourself as who you are during this present moment. If you find you still cannot see yourself past your past, then you still have some healing and perhaps some forgiveness to do. Or if you find that certain present situations are your focus then this is where you can try to solve the issue to your problem by then asking why this is not sitting right with you. You can also do this by looking at a photograph of yourself.

PRAY TO THE HIGHER REALMS. We are all in need of their assistance in our lives and that's why essentially they are at our availability 24/7. When you seek their help, whether it's from

Source, Angels, Spirit Guides or your departed loved ones or Ascended Masters, be specific of what it is you are asking help on and why. Make sure you are asking the right questions. Don't be ashamed of this moment. Let all of your debris of your past or present situation fall to your humble feet while embracing their unconditional love, ultimate wisdom and supreme guidance. Ask them to give you the tools, and courage or whatever you feel you need to overcome your pains successfully. They will listen adamantly and will respond without delay. After your plea, take time to see what responses you receive. If you find you are not getting the answers or help that you desire, then it very well could be a lesson that you may have to learn to overcome yourself depending, again on what the situation is.

READ SELF-HELP BOOKS. Taking the time to read experiences from other people that have been in similar shoes enables your inner self to no longer feel alone. Thanks to the internet, public libraries and thousands of books available on our tablets, one never has to leave the comfort of home even. Suggested books would be people of both the professional field and those of personal experience. Both are powerful messages of how to look at your situations personally as well as objectively. Reading can give more insight into how to overcome emotions or enlighten a thought which may lead to clarity which then grants the gift in acceptance of a certain person and or situation.

SEEK PROFESSIONAL GUIDANCE OR HELP. There is no shame in going to someone that knows your situation on a level that is grounded on countless success stories. The professional of the specific field you need guidance on will give you the best results to overcome your situations, pains, regrets or resentments, which will propel you to discover more with tools and strategies that are specifically designed to get you the best healing possible.

No matter what our history is, we are granted the gift of the present, to take our lives back, taking charge in our *now*. We are connected to Source, God and with this beautiful connection that we have inside of us, we are granted the power from within to withstand even the most doubtful of odds. Life is meant to be taken with love, with appreciation of the moment we are blessed with *now*. Even the breath that you're breathing right *now* to read this book…that's a *miracle* in itself. And by sharing my story which is in truth, a crumb of my life, I believe that this piece will grant you more hope in a better tomorrow for another better today. I too understand the indescribable-ness of pain emotionally, physically, mentally and psychologically. Yet I have learned even then, I still move forward because to me, there is always another person out in the world right now, experiencing something much worse as the *experiencer* of their own life.

"We are given the gift of life, and Spirit and your departed loved ones wouldn't wish for us to squander that gift another day."

I am not a psychologist, therapist, or a clinical professional and I urge if you, or someone you know is dealing with addiction, to please seek professional help. Each individual case is special, and must be taken care of with unique techniques that are specifically beneficial for the person in need individually. This is only based off of my own personal experiences. I do not relay in anyway, that you, or another person's case, does not need to seek professional treatment or care.

THE HIDDEN BLESSINGS

When I was sixteen, I was taught quickly to take my body very seriously, after having a near death experience from an anaphylactic shock reaction to beef out of the blue. It has been over ten years since I've had the pleasure of enjoying a good burger without having to say, "… and hold the beef." Even though I thought that it would be such a curse to never be able to enjoy one of life's simple pleasures, I somehow knew inside it would teach me discipline and gratitude for life. And although I spent days crying in my soup about it, I knew I had to accept it. I was woken up with the realization that I would have to say goodbye to beef forever. This is something I couldn't change no matter how badly I wanted to, but in the end it gave me the gift of adaptation. I knew somewhere deep inside, that this was a blessing in disguise.

Over the course of time while watching my family indulging in their hamburgers, while I was stuck with buffalo, I began seeing the changes allow me to grow into myself more. For I didn't realize it at the time, but later it allowed me to understand that things are going to happen that at first may seem unfair. And even though at first I responded with, "God hates me! I'm never gunna be able to be happy ever again," eventually, I looked at it as, "God gave me what I can handle and apparently He thinks I'm a badass." Being truthful, I can't stand the, "I hate the world", or "the world hates me" kind of people. Reason being is because they're missing the bigger picture of why things happen the way they do. Sure, sometimes we aren't meant to understand why certain things happen, but it certainly doesn't mean that all of a sudden God hates you. These types of people always focus on the negatives, rather than on the blessings in their life. Life isn't meant to be boo-hood over. If you lost a loved one, yes by all means mourn in your own way and time. We are meant to process those emotions. But…to those of you that are the, "damned if I do, damned if I don't" about everything…then you might as well sign your growth from life experiences away forever.

Understand, it doesn't mean that this type of person is a bad or a negative soul, more of, this is how they choose to perceive life and the blessings.

Choosing to live this way is not ideal in Spirit's eyes. Not to say that bad things aren't to be upset over for a fair amount of time, but Spirit's message is not to focus on the bad, but on the *potential positives* to see the bigger picture.

A man spoke of this exact perception on his own daytime television show, the *Steve Harvey Show*. *Steve Harvey* is a well-established author, radio & television host, father, husband and founder of numerous programs, helping people all over the globe. But even after all of the major success in his life, he has always remained to be a man of integrity, guided by his faith. Never does he stop his mission to help people in establishing their true purpose, and most of all, when it comes to finding love. And on one of the episodes of the Steve Harvey Show, he made a part of his mission known.

Steve was speaking about how people in the dating world wonder why so many spouses cheat. A woman who was a guest on this particular episode was asking Steve for dating advice, on how to get back into the dating world. While confessing, that all she kept focusing on, was the fact of how much time she wasted investing years with a guy that cheated on her.

But Steve said something to her that forever is engraved in my memory box of useful inspirational messages. He said, "You're so focused on the fact that this guy cheated. And I know that was hard, and it was unfair to you, but you gotta stop focusing on the fact that he did that. You're so focused on the time lost, when you should actually be thankful for the time saved." His words were not only incredibly true to the importance of time saved, but more importantly of how much we tend to get so caught up on the fact of time lost. When in truth, we should be thanking the Universe, Spirit and Creator for giving us the time back! No longer will the woman be wasting more of her invaluable time on this cheater, and is now blessed with more time to focus on someone else that is deemed worthy for her.

Even in our worst situations that may come across as completely unfair, we are deeply supported by Spirit. We are encouraged to view the unexpected changes in our lives with a humble acceptance which is for the best of ourselves in the long term.

I have always been the type to say, "I'd rather know the guy is not the one for me sooner, rather than later." But even then, we tend to get too caught up in the time invested, no matter how short the relationship was. Instead of focusing on the concept of time, focus on the messages that could be lying out before you. Doing this, we are then allowed the chance in seeing the bigger picture, while receiving the gift of the experiences fully.

RECEIVING LIFE'S PRESENTS

Life's sucky moments are usually where we need to stop and reanalyze what is to be expected of us in the situations, and why. One of the best pieces of advice I heard was from *Theresa Caputo* as seen on *TLC's The Long Island Medium,* saying, "Whenever something bad happens in our life, that's when we should stop and find out what lesson is from the situation that has been placed before us." When you stop and focus on the bigger picture, that is when you start to ground yourself in the present, really appreciating the moment with which you are blessed while embracing the lessons given.

Spirit states often, *"In life experiences one must embrace the beauty of the here and now."* Once you start to hone the present, that is when you will start to really see the bigger purpose of your life and why you are here.

That is why it is called the, "present" because that's what life's moments are. They are Divine treasures for us to fully embrace with gratitude, for the experiences and the lessons that come with them. In life, we come across situations that never usually seem to make sense, and believe you me, I know that feeling. But when we can push aside the need to understand the *why*, and search the *why not's*, then we're more easily acceptable to the lessons that come with the experiences. Each experience, each piece of "bad luck", has a lesson tied to it, and with each lesson, is the gift of more wisdom gained.

Through the gifts of life, we are generously given more opportunities to adapting to a better version of self. We are able to take life by the hand, release our worries and embrace the joy that comes with spending time with those that we love in the now. Now is all that we have any control over and no matter how much you may wish your past were different, or wish to see the future possibilities –what truly matters is the crucial in depth moments we have today. This *very* instance you could take life more graciously by smiling more often with strangers you encounter or by taking the time to listen more intently to those that seek your opinion or ear. We may only be our human bodies in this moment but we are not without the power of controlling us in this *very present time* and truth be told –that's one of the *most precious* gifts we will ever have the free will to embrace without limits.

Whether you have lost a dear loved one, or are going through a situation that seems unfair, Spirit whispers to look into your heart, viewing the bigger picture. Take in the new, the now, so you can take in the knowledge of a new way of living. Take in the present, to accept more of the amazing gifts that are hidden within the now. They encourage you to look into the new with an open heart, and an open mind, in order to fully embrace life and its potential lessons.

Embrace Where We Go In Spirit On The Other Side And The Unbreakable Bond

As the old saying goes, *"When one door closes, a window opens."* And I'd like to add...*but before we can open the window, we must be brave enough to lift the blinds...so as to take in the light of today.*

God, Source, Creator

I find it incredibly interesting that the day I decided to write this portion, of all days, is on a Sunday. Not like I planned it that way. Coincidence? Nah...I don't believe in that hoo-ha. But what I do believe, is that when there is a Universe that is ever evolving, so is our timing for everything to be in synch.

WHO IS GOD?

When my personal conversations with God take place, as they do now, I speak from the heart. Just like as if He were my old time friend from grade school, and I believe it should always be that way. The idea of talking to God was always more comfortable to me, than the idea of prayer. This is just my take on it, and how I feel the most vulnerable. Everyone's approach to God, or the idea of God is always going to be different, based on experience and perception. Including the way we perceive Him. There is no right or wrong way when approaching God, which is just my understanding based on what I have learned from Spirit.

When people think or picture our Source, Creator, many imagine a man like Zeus, with a trident ready to strike lightning down. Or some will picture an energy being, with immense power that will judge you if you don't bow down, praising His every move. But I can tell you exclusively, that's *not* God at all. I can't express this enough. Our Source, Creator is indeed a beacon of light, but filled and fueled by *only* love.

"There's a fine line between building a relationship with God vs doing rituals out of fear or discipline. Love is His goal, not how much you worship Him."

I respect all religions, and other people's personal beliefs, and most certainly respect how you choose to serve and honor Creator. However, Spirit continually shares with me, that God is not one that judges so harshly. I have learned from God that no matter how much you may get angry, confused, or upset with Him, He will always respond to you out of love. I don't care how bad you have been, there is nothing we can do, that He has not *already* forgiven you for. His love is immense, powerful and desirable. Personally from my experience, God doesn't think Himself so highly, even God takes Himself to a humble place. Simply because, He knows that if He wasn't, we would never feel comfortable enough to be vulnerable with Him. I cannot imagine a life without His love to be honest with you. The idea alone scares me to death. His love is the Source of all that exists, and all that ever is. He is the light that brings you hope and the love that you share within yourself, and others.

The image that God wants us to envision when we see, or think of Him, is to never be afraid. He wants us to always remember, and to know that we can always go to Him for everything, no matter the size.

The impression that I have acquired from Spirit about Creator, is He is *simple*, *loving*, and so *merciful*. He's not so serious like so many proclaim. I don't understand this mentality that so many believe, that He is this judging being that doesn't forgive. That's no true at all. He is all of the love that you could possibly imagine, and then multiply that by a million! He is the answer to all of your problems, and is the light guiding you on your path. Source knows everything about you, because He made you, because He loves you. He made you because He *strongly* believes in you.

PERFECTION IS FALSE

Too often, I have met people that believe God expects perfection. *This is false.* God doesn't expect you, nor I to be perfect. But what He does pray, is that we do our best to love others, and ourselves, the best way we know how. It doesn't matter how much you go to church, or how often you pray, or how much you do to "earn" your way into Heaven. In fact, Spirit explains that you're always welcome in God's Paradise. The only person that denies you, is you. He will *never* deny you, no matter how bad you think you are, or have been in your life.

LIFT A PIECE OF STONE AND I AM THERE

What's got me all worked up, is what I dreamt of last night. I knew I was going to be writing this portion for you today, and strange enough I had dreamt of something interesting. I have *extremely* vivid dreams, always have since I can remember. But this dream was something unique, and what I remember for *sure* had to have been a Divine message from Spirit.

There was a group of men trying to hurt another woman, but I told her to hide. As the men came up, there must've been about ten of them, whom all were carrying an ax, and the leader shouted, "Where is she? You can't hide her forever!" I then saw myself lift piece of stone. I didn't do anything spectacular, but picked it up, and I could then see another group of people that came out of nowhere. These people were then protecting us. Once the angry mob of men realized who had shown up, they attacked. But this brawl wasn't like anything I had ever seen before, for it was like time had been moving fast and slow at the same time. As the men raised their weapons to strike me and this woman, the new group of people stood their ground, glowing, then with haste, countering each strike made. Every time the mob lashed out, the bright defenders were ten steps ahead. Strike –Counter, STRIKE –COUNTER, *STRIKE –COUNTER*. No matter how much speed the mob engaged, the defenders were ten times faster, quicker. Similar to a group of soldiers, like soldiers of God they reined. They never flinched during this battle of Evil vs Good. Never once did any of them lose their stance, but stood their ground. The sound was another memory I'll never forget either. For each blow was exceptionally loud like thunder. And as the fight enticed, each defender began to glow brighter more, together as one.

They were so fast it was *beyond remarkable*. I was witnessing them move like the speed of light. They didn't hurt the angry mob, merely preventing them from coming closer. Then, without delay, a second group again appeared out of nowhere, and formed themselves into a circle. Sitting down, this quiet circle began to pray to Creator. As they began their prayer, the negative mob dissipated entirely within the wind. Each ax, each person, each gasp of breath, gently faded into the atmosphere effortlessly.

I can still recall how I felt when one man outstretched his hand, to stand me up after such a glimpse of Angelic power. I can still remember their serene smiles. Then within seconds, from the wind, a flock of butterflies gathered around us, surrounding all that stood there. Each butterfly was bright in different colors, greeting us with sweet gestures of their hellos.

I have no doubt that Creator brought me this dream, and possibly a visit into the Spirit Realm, for me to take note of their grand protection, love and loyalty. But more importantly, the fact that all I did was pick up a rock and the next thing I know, God's love was there without delay.

This has to be said, God doesn't require you to go to church. Does this stretch it a bit? Yes. And that's because this is what I have learned from Spirit and God Himself. I know this is taking it quite far, but Spirit has taught me that no matter where you are, you're always in God's palace of glory. It could be your backyard, in the clouds, work, or wherever you are. Not to say that church is a bad thing, *not at all* am I saying that. In fact, it's a beautiful place to spread the love –but to remember that His love isn't based on what church you go to.

I cannot tell you how many people have asked me what church I go to, or if I go to church. And each time I say, "I believe God is with me, no matter where I spend time with Him." the person usually then discontinues the conversation, or worse, they try to get me to go to their church. I have to say this again, God doesn't focus on how you praise

His love, but on *why*. I have learned throughout my life walking, talking with Spirit, Angels and our Lord, that He is not about how you worship Him, but *why*. His focus is your heart, not your works. This is not to say that church is not a good way to worship Creator, but what I am saying, is it's not the only way. We are allowed, as God puts it, to *worship His glory in whatever way that we feel comfortable that is good.*

LOVE FOR HUMANITY IS LOVING GOD

We are here with a Divine responsibility to look to our fellow man with love, and the utmost respect. Even those of some of the highest levels of respect, such as Mother Teresa communicated this often. She believed that unity with God was through other people, in order to not forget why we are here. She couldn't have been more spot-on. This woman, not only devoted her entire life to the poor and the hungry, but for God, and to spread this loving message to everyone she came into contact with. And even though she knew this, and devoted all of her life for this message, there are still many out in the world, that have sadly forgotten this spiritual truth.

Our Source, Creator LOVES watching us love each other. His brilliant light sparkles with everlasting beauty, and shares this good news with all of the Angels, and our departed loved ones on the Other Side. The message from God is, and will remain to be to, *"Love fellow life with the utmost respect."* I don't care where you come from, for we are meant to hold hands in unity, loving the moments we have without regrets, with appreciation for the experiences. It is of course, easier said than done. I get that. However, I was raised with the old Southern saying, "You catch more flies with honey, than you do with vinegar." Not that I want to attract flies, yuk! But to attract love from love, which goes back to the Universal Law of Attraction. The more you give, the more you receive what you give. Which also goes to the core of your thinking, and inner feelings about others and yourself. The more you are here for love, the more often you will discover how much love you can receive in return. And the more you give love to others, the more you will find that you are loving God.

We are all a piece of God, we are actually looking at God in each one of us. Did you know that? I didn't for a long time, but when I learned this spiritual truth from Angels, and my Spirit Guides, I was more often finding myself respecting each person. Love is something you *are*, not something you just do. I cannot express this truth enough, you don't want to just act in love, but live as the expression of love.

We are all a small spark in God's eye, and He is our energy that fuels us alive here today. The more you are embracing yourself, and our fellow man as a whole, that is where you are loving God.

CREED IDENTIFICATION

When I met with my friend Chad in Heaven, he told me as I gazed upon its unspeakable glory, *"We are all God, and God is all of us."* I then asked, "But wait, so are you saying God is not a person or a being?" He confirmed with a nod then added, *"He is a Source of everything that is massive intelligence and energy."* In shock I said, "So you're saying that all of the spiritual, religious beliefs are actually wrong?" He then responded by saying, *"God is not bound by a set religion or belief. It was man that created this, not Him. He is the light inside all of us, the love that surges inside everything and everyone for all eternity. They are not wrong, just misinterpreting what is the whole truth."*

In short, I learned that Source is not to be identified by a set religion or a closed belief. It was mankind through our own thoughts that identified Him to these many labels, not Him. In retrospect, religions have a tendency to separate by identifying oneself to a confined set of beliefs thus creating a division which then only propels one's Ego through this unawareness. Many "religious" people are confined to a level of thought, and this thought that is defined by one belief, conducts the separation that was produced from the thought. The thought I speak of is the thought, belief of one "truth". Source is not one truth but is all truth. He is not to be bound based on one set of ideas or limitations, but is the *whole truth*. It is the thought that is identified with one's own "truth" that makes it confined, that which causes the separation in the world, which is not Source's desire in any length. This unconsciousness, the thoughts in believing that Source is only "one way of truth" or to be labeled as "My God vs Yours" is only the mind being led by this collective separation. When another says this to me, I simply respond with, "There is no my God or your God, but one of all that is and ever was. He is everyone's regardless of belief, or faith and religion."

Does this mean that following a religion or a belief that speaks the closest to you is a waste of time? Is purposeless? Not at all, for it's another wonderful way in being able to feel closer to Creator, to feel the true inner connectedness that is boundless by form and endless by time. His advisement is to remain consciously aware that He is not to be labeled or to be identified by a religion but is of all that is and ultimately will remain to be that coexists within the course of the Universe.

WHAT IS GOD?

I used to ask this question all the time. What is God? Truth be told, even as a Medium, I don't always have all of the answers. So likewise, God isn't offended when we ask this because He understands our desires to know.

From what I have learned, God is the entire Universe. The ultimate intelligence that is interconnected to all that coexists within the whole Universe that is forever eternal. Creator is the Source to every answer to your question, is the guiding light to end your doubts and fears. He is the velocity of energy that lives inside of you, in what makes up your Soul Print. As you are connected by His energy, you too are also a piece of Him. We all are a piece of His creation that is to be the vessel of that supreme intelligence, healing, unconditional love and wisdom. He cannot be in existence without us, for He is a piece of us as we are a part of Him. Which is why connecting and building a relationship with Him is important to an epic proportion. So to say, He is not an entity that is physical in form, but is the ultimate Source of what is true and founded on supreme Divine love.

He is the being that lives inside of you, the love that you hold for your mother, father, sister, brother, neighbor, boyfriend, girlfriend, husband, wife, dog, cat, etc. He is the light that shines in your eyes, and the smile in your cheeks. We are all a part of Him, which is why He is able to see, and know us so well individually.

For a brief moment, I thought that I wasn't worthy to do what I do, but

I still wanted to believe I was worthy. So I told God I wouldn't write this book until I had a vision, because I couldn't do this without some kind of personal truth. Sure enough that very night, I fell asleep, then quickly found myself in a higher state of consciousness. My body was asleep, but my mind was still awake, and without hesitation I felt a sudden but gentle pull. Without delay, my soul floated from my bed, leaving my physical body behind. Flying past millions of stars, even galaxies I flew into space, to the point it felt like lifetimes had passed in seconds. Before I could even process what I had been experiencing, I was standing before a bright light that was of pure brilliance. The light of God is not bright like the sun, but built from energy, and massive amounts of it, which aids in seeing Him. You don't age when you see God or higher Deities, that's a myth by the way. Not to also forget, He relays that He doesn't possess one gender like a human but is of both male and female energy frequencies. He is the Divine Masculine and Feminine. And even though I say "He" and "His" most often, God is balanced in both nonetheless. He likes us to imagine Him as a Source of all that is Creation, being anything for anyone, and everyone.

His feeling only gave me love, with a strong sense of security, giving me the reassurance that I needed. I could feel my emotions as a whole, along with Creator's love. Being in the presence of Creator is one of slight humility and in a place of ultimate unconditional love guided with Divine wisdom. His power does not intimidate you, but brings a personal relationship with Him in an intimate way. I can tell you from this experience, that His love for us so *extremely lovely.*

Creator is the healing, the answer to all that is love. He is the energy in your strength to get up after you fall. He is the faith in you to keep going. He is the tears you shed when you lose a loved one. He is the truth to all that is forever pure, holy and radiant.

I truly wish I could tell you exactly what God is, but honestly it's literally impossible to put His glory into words. His love is *that brilliant*. His being is *that magnificent*. But He does say, the best way to imagine Him, is to picture the sun warming, not just your body, but your soul, and your inner child.

Imagine His love wrapping you up, holding you safely for the rest of your existence. If you can imagine this, even a little, then be rest assured, this is the place where you will *always* find Him.

WHERE IS GOD?

Creator is not bound by one location that would be considered, or labeled "holy". Instead our Creator insists that He is within everything, and everyone that was, and forever is energy. During the point where I was learning about God, trying to comprehend who, and where He is, Spirit would remind me of this spiritual truth.

Being here on the lower, physical Realm, we can understand that God and our departed loved ones, are wherever we are. However, when it comes to being on the Other Side, God is on the highest level of energy, which is also on the *Seventh Realm*. This Realm as we discussed before, is the highest level you can go, which is where you will find the highest level of wisdom, truth, and unconditional love. But even with that, Source insists that regardless of where you are, no matter the dimension, He will always be there for He is all that is energy within the Universe.

There have been moments where people would wonder where God is, when bad things are happening. God was and forever will be by your side no matter what. He has never left you, and never left anyone who has ever doubted Him. In God's eyes, He sees and knows all, and as long as you remain in existence, whether as a human, or in Spirit, He will remain to love you eternally.

In order to know He is with you, is to ask for a sign. Like I had mentioned before, when you ask Spirit for a sign, make it open and simple for them, in order to give you the reassurance in their own creative way. God too, can apply His own skills and creativity for us when we need it the most when asking for a sign. I can't tell you how many times I have received *amazing* signs from God, but I can certainly share that each and every time is *heartwarming, surprising* and *powerful*.

There was a segment I had watched on television, about a man that was distraught from losing his entire family, including his wife, two young sons and dog in a horrible fire and shooting that his own daughter had started. His daughter premeditated this gruesome shooting on her own family members, including her younger brothers and then left them for dead, by locking them in the house that was engulfed in flames. By the grace of God, this man was able to survive the fire, but was left to watch his house and family die in the flames. His pain was so overwhelming for he felt betrayed, hurt, and mortified by this, and didn't understand how in the world God would allow his own child, his own flesh and blood to commit such a horrendous crime on her own family. In his story, he described how he had witnessed the worst of the worst, and just when he thought all was lost, he found a burnt piece of parchment that was a verse from the Bible. Even more remarkable, is this parchment could have been anywhere, but instead, it flew to his lap the second he fell to the ground in utter anguish. The message here, is that no matter how much you may feel you are completely forgotten, ignored, or abandoned, always have faith that His love is never far behind. This parchment he found spoke to him personally, to his heart and gave him peace, reassurance and the love that he so desperately needed, in order to know that he was not facing this alone. I find it deeply incredible, that he was able to keep his faith in love, and in God, even after something that most wouldn't dare to imagine. I don't know about you, but that's a *strong* example of faith, and God's presence even during our worst of fates.

Creator will impact all of us in many ways, and most of all, very personally. This man received the gift of peace, and reassurance through a scripture in the Bible. This was how God was able to speak to this broken man at the time. He was able to hear and accept God's message more effectively, allowing him to know that God was there going through this with him.

Like I have said, the Bible, going to church is not required, BUT… that's not to say that it's not good for you personally or spiritually. I find nothing wrong with it, and greatly encourage you or anyone to attend their local church, and read their favorite scriptures, if it speaks to you personally. We all have different tastes in personalities, and in things that speak to us individually.

With that, no matter what you go through, there is always a light at the end of the dark tunnel, where God is watching, forever guiding you. He is never without knowledge of our situations, no matter the size. Spirit shares, that when you feel there are moments that you need God's loving messages, to ask from the heart. The more you ask, the more you shall receive in Divine timing.

GOD'S EARS

Creator does not hear only by words, but by your heart, by your level of love, hope and faith. When we reach out for His Divine love, and security, and maybe even direction, He asks us to do so with vulnerability.

Approaching Creator, Spirit encourages that we have nothing to fear. His love for us is no different than from our Angels, and our loved ones on the Other Side. The approach from God is simple, delicate and assertive. His words are pure with undivided attention, and direction with leadership. Our Angels plead for us to understand this truth, for their messages are direct from Him.

"All of man is bound by me, and all of Me is bound with the course of man. We are not separate, but joined together in Divine unity that is fueled by love."

-God

From birth, all the way to our passing, we are in Divine alignment with Creator. His image is to allow us to continually grow, evolving closer to Him, which will allow others in life to grow. With this unbreakable bond, we are capable in hearing His love in our hearts, and even within our mind's eye.

The process when communicating with God, to us appears very simple. When we pray, we think that we are simply speaking to Him, but other beings that are in direct contact with God, at times may send those prayers to Creator. So, behind the scenes, we are actually working amongst an entire team such as Angels, our Spirit Guides and departed loved ones when communicating to God. This isn't to say that when we pray to God, we actually aren't, because *we are*. In the scheme of things, we're actually working together in order to support one another, even on the Other Side. In truth, if you wanted to have a private moment with God, you can, by simply only speaking to Him. But when it comes to asking for something such as a sign, then that is when our Angels, Spirit Guides and departed loved ones may also intervene.

GOD'S EYES

The way Creator can see us is Universal. Can you imagine being able to be in every place, at all times of the day, all over the globe? I sure as heck can't. Spirit has shown me that He has this unsurpassed ability to be there for all of us no matter the time, day or location. God is not limited as we are here in the physical world. In fact, when you and I are to cross over, we are also able to be there for our loved ones, just like Him. From what Spirit, and Angels describe to me, is God is not limited to time. Having the advantage of being able to be the subject of time to say, and manipulate it to His timing instead. I'm sure you've heard the popular phrase, "It's all in God's timing"? This also goes in tune to the fact that there's no sense of past or future on the Other Side but only the presence of now. This not only grants God more leverage in aiding us in our lives with Divine love, and guidance, but grants Him the undoubtedly impeccable ability, to be on time for everything and for everyone.

GOD'S VOICE

Hearing God will be different for everyone. In my experience with hearing God's messages, it's much more different than Spirit. The difference is His level of wisdom, security and certainty. It's almost hard to describe. Before the moments I have been the vessel of truth for God was something I have never understood, till the moment I heard from Him out of my own mouth. He is the voice of reason, hope, love, serenity, and certainty. Even as a Medium, I cannot doubt when the moment His words come through, for all of His energy is nothing but pure love. His voice will feel as if only *love* is your voice, and *truth* is your message. Again, it's *almost impossible* to describe, but you cannot speak from Him without being *overwhelmed.*

Going back to the moment when I was speaking with my friend, about why God brought Mediums. The reason why God came forth, was simply because she has been devoting her entire life to Him, and has been confused by the whole process. I know she needed His loving message more than ever, and when He came through, I *knew right away* it was Him. The moment one is to speak from God, will be a moment that even you yourself will have to question, Was that *really me?* His moment of speech is not something you force, but a process to which He will do on His own accord. We cannot force God to speak for us, or to us, and most especially through us as the vessel. Only when we either need, or are ready, will it be the time to which we will sit, and simply listen to what He has to say.

"God doesn't need words for a message to be sent. In order to hear His loving guidance, is our will to hear, and our hearts to love."

When you hear God's words, no matter who He is speaking through as the vessel, everyone will stop, and listen with attention, for He is the voice of truth. Some will question this, but the truth is, He can channel through *anyone*, and *everyone* if He chooses to. **He's God.**

There are people that will relay that they are speaking from God, but be clear —God's words are always filled with love, and Divine guidance. I cannot tell you how many people will say they're speaking from God, but then you hear that everything out of their mouths is negative and judgmental. If this is the case, gently redirect them to this spiritual fidelity, allowing them the chance to see with their hearts with awareness.

Love is God's voice, nothing else. And if anyone were to try to tell you different, then they are misunderstanding the absolute message of Creator. I'm just saying it like it is. And if that means maybe I'm coming off a little forward, then maybe *it's time it's said.*

There are times where Creator won't use, or need words to communicate with us. All He will need is His love to swarm into your heart, and blanket your soul with tranquility. God doesn't need words for a message to be sent. What we need in order to hear His loving guidance is our will to hear, and our hearts to love.

HIS LITTLE BIG HELLOS

When we seek guidance, or reassurance in our lives, He relays that we only need to keep our hearts and minds open. In order to take notice of His loving messages, we are asked to remain open to endless possibilities of what His messages could be.

Just during this chapter, working, rewording, going over and over this…I was beginning to feel lost. A little unsure of whether, or not I was on the right track, so I asked Him for a sign. Little did I know that when I would receive my sign, I would be getting them in the most random moments. The bigger thing to remember when receiving messages from Heaven, is that it will always be when we least expect it. I can guarantee that no matter how much you feel like you're waiting, and waiting for something big to happen, it will always be something you could never expect, and it will almost *always* blow your socks off.

Some like to say these are God's little whispers, which I can state, *they absolutely are!* When you ask for a sign, be sure to pay close attention to things that you normally wouldn't. Even the littlest things such as notes, numbers, dreams, insights, thoughts, visions, advertisements, or even a kind word from a friend, or stranger can be messages from God.

HIS PRAYER

Creator's goal, and ultimate dream is for us to love others as we would want to be loved. It's that simple, but the sad truth is there are individuals in the world that seem to not know how to do this. If we just stopped all of the negativity, and focused on how to be happy, instead of being right, we would find a huge energy shift in our Universe.

"Our prime purpose in this life is to help others and if you can't help them, at least don't hurt them."

-*Dalai Lama*

His energy aches when He has to witness us lashing out at each other, over things that could be resolved if done out of love, with love. Our path for true awakening in life as a whole, is only going to happen if we stop and reflect on our reactions to things. By the way, did you know that God doesn't react at all? He doesn't. He responds, but does not react. His approach to us, is to show us love, kindness, even when we are angry, or confused with Him.

Reason being is simple. If He reacted, He would only be a hypocrite, and would not be the Divine example that we all need so desperately.

I'll never forget a school paper I did for an English class back in my freshman year of High School. The teacher wanted us to write about what we were most passionate about, and how we felt about it, and why. I wrote a paper which was something not only was I passionate about, but was being truthful, based on my Lightworker eyes towards the world. It was about how the world was hurting each other, and how people today don't stop and do anything about it. How we are killing our children, stealing from our grandparents, robbing food from the poor, and murdering our prom dates. It was about how no matter how sweet people try to appear in real life, they were actually not the people they said they were. How even though the world itself is so beautiful, the people in it are destroying its integrity.

The class was quiet. My teacher followed with how it wasn't as positive as she had hoped it would be. For a long while, I figured I was being too depressing, but the fact was, I was seeing the world as it really is, and *no one* wanted to admit that these things are actually going on every day. I would sit by myself for hours, wondering why it was so wrong to talk of the truth. It wasn't like I was emo or anything. In fact, I was a joyful person with decent grades, and only did what she had asked. I spoke from the heart, but in that moment I started to learn that most people are afraid to admit this harsh reality. Not to say that no one will stand up to bad people, but the truth without the sugar, is that *very few* will. I'm small in stature, and uncertain of things more often than I would like. And even though I understood where this teacher was coming from, it still wrenched deep inside of my soul, that it felt like it was being brushed under the rug. Not sure why I was passionate about it at the time, but the only answer I have to it, is that I felt this strong urge inside, that there's an astounding number of injustices in the world.

This ties into the fact that no matter who you are, you're meant to do something great, and stand up to even the impossible. There was a moment when I was in a movie theater, watching *The Last Samurai*, starring *Tom Cruise*. And during this film, I was told by a foreign exchange student from Japan, named Saho that it was common for people in her hometown in Japan, to look the other way when bad people were doing bad things to other people. I was in *shock!* I asked her, "But, if you all gathered together, then the bad people could be stopped." Then she added, that people would hide their faces or look the other way, to avoid the possibility of getting hurt themselves. I was truly saddened by this. Not only does this mean, still to this day, people are afraid to step up for the good of others, but for the sake of love of man. Of course this isn't to say that all people in the incredible country of Japan are all like this. But what she did express to me, was this was in a bad area of her hometown, that she would witness this often. This was her own opinion based on how she viewed her hometown.

Now, I'm not saying you need to be the hero, *please don't* if you feel the odds are truly against you. But, without a doubt I firmly believe that if there is something bad going on, you are granted the undivided responsibility to stand up for the truth. Yes, it takes a lot of courage to stand up, I get it –*trust me* I know. But the fact from Spirit's message is that no matter what, we are here to love, honor, and *protect* each other.

Even I have been faced with defending another. I've been hurt physically, emotionally, mentally and spiritually, but regardless of how much you may feel like you aren't big enough, strong enough, or smart enough, God will always be the one to back you up. There was a particular unforgettable instance where I was faced with having to defend my younger sister Heather against someone that was threatening her with a knife. Immediately, without hesitation, I put myself before her, becoming her human shield. Then the table had turned and the knife was on me. Of course I was afraid. I'm only five foot, standing up to a guy that weighs double my size, not to mention a vast difference in muscle mass. But in the moment, I didn't care. I only could think about protecting my sister. Keeping her safe, even if that meant me being beaten to a pulp, for my focus was on loving her no matter the case. I had never had to face such a situation like this before, but I knew that I would also never forgive myself if I hadn't done something to protect her. The miracle, was even though this man said he would, "F" me up, I stood my ground, and told him that what he was doing was wrong. His hand was shaking with such enraged anger, and even though I was secretly sweating inside all of me, I knew that I had to stand my ground, keeping my eyes steady on him. It felt like something out of a movie. *Never* before had it felt like time had stopped, it was *terrifying* knowing that at any moment I could have lost an eye, face or life. The instance he dropped the knife, I knew that moment, God was there giving him peace in his heart to stop.

This is the reality that God reminds us about. It brings pain to my heart, when I hear of a mother drowning her own baby. Or how a husband decided to kill his entire family, and then end his own life. We are faced with such dark times, and the darker it becomes, the brighter we must be. In our time of need during these terrors, we must be able to be that foundation for others in our communities, and even in our own homes. Strengthening the bond between parent and child, mother and daughter, father and son, friend or foe, we are all responsible in being able to drive the course of humanity as a whole. It is up to us on how we will drive our world, by taking the wheel of empowerment and enlightenment with unshakable courage.

GOD'S FOCUS

We are here to give, and let the Universe allow us the opportunity to receive in "good" time. We are here for joy, and to bestow that joy to others. Our fair share of love is not just to focus on ourselves, but on everyone and anyone we come into contact with.

His message is to capture the beauty that is in your child's eyes when they giggle. His message is to give a few dollars to the unfortunate souls that seek food and shelter. His message is to give up your time, and patience, to visit your elderly parents, and assist them with their dinner preparations. His message is to give guidance to your teen that is dealing with bullying at school, and help him/ her, to know they're never alone. His message is to stop judging one another, and start loving one another. His message for us is to allow ourselves to take time to save our planet from ruin, and to pick up the trash we left behind. His message for us is to stop yelling, and start listening. He wants us to not make war, but to make love, through forgiveness, sharing, and through mutual respect. His message is to be the savior for others that are in danger. His message is to remember the act of unconditional love.

Enjoy the simplicities you are given in this life, and embrace all that Spirit, Angels, and God have to offer here, and forever in Heaven. Our Angels, Guides and loved ones on the Other Side are here to give us the reassurance in these modern times. They're here to help us to remember what we had so long forgotten.

Even in the darkest hour, we are able to find the light at the end of the tunnel, in order to discover the enlightenment inside all of us. We are empowered by massive amounts of love from Creator, that which allows the grace of an ever evolving world. We are limitless beings with the endless knowhow forever guided with God's love, grace, and mercy by His light without delay. His love for you, is to remember that no matter who you are, no matter how much others can't find the joy in your company, you're always welcomed in God's. You're forever the joy in His beacon of life, and the laughter in His glow. He pleads for the world to take a step in the direction of faith, and remember that you are the Source of all that is love, and *with love, anything is possible.*

"My dream is for you to love without the course of judgement from the world's views. My focus is on you, and for you to understand and know Me. My love for you is eternal, that which cannot be destroyed. Love as you would love yourself. Love others the way you dream others would love you. If you do not receive the same love in return, know that I will never love you in the same, but stronger, longer, forever lasting. My devotion is for you to know Me, for I Am the way to all that is the whole truth. In sickness and in health, for richer or for poorer, for as long as you shall live, love thy neighbor."

- Creator, God, The Source Of All That Is Love

aith

Faith in society has reigned alongside man for centuries. Many are gained the insight of faith, by being dealt with odds that are undoubtedly against them. But with the little push in the right direction inside of them, they are able to keep moving forward, completely unaware, that an unseen force is guiding them along the way. Most often, the word, "faith" is defined as having confirmation, trust, or a strong belief in something that is there or in a set religion. To specify, faith, is not to be mistaken as an identified set belief but on *having the certainty in something unseen.* Some ask, "How can you have faith in something you can't see?" My answer is the same now, as it was then… "I just know." Long before I ever knew of my gift of discernment, or of my NDE experience, my strong belief in the Other Side, and in God was always solid. Never did I realize that my near death experience was factual, as I kept denying that it had actually happened. Sure enough, years later, flashbacks came back, arising the memory of that actual event that shouted this a factor. And even for years without memory of the near death experience, nothing else really laid proof to me that God did in fact exist physically. Instead, I just somehow always knew in my core that no matter what the world said, we are always here for a reason with faith in something bigger.

LET FAITH LEAD THE WAY

Let's be honest, there's not much to say when you tell people that you talk to Spirit for a living. I can't tell you how nervous I get whenever I'm meeting someone new. The conversation is going smooth, people are laughing, sharing their positive energy, but then those seven words I dread the most come out: "What do you do for a living?" Of course, I will think of the best approach in telling what I do, when I say, "I'm a Psychic Medium." Then I love it when I get the quizzical look followed with, "What's that?" I am *amazed* at how many people actually have no clue what a Psychic Medium is.

Now before I go on, this isn't a profession, as much as it is a way of life. Being a Psychic Medium is not a career that I woke up and just decided to do one morning. Especially with the amount of skeptics, and religious debaters, it's not something many would consider to be socially acceptable.

I've never been good at fitting in. In almost every setting, I've been dealt the hand, "outsider" for a majority of my growing up. Little did I know, it would be a part of the bigger picture in what I was meant to pursue later on. I was made fun of constantly in every grade of school, and quickly found myself with very few friends. But along the way, it was teaching me the importance of solitude, and the company of people. Forced to be comfortable with my own company, was when my abilities started to emerge to the surface. While completely unaware that I was actually talking to Spirit on a regular basis, when I thought I was merely talking to myself, or God out loud.

And even though I appeared "normal" on the outside, I knew inside there was something different about me. Likewise, we all have a deep sense of knowing of who we are, and who we are born to become in this crazy place we call Earth. Although we may not understand all of it in the moment, later on we always find people that say, "It all makes sense now after looking back." Life is meant to give you a grander proposition, which is to challenge your level of self-certainty. I always say, "I will depend more on something unseen, than on something I can touch." The world that we have come to understand is so vast, so large, yet we humans still somehow believe that this is all that exists. But I can tell you without flinching, "If you have faith in something you can't see, or touch, then you're more awake today than you were yesterday."

With faith, we are able to establish a life that is set for us. We are able to be in alignment. Our natural soul vibration becomes in synch with what is our soul DNA. We become the unlimited beings that we were created to uphold, while being guided towards the best version of ourselves. We don't have to know what is going to be, but believe that God, Spirit, and our departed loved ones will lead us in the right direction without fail.

FAITH IN THE POWERFUL UNIVERSE & HIGHER POWER

Have you ever found yourself in a hole, because you just lost your job? Or you're in a financial rut, and have no clue how you're going to pay your bills? Then out of nowhere, an unexpected check comes in the mail, and you are saved, and as happy as can be? Or, you get a call from a friend who says, "Hey, I just fired my last guy, because he was seriously unreliable. I need someone that is. Would you like the job, even if it's just temporary?" I bet this has happened to you in one shape or form, and these miracles aren't meant to be misunderstood as, "coincidence", but as a Divine blessing from Heaven.

"Everything happens for a reason, even when we are not wise enough to see it. When there is no struggle, there is no strength."

-Oprah Winfrey

I can't say this enough, there's no such thing as coincidence. See…when we need something, and Spirit knows this blessing would be in our best interest, they will stop at nothing to make sure that we get what we need. In all that is Divine in the timing of God, and Spirit, everything will be brought to us, when they know that we will surely benefit the most from it with gratitude.

Back in 2010 I used to work as a cashier for a thrift store for a little over a year. I enjoyed what I had learned and with what I had been granted, for I met some of the most influential people in my moments of weakness. During this timeframe, I was dealing with being a young single mother, struggling to keep up with my rent. I would work from ten to sixteen hour shifts around the clock, because I really needed the extra dough. I was overworked, most *definitely* underpaid, and most days too exhausted to spend quality time with my daughter for all I wanted to do was sleep the instant I got off the clock.

And one of these particular months I was facing the stress of not being able to make my rent payment, and I really don't like being late on anything at all. I was raised to earn what I either wanted, or needed. Not of custom to ask for anything. So me being stubborn, and because of being told to work hard, I didn't tell anyone of my situation but to God. I thought that if anyone would make it happen, it would be Him. I didn't pray for a lot, just enough to get the rent paid.

Then one day, I had just gotten into work early. I was going through a giant stack of purses and bags to bring out on the shelves for the customers. As I was working, I then came across one purse that was old and tattered. This thing was beat up, gross and ready to be thrown in the garbage –which is exactly what I did. But then some weird, random feeling stopped me, and I heard the words, *"Don't judge a book by its cover."* I didn't know where this thought was coming from. After much contemplation in my head, and thinking way too much, I finally decided to take it out of the garbage. Looking inside it, convinced me then that I wasn't crazy, for what I discovered brought chills up my spine. For inside this beat up purse, within a small pocket that so easily could be overlooked was where three crisp one hundred dollar bills rested. What was even more insane, was lying beside these abnormally clean bills, was a picture of Jesus Christ. I was *speechless*. I can still remember the moment I gasped for air, as I stared at these bills in utter shock. My mind was racing with thoughts..*"I just prayed not two days ago!!"* *"How's this possible??"*...

As blessed as I felt, I still did the right thing, and brought the money to my boss. I let them know what I discovered, and the manager waited for someone to come back to claim the money. About seventy-two hours later, my boss brings me into the office and gives me half of the money (because nobody claimed it), while the other half went to the store. They were pleased with my loyalty, thus allowed me to keep half. What was even more impressive, was the amount I was given. The total I had needed to pay the rest of my rent that month, was the *exact* amount my manager had given me.

What I feel is that not necessarily Spirit may have manifested money out of the blue into the pocket of this purse. (Not that they can't) But that, more likely, someone decided to donate this money to someone who they *felt* would need it, and fortunately that person that needed it was me. Because we are all in the same energy field, use, live and exist in the same energy from Source, we are able to *feel* when someone needs something. Even if we don't know for sure why, but *feel* we need to do a random act of kindness is the Universe at work. With this unknown person responding to their *feeling* to donate, I was able to receive my gift from the course of the powerful Universe that is ultimately connected to Source.

I don't expect you, or anyone to take belief in this "coincidence", but the fact is there's no such thing. We are all in union with the Universe, and with the answers we pray for. The higher Realms hear our prayers, and even if they may take longer for us to have them answered, doesn't mean it is less real. As long as there are people on this Earth, there'll remain to be repeated unexplained "coincidences."

See, when you find yourself in a tough circumstance, or stuck in a hard place, means that not only will it be a test of yourself, but a test of your faith. The amount of unconditional love, and endless guidance will never cease.

We're here to learn how to love to the fullest, even in our worst circumstances. That is our test here. We have to remain strong in all that is brought before us, and the more you remain faithful, the more you will recognize how Spirit will help you up.

FOR A DIVINE REASON

Now, there are moments where you may be thinking, *"Wait a minute, but what about those times where it seems my prayers aren't being heard?"* Good question. Prepare yourself for this answer, for the amount of ownership can take a lot for some. The reason this is, is because Spirit has to let us learn life lessons, as we continue on. Whether we're learning something large, or small, it all matters in the eyes of Spirit that you have mastered those lessons through your experiences as the said *experiencer.*

"God doesn't make mistakes. You are exactly where you are supposed to be right now."

-Steve Harvey

This is usually the toughest part for people to accept, and that's *okay*. Did you ever have an instance, where you had to do something more than once, in order to learn it? And then when you finally figured out that the original plot wasn't working, what did you do? You changed your approach, or changed your strategy, and possibly timing, right? Of course you did. All of our lessons take time to master, and they're here to guide us to be the best version of who we are. Spirit knows when they have to step aside, and allow you to figure out your life on your own.

They won't leave you, but remain on the bench of observation, to view your progress. When they feel there is a need to intervene, and influence you to make wise decisions, or give you a clue to your answers, that's when they may guide you in the right direction.

When we are enduring darker moments, it's time to really appreciate all that we have been blessed with the most. This is something that a lot of us tend to easily forget, for we can get too caught up in the moment, becoming convinced in the lie, that we only deserve the negatives that happen to us.

Keeping ourselves focused on the bigger picture is indeed important, and is greatly encouraged. But we are greatly reminded to appreciate what we are blessed with, while visualizing your targeted goals in life. Yes, Spirit understands our hardships. They understand that mourning through difficult times, gives us the relief that our bodies, minds and souls need in order to remain balanced. However, Spirit emphasizes specifically, to not forget during these times, that everything happens for a Divine reason…even if we can't see the reason in the moment yet. The moment when we begin to realize how much Spirit actually takes part in our lives, the smoother it is in accepting situations with faith. It can be incredible when we learn this with grace, and start to truly embrace their love and guidance without fear. Everything is Divine in the timing of God, and the Universe. Allowing everything, and everyone, to blend harmoniously together, like pieces to a giant puzzle. You may be a small piece to that puzzle, but you play a very large and important role in order for that puzzle to take its full form effortlessly.

THE RISE

Every dark experience we endure is not to be reprimanded by Spirit, but to be respected, for that is what causes us to grow to be the better version of ourselves. We can either be a victim, or a victor in the eyes of our life, and it is us that decide whether we choose to be destroyed by those moments, or created. The true beauty in all of our dark history, or our dark lifestyle, is having the power to overcome all that is brought to us, battling it down without fear in our hearts. What a better way to learn on how to live, than to be smack down in the middle of it? I always say, that if you want to be a master at something, then you should experience it fully, without any limitations. Think about it. Really think about it. Do you ever meet those people that say, "Oh I know how you feel." But then you think… *"No you don't."* You have never been down the road I have. True. Which is only more reason to be a master at life, is to be in it at full force. This isn't something to shake your head at, and put your face in your hands, with fear or shame. Life isn't about how you were beaten down, but *how you got back up.*

My life growing up wasn't easy. I endured moments that became very negative experiences. I was forced into situations that I didn't want to be in, and was subjected to large amounts of humility, feeling as if I had no dignity left. But I had a choice. To either be a hero of my own life, or to be a slave to my history. We all have something dark in our lives that we may wish to change, but if you ask me, I wouldn't have it any other way. I only pray for love, and for courage to endure a difficult life. I am here to put my hand on your soul, to tell you that I know what it means to feel absolutely alone, feeling unloved, unworthy, and how you may feel as if nothing you do is ever good enough. But the truth is, you were *born good enough.*

Hitting rock bottom, you really start to discover more about yourself, and of your authenticity soulfully. This goes without saying, that *life isn't about being great, but how you became great in the first place.* It's not about how much money you have, or how famous you are, nor is it the cost of your material items. *Life is about embracing you, and others without judgment, and with love, grace, honor and mutual respect.*

The point here, is no matter how much you may feel your past or current experiences seem unfair, always remember that nothing happens without a Divine reason. All life experiences we endure may not be what we bargained for, but do not proceed without a cause and effect. Thus, enables us a Divinely beautiful opportunity, to allow faith to lead us out of the darkened tunnel you may be laying in for far too long. Faith raises our vibration, our self-worth, self-belief, and values within ourselves, and others. Without faith, so many people wouldn't be able to survive another day if they didn't *believe* deeply within themselves that they *deserved* to.

Faith is a Divine gift in the Universe and God. It's a deep understanding and an acceptance that you will walk in your journey with hope and assurance, that you will forever be supplied by the Universe in Divine timing. And even if you experience a great loss, whether it's through people or materials, you are gifted the affirmation that all will return in a new form.

You will become a person that is more certain that everything occurs in full circle within the Universe. And as you begin to accept this beautiful gracious gift, we then can have a higher confidence in our lives, and in ourselves. As this Divine confidence builds, so does your energy, your vibration that echoes through your body that surrounds your soul.

FAITH IN THYSELF

We all come face to face with our worst enemy, and that's ourselves. We are not here to be beaten down, but to learn how to overcome the battles without fear in our hearts. Even though you may feel as if you are eternally alone, overwhelmed with your emotions, doesn't mean you aren't still being tested. We all have to confront the truth, and learn how to master the real reason why we are here. When we can stand in the mirror, and look at ourselves with respect, and not with weakness, that will be the moment where we're seeing the way through the trials. The beauty in it all, finally seeing the bigger picture.

Looking into the eye of our enemy without fear, but with courage, is what Spirit helps us do. A lot of the time, we may not even realize it, but when we start to cancel our self-doubt, it's because Spirit is helping us to do just that. They don't want us to be disappointed in ourselves. Instead, remain proud of our progress, especially if we can recognize how much we have overcome. Expressing there is always a light at the end of the tunnel, does sound pretty cliché. But the examples you witness with family, friends, or strangers, remain to be an inspiring role for humanity today. It cannot be said enough – *life isn't about being beaten down, but about building you up.* You were placed here to learn the lessons you are learning, and to know how to wrestle your battles with strength, and faith inside of yourself to be able to.

A truly inspiring person that comes to mind is a woman named

Michelle Knight I had seen on the *Dr. Phil* show, in November 2013. With television host *Dr. Phil McGraw*, she explained her horrifying experience of being kidnapped at the age of 21, and brutally, sexually abused for more than a decade by a gruesome man named Ariel Castro. Treated worse than an animal, neglected, chained, raped, miscarried five times, and beaten on a daily basis, yet despite all of this Hell she and the other victims went through, they were determined to get out. Michelle's focus was always to survive no matter how bad it was. Her inner belief, and faith in seeing another day was all she could dream about. The day they were able to feel the taste of freedom, after this tragic experience of what must've felt like an eternity, is something I *can't even* comprehend. I can't imagine this kind of heartbreak! Not only did her story create enormous amounts of tears from my swelling eyelids, but became a global inspiration for *all.*

These kinds of people are *true heroes* of their own lives. There's no mistaking that she was meant to endure this kind of experience, because of her *undeniable* strength, endurance, high level of tolerance and a strong will to live. My hat, my heart, and soul bows down to people like Michelle Knight, for she truly puts the *fight* in Knight!

Your hope is not going unheard, nor unnoticed by God, or your loved ones from the Other Side. They're with you continually, so much more than you truly know. They never leave your side, and are with you fighting the good fight, alongside with you. They hear your pleas, your laughs, your sorrows, your fears, and your inner demons.

Maybe you are a little rough around the edges, but for a grander purpose to keep going through it all without fear. No one will understand you better than you. No one can play your role in your life than you.

And it is up to you on whether you want to remain strong, or to throw in the towel. There are so many people you read, or see on the news like Michelle. Some that were slaves at one point in their lives. People that were taken away from their home of safety, faced with a horror that is completely unspeakable. When you hear in their voice of their terror, it moves your inner self to a place that is *unbearable*. I can't imagine such a terrifying Hell. Yet, after all of their anguish, they somehow survived to tell the tale. I don't even believe it appropriate to call it a tale…but more of an experience that left them with serious amounts of wisdom attained. People that have to carry memories that only make you wish to pick your brain apart, are the people that speak *true* faith. Somehow, even after all of the hell they endured, their faith in a better tomorrow got them through another day. Believing that somehow, they were going to make it out alive. Whether the hell was emotional, mental, or physical, all leave a special scar that only faith and unconditional love can heal. If you are one of these brave souls, my hat tips down to you. No one should EVER have to go through such a damaging infliction.

Even the word, "experience" carries support of other words that go sweetly with a delicate topic such as this. "Experience" is also similar to other supporting words, such as "brave". What a perfect match that is. An experience doesn't come without the word, bravery, and that to me speaks louder than anything. To follow, another word that catches my attention to, "experience" also comes the words, "encounter", "knowing", "suffer", "understand" are just a few. Each time you hear the word "experience", I want you to envision the rest of these words with it. No *experience* comes without *bravery*, and no amount of *bravery* comes without knowledge. And with knowledge comes more wisdom.

Each experience, whether good or bad, we are embracing something that can allow us to teach others what we have learned. Being the walking example of, *"bravery."*

"Defeat is a state of mind; no one is ever defeated until defeat has been accepted as a reality."

-Bruce Lee

The people you hear about that were tortured, beaten, and lived to tell their story, are just another prime example that they kept their focus on surviving so they could again experience living. Being able to live another day in freedom, and happiness was their sole focus. They kept their faith in themselves, knowing they're able to live for another day, as long as they *believed* they could. Doesn't mean they won't endure horrific memories of their past, but it does mean that as long as they kept their faith, that something better was on the way…they were blessed to keep going.

Having faith in ourselves to keep going through the hard times, is one of the pushes that Spirit greatly encourages. They would *never* allow us to go through something difficult, if there wasn't a Divine reason for it. Of course, the experience that Michelle and the other women went through was not in God's Divine plan but due to Ariel and his choices, (free will) to do what he did it became a reality. But even so, God wouldn't have allowed Michelle to sign up for this experience in her *Soul Contract* prior before coming here, if He, and her didn't believe she could surpass it *indefinitely*. It's our choice to take the experiences as a lesson to overcome or not. She made the choice to keep going, she didn't give up –but I'm positive there were many moments where she wanted to. But thanks to her high levels of faith in her own endurance, and Spirit, she was able to make it out and I forever wish her and the other women the *absolute best.*

Having faith in our own innate abilities to overcome anything that is laid out before us is one of the reasons to why we are here. We are being constantly tested of our endurance, our will to be brave, our tolerance levels, our thinking, our creativity, our self-worth, our self-belief, of our unconditional love in ourselves and in others. Without faith in even ourselves, we would not be able to continue life when it gets tough. We have to have the faith in knowing that whatever may come our way, we can handle it the best way we know how. With faith in yourself as a spiritual being connected to Source, Creator, we are granted the undeniable ability to surpass *anything.*

FAITH IN HUMANITY

Having faith in humanity, for a long time, I didn't know how to do. I used to believe that believing in the concept of man, was a waste of energy. I would look at the people around the world with constant sheer disappointment. I was *wrong*. Humankind is one of the major reasons of why we exist. If I were to give up on my faith of humanity, then I would also be giving up on myself, and that *ain't happenin' anytime soon.*

Humans are a very complex mammal. We live our day to day lives with our own agenda. Some working to live, while others are living to work.

Some live to build a better tomorrow, while others strive to build a better today. It all fits in the grand scheme of our animalistic nature that we call humanity.

Yet, I sometimes ask myself, if we could be doing so much better. Within all of the world's chaos, I still dream of a better now and tomorrow. I dream of what it would be like, if instead of Heaven being on the Other Side, it was here. Here on Earth, where we all worked together harmoniously, but of course that's not our reality. *"Can't live in the clouds forever, Minda,"* I have to remind myself. But wouldn't it be nice if we could? What if we all could? What would it be like, how much the world would change, if we all gave back to each other. If we all gave a piece of our time, our money, our patience to help another person, how much sweeter life would become for many. Of course, not all of us will, not all of us do.

Consider the amount of energy change all over the globe, if we all just stopped fighting. Sadly, not all will think this way. It took me many years to realize that no matter how much I wanted the world to change, it wouldn't —at least not until we all consciously chose to do so by our own free will. It is a conscious decision one makes inside of themselves. To believe that if we took the time to help one person a day, we could be creating an energy change within the world at the very moment. Having faith in humanity is something I believe we all should possess. Having faith with the power of love, we can slowly create a new beacon of hope, drastically altering the globe.

"The world is not dangerous because of those who do harm but because of those who look at it without doing anything."

-Albert Einstein

Possessing faith in humanity, permits the individual soul to believe in the reason of man. To believe that a random hero will save the day, or will give you the directions you seek when in unfamiliar territory. It permits you to hold a strong belief that we were not created in vain, and were created to uphold direction within a Divine Universe.

Life is about embracing all of what life has to offer, including the people that reside in it. Humanity is what gets you and I out of bed to tackle a new day with a deeper purpose. It is the reason doctors, nurses, and soldiers risk time away from their families, to rescue a stranger in need. It is the reason teachers at our local schools guide our children to understand the mysteries of the world. Why organizations take time to raise money, and donate their time to help people suffering from cancer, diseases, starvation, homelessness, etc. It is the reason why people in our armed forces will give their lives for someone they have never even met, because they have faith in something bigger than themselves. Having faith in humanity, gives a person a broader, deeper sense of hope in a better tomorrow, a better five minutes from now. Without faith in humanity, man would be forever lost in the chaos that we endure. We must believe in our fellow man, in morality, and in love for all. *The day we give up on humanity will be the day humanity ceases to exist.*

God hasn't given up on man. He hasn't given up on the better version of us, and never will. We are made from Him, and He is made from all of us. If our Lord stopped believing in us, He would then be disapproving in His own existence, and that just cannot be. Spirit loves us more than we can comprehend, and have a strong belief in teaching the betterment of our souls. Carrying us in the bosom of hope, birthing a light inside all of us,…so that we may see a better world.

A PRICELESS GIFT

Each conflict, no matter the weight, comes with an invaluable lesson. With those lessons, comes the gift of more wisdom, knowledge, and unconditional love. As long as we hold faith, believing that there is a Divine reason for why we are to learn what we are learning, the easier we will notice Spirit's loving messages. They are with you during *every* moment, no matter the impact.

Have faith in their presence and in their unconditional love, forever guiding you to the better version of yourself with faith in them.

With the gift of pure unconditional love, we are forever entangled with the Universe and our departed loved ones. Their presence is near you more than you may ever know, and their love for you is louder than the whispers they may be able to bestow. Each moment with you is a treasure to them in Spirit, and each treasure they receive is taken with the highest levels of gratitude and appreciation. They love and miss us just as much as we do them. They are just as excited to speak to us, as we are when hearing from them –did you know that? It's true! They love and honor us *so much*, and *never* want to miss out on a good chance in saying so.

With experiencing grief from our greatest losses, there comes the gift of seen or unseen gains. With each loss we are gifted the beautiful gift in appreciating what we miss. Yes, it's hard, and I can tell you undoubtedly, that no matter how much time passes, the grief from losing a loved one will never cease. Because that love is there, the pain, that undeniable void will remain within our hearts. But, thanks to Spirit's wonderful gift in reassurance through people; instances, and through millions of messages in our lives, it can make the grieving a little bit easier. Not a lot, but just enough to help us move forward each and every day.

Their wish and reassurance for you is to remember that they are never far away, but just in a different place. They're not gone, just in a different form, a form that we all will be when our time comes. Each of the souls that I have had the pleasure in connecting with, were more than just a gift in experiencing this obvious truth, but truly an *honor* that I will forever cherish for all my life *here*, and in the *next*. They have proven to countless clients and friends, whom I have met along my journey, that no matter how long they have been departed, their soul is still sharp and witty as ever. Whether they were strong willed, stubborn, selfless, or shier than ever, they're remaining to keep up their stamina, while forever growing in Spirit on the Other Side.

Spirit's deepest desire is for all of us to keep them in their memory, to remember the happier moments that we shared with them. They wish for us is to capture life forever with grace and gratitude for the old and new experiences. For the present is the most bountiful of times, where we are granted the token of creating new memories with our *now*.

Embrace Where We Go In Spirit On The Other Side And The Unbreakable Bond

Your departed loves one are forever watching you in their natural, Spirit form…forever loving, guiding and protecting you from Heaven.

Be strong, be great, and never allow a shadow to prevent you from showing your true light inside.

We are all guided to tackle all,

and to uphold all we are faced with.

Never doubt your own true spiritual value,

for Spirit never does in you,

and you're to always remember this is so.

They're here to take your journey with you,

and to guide you to the truth about yourself.

To show you that you're strong, that you are unconditionally loved,

and are never alone.

Trust in their love, in Source, and in yourself as an everlasting spiritual

being fueled by love. The more you do...

the more you will be guided the way back to the light.

The Unbreakable Bond

The loss of a loved one is a pain that many would agree is an experience that no one should have to accept but the flip side to the coin of "death" is it's only the *beginning*. The afterlife is just another Realm at which is our calling that all are destined to be a part of sooner or later.

When we depart from here to there, there is no longer the pain that is accompanied with human emotions. No more of the grief that we harbor due to past resentments and regrets but only the true serenity while faced with effortless peace and happiness. And as we are all made of the same energy that is connected to Source, Creator we are all gifted with the precious token of a bond that will *never* break. Never will this tear, rip or become destroyed by time, distance, emotions or lack thereof.

I used to fear the same. When I lost my dear friend Chad I used to believe that somehow we would never be together again and the friendship we had was no longer in existence. Him being my Master Spirit Guide and Twin Flame, knew how I was feeling and dealing with the emotions that I had.

More importantly, because we are all made up of the same energy as our loved ones on the Other Side are, they are forever bonded with us as we are with them.

I still remember this like it was yesterday. I had been crying for hours every night for months while feeling his holy touch caressing against my solid cheek compared to his soulful essence. And one particular night I literally wept myself to sleep. Once my eyes had officially closed that's when I suddenly found myself sitting on a couch with Chad on the floor kneeling before me. Without hesitation I touched his face ignoring the tears running down my quivering cheeks like a river with a cause. He gently took my hands in his, placed them upon my lap and listened to the anguish flow from my mouth like the river from my eyes. The more I blurted the tighter he held on, letting me know without words he was present in this moment. I can still remember his grip, the physical illusion of who he used to be before now. Still able to recall the very buttoned shirt he used to wear. So lively he was. *So real,* I almost believed he could come back to life as the man he once was at any moment. My dear friend's presence was so lucid, I almost didn't notice the other souls that were also present. Even my grandmother, Granny Pat was here with us who had been departed for more than ten years. Then, in that instance I knew I was experiencing a rare spiritual visit where I had appeared to be in a different dimension.

Still holding my hands he said to me, *"Melinda, you must know by now that we are forever linked together and no matter what I will always be with you."* This was six months after he died and going through the mourning of his passing. Trying to grip the loss in accepting we would never be what I had hoped. But thanks to what he said next, I knew this was something that all had to hear, not just me. As the passionate smile birthed from his eyes he confirmed, *"We are always together no matter how much you may feel we are apart. No matter what, our bond is stronger than you could ever imagine. Not even God Himself could break our bond because that's how much He loves us."*

The unbreakable bond that we all hold with our loved ones that have departed from this physical illusion, will remain the same level of solidity the instance it was created through love from Source. The bond will *never cease*, never deter from the true purpose that is meant for all in this incomprehensible extended Universe. Extenuating, the unconditional love you have from your departed loved ones, the memories that you created with them, undeniably will outlive anything physical.

Taking in the new, whether it's people, relationships, environments or material items is another opportunity towards growing into the loving soul that you were meant to uphold. Their love and wish for you is to move forward with their memory in your heart without guilt. They bring new people, opportunities, environments and even experiences for you to embrace life fully without limitations. While moving forward in your life their reassurance is their love can never be replaced, tarnished or diminished but are only in a better place honing their true form while forever loving and guiding you in Spirit.

ove

Love is the one Universal language that every person, animal and any sentient being can understand and indeed appreciate. Apart from the language gaps, culture differences and beliefs, there is no greater power within the physical world, and the world on the Other Side. Because love is such a benevolent ingredient to every solution to every situation, I have decided to take this time and instead of describing it myself to you…I will share quotes from some of the greatest positive influencers. Every word we say has an effect on others around us. As long as we use our words, actions, and intentions for the best of all concerned, we can see *powerful* and inescapable positive changes around the globe.

With very little words, much inspiration can go a long way. Spirit encourages us to live the bright vibration that is love, and with these quotes, I have *faith* they will provide an optimistic start…

"People, even more than things have to be restored, renewed, revived, reclaimed, and redeemed. Never throw out anyone."

-Audrey Hepburn

"No one is born hating another person because of the color of his skin, or his background, or his religion. People must learn to hate, and if they can learn to hate, they can be taught to love; for love comes more naturally to the human heart than its opposite."

-Nelson Mandela

"Only do what your heart tells you."

-Princess Diana

"Evil begins when you begin to treat people as things."

-Terry Pratchett

"In a gentle way, you can shake the world."

-Mahatma Gandhi

"To give someone a piece of your heart, is worth more than all the wealth in the world."

-Michael Jackson

"If you judge people, you have no time to love them."

-Mother Theresa

"When the power of love overcomes the love of power, the world will know peace."

-Jimi Hendrix

"Have the courage to follow your heart and intuition. They somehow know what you truly want to become."

-Steve Jobs

"Be the change you want to see in the world."
-Mahatma Gandhi

"There is no need for temples, no need for complicated philosophies. My brain and heart are my temples; my philosophy is kindness."
-Dalai Lama

"Peace is not merely a distant goal that we seek, but a means by which we arrive at the goal."
-Martin Luther King, Jr.

"It has become appallingly obvious that our technology has exceeded our humanity."
-Albert Einstein

"The greatness of man is not in how much wealth he acquires, but in his integrity, and his ability to affect those around him positively."
-Bob Marley

"We teach people how to treat us."
-Dr. Phil McGraw

"We make a living by what we get, but we make a life by what we give."
-Winston Churchill

"What is love? Love is the absence of judgment."
-Dalai Lama

"You know, all that really matters is that the people you love are happy and healthy. Everything else is just sparkles on the sundae."

-Paul Walker

"Water is the softest thing, yet it can penetrate mountains and Earth. This shows clearly the principle of softness overcoming hardness."

-Lao Tzu

"If you wish to experience peace, provide peace for another."

-Dalai Lama

"Wanting to be someone else is a waste of the person you are."

-Marilyn Monroe

"A life not lived for others is not a life."

-Mother Theresa

"Darkness cannot drive out darkness: only light can do that.

Hate cannot drive out hate: only love can do that."

-Martin Luther King, Jr.

"I destroy my enemy when I make him my friend."

-Abraham Lincoln

"For where your treasure is there will your heart be also."

-Jesus Christ – 21 Matthew 6:17

*H*igh Vibrational
Affirmations

The experience of being human can bring us down at times, and in certain cases we could use a little pick-me up from Spirit. Here you can go to words that will sweeten your day or mood, in order to remind you of how wonderfully gifted, loved, and eternally blessed you truly are…

---

1) *I am loved unconditionally by Creator.*

2) *Everything happens in Divine timing.*

3) *I am supplied to by the ultimate Universe*

4) *I know that God will never deny me.*

5) *Heaven is meant for me, and I am meant for Heaven*

6) *As long as I hold faith in God, Spirit and in the Universe, I will always live in abundance.*

7) *My love from my departed loved ones will never cease.*

8) *I AM eternal, I AM infinite, I AM connected to Source, Creator.*

9) *I am living to learn unconditional love.*

10) *My ultimate Divine goal is to surpass my lessons with grace, gratitude and appreciation for myself and others.*

11) *If I need guidance, I know I can always go to Angels, Spirit and to*

Creator.

12) I AM an infinite being created and fueled by absolute love.

13) When unfortunate things happen, I will process emotions without shame.

14) I can go to the Source, for the answers I am seeking.

15) I am forever loved by Creator, no matter my mistakes.

16) I am learning that it is okay to learn as a humble Spirit being in human form.

17) Without Creator's forgiveness and mercy, I would not be able to learn the way that I am.

18) My departed loved ones are not dead (spiritually) just in a different form –their true form.

19) My purpose here is to learn on how to love others and myself without judgement.

20) I know that I am Divinely protected by my Spirit Guides, Angels, departed loved ones and Creator.

21) I will forgive myself and others because I deserve the freedom from despair.

22) Without fail, I am certain of my connection with the Divine.

23) I can call on my departed loved ones whenever I want, without guilt or shame.

24) My departed loved ones miss me just as much as I miss them.

25) I have a place I can call Home in Heaven, Paradise.

26) I am an infinite being with immense power that is fueled by Creator that is interconnected within the supreme Universe.

27) With Creator, anything is possible.

28) I will no longer be fearful of crossing over to the Other Side.

29) *I am brave, I am courageous.*

30) *I am aware that my dreams of my departed loved ones are actual visitations.*

31) *I am free to worship Creator in any way that is deemed positive in the vibration of absolute love.*

32) *I am eternally powered by love.*

33) *I am Divinely connected to all that is energy.*

34) *I am a part of what is an ultimate, infinite Universe.*

35) *I have the undeniable gift by Source to make the impossible – possible.*

36) *Angels are always there for me when I need their supreme love, protection and guidance.*

37) *Source's unconditional, absolute love is limitless.*

38) *There is a surge of power through me that is ultimately positive in love and light.*

39) *My living is Divinely purposeful for all in the Universe and Source.*

40) *I am given the chance to allow lessons to guide me to higher wisdom.*

41) *I am allowed to grieve in my own time without judgment.*

42) *My love for my loved ones will forever be in existence within the Universe and praised by Heaven.*

43) *My departed loved ones talk about me in Heaven positively.*

44) *If I am lost, confused, or sad, I know I can go to Source, Angels and my loved ones for their unshakable guidance and support.*

45) *I am the only one of my kind of Soul Print –I am a rarity in the Universe that can never be replaced or duplicated.*

46) *I am a special love that is forever molding to a more beautiful me.*

Embrace Where We Go In Spirit On The Other Side And The Unbreakable Bond

47) Others love me unconditionally, even from the Other Side in Heaven.

48) My skills and passions are Divinely guided by Creator and Angels.

49) People need me.

50) I am FOREVER welcome in Heaven.

51) I am slowly understanding and accepting my self-worth.

52) Should I ever need an ear to listen, I know I can call onto the Higher Realms –Ascended Masters, God, Spirit Guides and Angels.

53) My dreams are a Divine connection to Spirit's love.

54) Without my heart, I would not be the good person that I am.

55) Freedom is the person that speaks truth from the heart.

56) I can forgive others' wrongdoings with faith that I deserve to be healed.

57) Just because the world may reject me, doesn't mean God will or does.

58) I can take notice in Spirit's loving messages in unlimited ways.

59) Source is the answer to all things.

60) Everything happens for a Divine reason, even if I don't understand the bigger picture yet.

61) I will hold faith in a better now.

62) My departed loved ones hear me whenever I talk to them.

63) I know my departed loved ones are not lost, but Divinely residing in Paradise patiently awaiting for my arrival.

64) Should I ever lose a loved one, I know they will be guided and protected by Angels and other fellow departed loved ones.

65) I will hold hope in love.

66) Should I ever get lost, I know who to turn to.

67) *I know now that it is okay to forget and let go.*

68) *It is okay to go to God when I need reassurance.*

69) *I believe that I am forever loved by something greater than myself in Spirit.*

70) *I will not believe in my inner negative voices any longer.*

71) *From now on, I will do my best to only speak loving words to and about myself.*

72) *It is okay to not always be right.*

73) *The beauty to living is learning how to love in life with others.*

74) *I know Angels are always with me.*

75) *I know that I am not my situation.*

76) *My calling in life is what others need in order to discover theirs.*

77) *A life without love is not a life at all.*

78) *Every hardship is a Divine experience to be learned from.*

79) *All of my life is not in vain, but a Divine line of lessons to master.*

80) *I am loved for all eternity.*

81) *Absolute love from Source is not measured nor identified by sexuality, gender, age, height, weight, riches, popularity, creed or color, etc.*

82) *All people that I come into contact with is another form of contact with Creator for we are all a part of Him.*

83) *Energy was never created nor destroyed –therefore my soul is eternal.*

84) *Love cannot exist where there is hate, and hate cannot exist where there is love.*

85) *Love is like wind. We cannot see it, but when it's called, it will be*

stronger than any force there is, overcoming all that cross its path.

86) Fear does not exist. Fear is only a matter of possibilities that are conjured within thoughts from the mind. As long as there is courage, fear cannot coexist.

87) I am aware now that as words, thoughts are a powerful tool within the Universe.

88) As long as there are other good people in the world, our human existence will prevail.

89) Harmony between colonies cannot come to a place of peace unless one is willing to put down their sword.

90) We are in a time where consciousness is flourishing over technology. These are the truths that are speaking about us for the first time in centuries.

91) It is not walls that need to be built to protect others, but open gates to welcome all.

92) It is only natural for an adult child to crave love from their parent regardless of age.

93) We are a Spirit that is in a world that seeks power. If we became a Spirit that seeks the power of love than the world would become a Spirit of one.

94) Harmony between two enemies can be the influence that can impact the world.

95) I must generate love from the interior before seeking it from the exterior.

96) The lack of love I receive is not what I, or anyone deserves.

97) The Karmic reactions I receive are bringing me in balance to come to a full circle to become one with Source, Creator.

98) *I am brave enough to take control of myself by choosing between reacting or responding with love.*

99) *Remaining consciously aware of the bigger picture at all times helps to be more aware of thyself.*

100) *If I have done something that would be unforgiving to some, I know that as long as I hold true remorse for my mistakes or low vibrational choices, I will be forgiven in Heaven by Creator.*

101) *I am confident in who I AM at all times regardless of the naysayers.*

102) *There is no creed when it comes to love.*

103) *The purpose for each creature living is to understand and appreciate the gift of absolute love.*

104) *Even though I am human and know I will still make mistakes in the future, I know as long as I remain aware of thyself at all times, I will at least do my absolute best to love others and myself.*

105) *Separating myself from others that are not in the best interest of my wellbeing or those that I love, is not me being a "bad", or "unloving" person.*

106) *Just because I forgive others for their wrongdoings against me, doesn't mean I have to allow them or their negativity to remain a part of my life.*

107) *I deserve bliss and happiness.*

108) *I deserve a spouse and friends that will love me for me and not what I have or what I offer.*

109) *I know that with God's ultimate love I can conquer all things – including addiction.*

110) *I am not what happens to me.*

Embrace Where We Go In Spirit On The Other Side And The Unbreakable Bond

111) *My soul value is not measured by how others treat me.*

112) *My worth is more valuable than all of the stars in the Universe.*

113) *No matter what others say, or do to me, I know that God will forever love me for me and never identify me by my choices.*

114) *I am fully aware of my past mistakes and am taking the high road to a better me.*

115) *I know that my child in Heaven is forever loved in Paradise with unshakable peace.*

116) *Angels are a non-judging being that knows no faults.*

117) *My life is the story that I create.*

118) *Without love the world will never know peace.*

119) *I know that I am never judged for my weaknesses or fears.*

120) *It is my job to accept my own levels of accountability and in doing so I know I am growing to a better version of myself in Spirit as well as human.*

121) *Being me is not lesser than the next person.*

122) *Beauty is not to be confused with physical appearance. True beauty is in the nature of the heart —not the contour of the face.*

123) *My love for others will never go unnoticed in Heaven and God's eyes.*

124) *I am being celebrated in Heaven each time I am loving another selflessly.*

125) *My departed loved ones will never forget me no matter how long it has been since their passing.*

126) *I know that my beloved pet is not lost on the Astral Realm but is enjoying the blissful peace in Heaven.*

127) *I know if I pray for a miracle for another stranger —it will happen.*

128) *Prayer is the power of telepathy through the love of being.*

129) *Thanks to God and the external and internal blessings each day, I know I am continually loved.*

About The Author

Melinda Lyons was born in Anchorage, Alaska and raised in the Last Frontier for a majority of her life. She is a proud mother of her daughter Josslyn Elisa, and her departed daughter Victoria Owen. Melinda does not align herself to a particular religion or tradition, but is in ultimate faith of the power of the Universe, Spirit and Source.

All of her life she knew in her heart that she was meant to help, heal and guide people to a deeper level of understanding. Never did she imagine her purpose would be to send love from the Other Side of the physical. But as her years stretched after her NDE (near death experience), so did her intuitiveness and Divine abilities. Thanks to many positive influences, and pushes in the right direction, her dream of healing has become a reality. More people each day, each moment are being Divinely healed, guided and transformed by Spirit, Angels and God's loving messages.

As a professional *Lightworker* & *Psychic Medium* –Medium first, Psychic second –Melinda has helped people from her home state to overseas. With more than 12 years of paranormal experience, and a higher level of awareness of Spirit, Melinda's developed relationship with the respect and understanding of the Other Side has changed the lives of many.

Embrace Where We Go In Spirit On The Other Side And The Unbreakable Bond

Melinda has been a guest on radio shows heard on *iHeartRadio*, while managing her own official website:

https://www.Lastfrontiermedium.com.

From her perfectionistic vision of creating a positive movement in the world, her ambitions drive her to create a new personable way in impacting each and every precious soul she encounters; alive and departed.

Acknowledgements

I want to thank some of the most influential and loving people that continued to believe in me. To my loving daughters *Josslyn* and *Victoria,* who are the light in my Spirit and the drive that supports my inspiration. Without you, *Josslyn,* I never would have grown up to be the mother and person that I was truly meant to be for you. *Victoria,* even though I was blessed to only have you physically for three months, I know that your soul is forever loving your bigger sister, and guiding me to be the best role model I can be. I love you both *more* than the human emotion can ever express.

To my loving family that has continually supported me in my new normal lifestyle. You all have gifted me with a new vision of a brighter future.

You've always encouraged me to keep going, even when the going gets tough. Thank you for your true unconditional love, *Carolyn, Heather, Patrick* and *Christopher.* Your continual loving guidance and support is my rock and I could never ask for better siblings.

Tiffany, there are so many words that I wish I could truly describe just how impacting you have been in helping me move forward without doubt in my way. Your unconditional love has been truly a dream come true, a pure example of what a friendship should be, physically and

Embrace Where We Go In Spirit On The Other Side And The Unbreakable Bond

spiritually. Whenever self-doubt begins to creep up, you always have the right words to say, to push me in the right direction. *Thank you* for being you, shining your light, guiding me to my next chapter in my life. *Forever* will I be grateful for this magnificent blessing, –that is your heart.

Haya, how could I forget you?... You've been one of the most positive influences that spoke to my soul to keep going when I lost Chad. Your belief in me never ceased, and I could never stop our friendship, and the power of your unconditional love. *Thank you* for all that you have done for me. From the hours of chatting late nights, to putting me in my place when I was stepping away from my higher self, you never steered away. Your heart and Spirit are truly moving.

Kathy, you hold a special amount of courage, loyalty, and unconditional love that is *truly* a *rarity*. Despite my countless screw ups, your solidity remained true. For without your pure heart, I would not have been able to continue this journey, and for that I will always keep you in mine.

Aunt Sharon, If it wasn't for you I wouldn't be in the place that I am today. You showed me a new road in my independence and for that I will forever be eternally blessed. Your love has and will remain a large part in my growing into the person that I am today and I will remain grateful to you.

Dad, you have a special place in my heart that no other "father" could replace. Your unconditional love is *irreplaceable*, and undeniably noble. Thank you for always keeping my chin up when I couldn't.

Mom, I know we tend to have our ups, downs. But despite the facts, I will forever keep you in my heart, as one of the most influential people.

You took care of us, sacrificed much of your time to raise five children. I will continue to *appreciate* your unconditional love.

There would be absolutely *no way* this book could've become a reality if it wasn't for the sacrifice and unconditional love of my *Master Spirit Guide/ Twin Flame,* **Chad.** The day I met you, I knew *instantly* that we would never stop communicating. You encouraged me to never doubt my first thought, and pushed me to believe in myself, no matter what others said. You took me to Heaven, introduced me to dazzling Angels, and tirelessly guiding me to discovering more of my higher self. Thank you for showing me what true absolute love means. I know without a doubt, you will forever help me through the rest of my journey; guiding, protecting, loving and laughing with me in Spirit.

Aaron, thank you for visiting me from the Other Side, and encouraging me to keep moving forward. I will always be *grateful* for our memories, friendship and laughs over silly things.

To **Spirit, Angels** and the other souls that have aided me in my journey – *thank you!* You're a *major* part to this magnificent long road, and I know I can always call on you for more answers to my constant questions. I am so *honored* and so *blessed* to have been able to witness your glory, and *can't wait* to see what happens next! The souls that have come to me in the past, and the ones that are planning to …I am SO HONORED to be able to be your vessel. If I could change it, I wouldn't! For the gift you have given me, and to many others is purely *priceless*.

Last but most certainly not least, **God**…you and I obviously go way…*way* back. I feel like I have not only known you here, but in many other lifetimes. *Thank you* for guiding me back to my roots. I can't even fathom the idea of taking another breath of air, without you present in my life. I am *eternally grateful* for your most gracious love, mercy, and understanding. You are the Source, the answer to every question, to every direction, for everything. My Spirit longs for you more each and every single second, of every day that I am here. I know you sent me here to help others become closer to you, and I can *promise*, that I will at least do the best I can –for I'm only your humble messenger.

And of course I cannot forget those that have supported me from the beginning, and to those that are new to my work with Spirit. And to those that I have not mentioned, *I haven't forgotten you.* **Everyone** that has been involved in my life, you're always a part of this major accomplishment, and yet I'm just getting started! Without your continual and gracious support, I *never* would've been able to make this book a reality. More so, to the **countless clients** –without your trust in my abilities, this book would not have been manifested. I am *eternally grateful* for your love, and trust in my gift as the vessel for your loved ones. *Truly*, no words can ever describe just how *honored* I feel in being able to be doing this for you and millions of others each day.

-Those that were not named in this book were either chosen to be anonymous by me or by the individual intentionally for the wellbeing of all concerned.

Embrace Where We Go In Spirit On The Other Side And The Unbreakable Bond

Made in the USA
San Bernardino, CA
27 June 2017